CREATING MULTICULTURAL
CHANGE ON CAMPUS

CREATING MULTICULTURAL CHANGE ON CAMPUS

Raechele L. Pope

Amy L. Reynolds

John A. Mueller

With contributions from
Timothy R. Ecklund and
Matthew J. Weigand

o

Foreword by

Caryn McTighe Musil

JB JOSSEY-BASS™

A Wiley Brand

Published by Jossey-Bass
A Wiley Brand
One Montgomery Street, Suite 1200, San Francisco, CA 94104-4594—www.josseybass.com

Jossey-Bass books and products are available through most bookstores. To contact
Jossey-Bass directly call our Customer Care Department within the U.S. at 800-956-7739,
outside the U.S. at 317-572-3986, or fax 317-572-4002.

Wiley publishes in a variety of print and electronic formats and by print-on-demand.
Some material included with standard print versions of this book may not be included in
e-books or in print-on-demand. If this book refers to media such as a CD or DVD that
is not included in the version you purchased, you may download this material at http://
booksupport.wiley.com. For more information about Wiley products, visit www.wiley.com.

Library of Congress Cataloging-in-Publication Data has been applied for and is on file
    with the Library of Congress.
ISBN 978-1-118-24233-9 (cloth); ISBN 978-1-118-41948-9 (ebk.);
    ISBN 978-1-118-42112-3 (ebk.)

Printed in the United States of America
FIRST EDITION
HB Printing   V10002950_080218

We dedicate this book to ALL who devote their scholarship and their lives to multicultural and social justice issues in higher education and beyond. In particular, we are especially indebted to Harold Cheatham, Jane Fried, Lee Knefelkamp, and Marilu McEwen. We are forever inspired.

CONTENTS

FOREWORD

THE UNITED STATES HAS BEEN a richly diverse country from its inception as a republic. However, in tension with its democratic ideals, those governing the nation have amassed a long and checkered history of legislating diversity out of American institutions. This began with our founding documents and continued through centuries of various ensuing laws such as the Naturalization Act of 1790 or the 1882 Chinese Exclusion Act or Jim Crow laws that re-inscribed white supremacy in the South after the Civil War. Women across colors, African Americans, Asians, indigenous people, Latinos, Catholics, Jews, the poor—all found themselves living circumscribed lives in the land of equal opportunity. Thus, exclusionary practices denied the nation the full and accurate rendering of its multicultural heritage.

The results have been visible everywhere—from who could vote to who could govern; from who could own property to which humans were considered property; from who could claim citizenship to who could bring their families legally into the fledgling or contemporary nation. Education suffered the same debilitating patterns, especially our colleges and universities. This book is about the residual effects of old habits and old legacies on educational institutions and how difficult these intellectual and behavioral shackles are to break free from. But even more so, this book is about the transformative role colleges and universities can play in a diverse democracy when they are purposeful about cultivating multicultural engagement, knowledge, values, and skills.

Historically, higher education became a site where inclusion and exclusion played out, whether on the same campus or in the development of parallel institutions marked for excluded groups that resulted in the creation of women's colleges, Catholic colleges, historically black colleges, tribal colleges, and more recently Hispanic-serving institutions. As anthropologist Renato Rosaldo said, "Conflicts over diversity and multiculturalism in higher education are localized symptoms of a broader renegotiation of full citizenship in the United States" (*Culture and Truth: The Remaking of Social Analysis*, 1993).

To demonstrate that acknowledging, understanding, and engaging with diverse others is not only the right thing to do educationally, politically, and socially, but actually possible to achieve, *Creating Multicultural Change on Campus* amasses in a skillful way much of the most significant scholarship on the matter. Higher education has been no stranger to radical transformations in this last half century, even though it is more typically mocked by its critics for being so bound in its ways and resistant to change. The democratization of higher education in the twentieth century is one of the century's most triumphant narratives. In 1902, only 3% of Americans had college degrees, but by the celebration of the millennium, some 75% of those who graduated from high school went on to college for some period.

But what kind of environment did these newcomers enter? And what skills did they and the old-timers—whether students, faculty, administrators, or staff—need to navigate productively in the multicultural swirl they all found themselves in? Too often the faces changed, but the syllabus and scholarship remained the same. Or the faces changed, but the policies and practices did not. Or the faces changed, but the deeper assumptions, norms, and expectations remained rigidly in place. This book pays tribute to the four decades of scholarship describing the theories of multicultural organizational change and individual development as well as the thousands of campus professionals who invented ways to tap diversity as an asset rather than a liability.

But its authors—Raechele L. Pope, Amy L. Reynolds, and John A. Mueller—who are scholars as well as savvy practitioners, tackle an even tougher question with their new book. They want to change not only individuals but also institutions, right down to the mortar between the bricks. Some thought it would be enough to change the students' faces. End exclusionary practices that shut some people out of a college education and we have solved the problem. But it did not solve the problem, as *Creating Multicultural Change on Campus* is proof.

So they have set about in a methodical way to offer some theoretical frameworks for deep-down change. They refer to it as second-order change. It is this level of change, layered on first-order change, that leads to multicultural institutions. Such institutions, in turn, offer students the very experiences they will need if they are to thrive and contribute to a diverse and often contentious United States and globe: experiences in grappling seriously with multiple perspectives, deepening their knowledge of historical and cultural legacies different from their own, and cultivating sophisticated skills in working collectively across differences to create solutions to messy, complex problems. The authors offer theories but wisely couple them with concrete practices, examples, advice, check-lists, and constant reassuring words that all this demanding effort is an evolutionary process with fits and starts and sometimes backtracking or outright failure. Their most insistent point is to keep at it.

Most refreshing is their assertion that relying only on individual change, while necessary, is not sufficient. We need new knowledge, aware-ness, values, and skills at the group level as well as the individual level. And even pairing those two, while necessary, is not sufficient. We need to invest in altering practices and understandings at the institutional level as well.

This final comprehensive approach that is, as they say, "systematic, planned, and sustained," needs also to encompass both first-order and second-order changes. These authors gently lead readers to not settling for anything less, while persuading us that such changes are actually pos-sible. They manage to do so despite orchestrated, richly financed anti–affirmative action movements, despite resurgent and virulent nativism, despite inadequate funding to pay for a college education, despite think-ing education is a delivery system of UPS-packaged courses that can land on your doorstep or in your computer to be consumed like a box of chocolates or a Harry and David fruit basket.

Pope, Reynolds, and Mueller understand that democracy is at stake in this multicultural experiment that began to go amiss several centu-ries ago. They argue with their book that the multicultural experiment can begin in earnest now with everyone fully present across the table from one another, curious, engaged, trading ideas, working together to figure out solutions for pressing common issues. But like our country and its laws, policies, and protections, colleges and universities need at the institutional level to be rewired. We need updated programming: 1776.2 or perhaps by now 1776.8. *Creating Multicultural Change on Campus* offers a founding document for how to do that.

CARYN McTIGHE MUSIL
Senior Scholar and Director
of Civic Learning and Democracy Initiatives
The Association of American Colleges and Universities

PREFACE

IN 2004, JOSSEY BASS PUBLISHED our book *Multicultural Competence in Student Affairs,* which focused on the principles of multicultural competence and described the integration of multicultural awareness, knowledge, and skill into the core competencies of student affairs professionals. Now, 10 years later, after much thought, we have decided that a different book is needed that expands our understanding of individual multicultural competence and provides a framework for creating multicultural change at the institutional level. Although we still believe that individual multicultural competence is a necessary prerequisite to effective and efficacious practice on college campuses, we also know that it is not sufficient to creating truly multicultural campuses.

This book is not an updated version of the earlier book, nor is it a prequel or sequel. Instead it is a completely different approach that examines institutional practices and uses planned change strategies to transform the campus. Our goal is to offer a deeper understanding of the institutional policies and practices that are essential for creating inclusive, welcoming, and affirming campus environments. It introduces theory, strategies to assess current multicultural policies and practices, and a practical framework for effective campus-wide interventions. More specifically, multicultural organization development (MCOD) theory and the multicultural change intervention matrix (MCIM) are explored in depth. MCOD theory, while grounded in organization development, provides tools and practices that can infuse multicultural principles into the everyday operations of higher education institutions. MCIM is a framework developed to help practitioners conceptualize and integrate MCOD theory into their work. This book provides practitioners with a rich understanding of both MCOD and the MCIM and how both can be used to appropriately and accurately assess the environment, identify or diagnose key issues, design effective interventions, and evaluate outcomes.

This book is not designed to be a "one-size fits all" or cookbook approach to creating a campus that fully embraces and enacts multicultural values and practices. Rather, it offers a conceptual framework on which multicultural change can occur at the micro (e.g., program or department) or the macro (e.g., division or institution) levels. Although books are available that discuss the need to create campuses that are supportive of underrepresented students, these important books tend to take a rather singularly student-centered approach, with much less attention given to practitioners, faculty, or institutional policies or practices. More recently, a growing base of literature has focused on how to develop multicultural competence among professionals working in higher education. What is needed now, and what this book provides, is a comprehensive focus on MCOD theory, strategies, and best practices for higher education professionals who are responsible for enacting multicultural change at the departmental, division, and university levels.

This book complements and adds a new dimension to multicultural competence by extending the principles of individual multicultural competence to organizational structures, policies, and practice. Although multicultural awareness, knowledge, and skills are important for all higher education professionals, these competencies can be even more effective in creating change when incorporated with an understanding of institutional barriers and organization strategies and tools. This book encourages student affairs practitioners, higher education administrators, and faculty to more fully explore what theories and strategies are necessary for creating long-lasting and meaningful multicultural change. This book also extends the profession's understanding of multicultural competence for higher education professionals and further clarifies the specific knowledge base and skills needed to create institutional multicultural change. By providing good practice examples using the MCIM, higher education professionals will have a more concrete and applied understanding of what it takes to create a campus that integrates multicultural values, policies, and practices into every aspect of the institution.

Before venturing any further, it is important that we explicitly share some of our underlying assumptions, which ultimately shape how we define some key multicultural constructs. Ten years ago when we wrote *Multicultural Competence in Student Affairs*, we highlighted the absence of a broadly accepted definition of the term *multicultural*. Although such unified language and understanding still does not exist, the term *multicultural* has come to symbolize a more universal and inclusive definition, which incorporates race, ethnicity, language, gender, sexual orientation, religion, social class, disability, as well as other differences. We believe that such inclusivity is a good thing. At the same time, we are also acutely aware of increasing pressures to describe our world as post-racial, post-gender, even post-sexual orientation. Many individuals cite the advancements that have occurred, including increased opportunities for women and people of color as well as expanded rights for lesbian, gay, bisexual, and transgender (LGBT) individuals, as reasons why extra attention paid to diversity is no longer needed. Our perspective is quite different. We have no interest in living in a post-racial, post-gender, or post-sexual orientation world, but we are interested in living in a post-racism, post-sexism, post-heterosexism world in which differences are celebrated and social injustices are eradicated. For that reason, we embrace both cultural specific and universal definitions of multiculturalism concurrently.

We also continue to believe that all of our social identities, including race/ethnicity, gender, social class, religion, age, sexual orientation, and abilities, shape who we are and how we view the world. All of us are multidimensional and experience the world, others, and ourselves in complex and dynamic ways. Part of our reality is influenced by our daily experiences with privilege, power, and prejudice. When we experience microaggressions that chip away at our self-image or bias that blocks our opportunities, our lives are diminished. When our privileges are unexamined and we lack complexity in our understanding of how power truly works and how we perpetuate bias and inequality even without trying, our connection to others is weakened.

With those definitions and assumptions, some related beliefs also need to be elucidated. We believe in multicultural competence and the attention it focuses on the need for all individuals to develop the multicultural awareness, knowledge, and skills necessary to work with individuals who are both culturally different and similar. However, whereas multiculturalism is essential to creating multicultural change in higher education, it is not enough. It is inadequate because of our tendency to either oversimplify complex concepts or to assume that everything is quantifiable or measurable. In reality, multiculturalism is a process and not a destination in terms of both developing our own multicultural competence and creating multicultural change on our campuses. Whether we are striving to increase the diversity on our campuses or address multicultural issues through our policies, procedures, or practices, these efforts take time and rarely unfold in a linear, always forward-moving trajectory. Additionally, when we discuss multicultural competence, the focus is often internal, including our level of individual awareness, knowledge, and skills. However, to create multicultural change, the focus must also be external and include topics such as campus climate, race relations on campus, recruitment, and social justice. Finding the right balance between ensuring that individuals have the requisite multicultural competence and providing adequate campus support, dedication, and infrastructure to create lasting multicultural change is essential.

The primary purpose of this book is to assist administrators and practitioners in their efforts to create multicultural change on their campuses. Specifically, it (1) offers a model of multicultural change for higher education practitioners who work in offices that directly serve students; (2) applies this model to individuals working at entry, mid-level, and senior-level positions at diverse types of institutions; and (3) presents specific examples of effective practice as well as provides useful case studies that will help practitioners apply MCOD theory to their work.

Audience

This book was created for higher education professionals, primarily those who work directly with students on a daily basis at college and university campuses across the country. *Creating Multicultural Change on Campus* is a practical text designed to provide insight, knowledge, and even some tools to help higher education administrators create effective and meaningful multicultural change on their campuses. This book is relevant for all higher education professionals and departments, especially those that directly serve students. Some of the essential offices (e.g., educational opportunity program [EOP], athletics, enrollment management, academic support) serving students are often left out of the campus conversations on creating multicultural change. That these offices become part of the dialogue and change efforts occurring on campuses across the country is essential for student success. This book will serve all levels of higher education professionals, from new and entry-level practitioners to senior administrators who work at diverse institutions that vary by size, location, type, and even investment in multicultural change. Higher education professionals also may use this book for their own personal or professional development to augment their own multicultural awareness, knowledge, and skills.

Likewise, this text may be useful for faculty members who teach multicultural classes or are involved in multicultural change efforts on their campuses. It is appropriate for graduate students enrolled in higher education administration or student affairs preparation programs. This book also may prove valuable for higher education or student affairs administration courses, particularly those focused on administration or strategic planning, which are attempting to infuse multicultural subject matter into course content. In addition, this book can be used in the diversity or multicultural courses that increasingly are being offered in student affairs and higher education administration programs.

Overview of the Book Content

This book is divided into three primary sections. Chapters 1 and 2 offer the conceptual and theoretical foundation on which the rest of the book rests. These chapters build a case for extending the important work of multicultural competence and offer MCOD as a powerful heuristic model for understanding, codifying, and creating multicultural change efforts on campus. Chapters 3 through 5 incorporate the framework of the MCIM and explore how to focus multicultural change efforts at the individual (Chapter 3), group (Chapter 4), and institutional (Chapter 5) levels. In this section each chapter begins with a few descriptive vignettes written to illustrate the realities of creating multicultural change at each level. Each of these chapters presents a theoretical framework or lens through which one can view multicultural change and then proceeds to explore the realities of the MCIM through a discussion of first-order and second-order change at that particular level (i.e., individual, group, institution). In addition to elucidating first- and second-order changes, the benefits and challenges to that specific type of change are addressed. Finally, a brief discussion of relevant competencies that are needed to create change and good practice exemplars are shared to round out each of these three chapters. Chapters 6 and 7 are the more applied portions of the book, offering principles, strategies, and tools for assessment and evaluation of multicultural interventions as well as concrete examples of successful multicultural change efforts already in place in different departments or divisions at three different institutions. Chapter 6 highlights the importance of assessment as part of the multicultural change process and provides examples of instruments and tools that can be used to evaluate multicultural issues on the individual, group, and institutional levels. Chapter 7, written by Timothy R. Ecklund and Matthew J. Weigand, is based on their extensive examination of the multicultural change practices of three distinct institutions. We are especially appreciative of their willingness to take the time out of their busy schedules to write a chapter in this book. When we decided we wanted some practitioners to take charge of this part of the book, we immediately thought of them, and we are so grateful for their dedication and the care they took. The purpose of these case examples is to help readers imagine how they might implement multicultural change on their own campuses and to illustrate some of the benefits and challenges of such interventions. The final chapter, Chapter 8, summarizes the key points, discusses the underlying themes of the book, and explores some of the inherent challenges and recommendations that are important to consider when enacting multicultural change on campus.

Acknowledgments

This book has been a collective effort, and its completion is the result of not only hard work but also the support and encouragement of many important people. First, we thank Erin Null, our editor at Jossey-Bass, with whom we have had the privilege to work on two different books in the past 10 years. Both Erin Null and Alison Knowles have been there to support and encourage our work and were exceptionally patient with us at every stage of the process. We are also grateful to the scholars who served as reviewers and provided us with insightful and helpful feedback to make our book stronger. Caryn McTighe Musil was ever so gracious in agreeing to write the Foreword to this book. We value her deep commitment to multicultural and feminist issues in higher education across many years and appreciate her ability to share valuable insight and set the right tone for readers who decide to join us on this journey toward multicultural change.

Our interest in writing this book grew out of our experiences as faculty members, scholars, and even consultants over the past ten years. As we explored multicultural change efforts on college and university campuses, we have come in contact with so many colleagues and students who have contributed to our own multicultural awareness, knowledge, and skills. Their insights, reflections, questions, and experiences have shaped and deepened our understanding of multicultural change as well as the unique context of higher education. We thank all of our students, especially those at the University at Buffalo, Indiana University of Pennsylvania, Teachers College—Columbia University, and Fordham University, who have given so much to us. A special heartfelt thanks to all of the students on our research teams over the past 10 years who have contributed hours of work and dedication to our various research projects, which has made it possible for us to continue our scholarly efforts. We wish that we could list all of your names and let the world know how appreciative we are, but limited space and fear that we would leave someone out prevent us from doing that. Please know that you are an important part of this effort.

Just as our work has benefited from the contributions and commitment of our students, we would be remiss if we did not thank the many professional colleagues who have encouraged and supported us for many years. Many scholars in higher education have studied issues of culture, race, gender, sexual orientation, and oppression. Their work has influenced us both personally and professionally. Some have been our mentors, some have worked with us side by side, and even more we have never met but still have greatly influenced us. We are also very appreciative of the many colleagues and friends that we have met through our work in professional associations, such as the American College Personnel Association (ACPA) and the National Association of Student Personnel Administrators (NASPA), who are so passionate about multicultural change in higher education. Your commitment and contributions inspire us to continue our efforts.

Finally, we are forever grateful to our families and friends, who have been there by our sides encouraging, supporting, and even challenging us so that we could continue to learn and grow about multicultural issues not just as professionals but also as human beings.

We have no illusions that we have all the answers about how to create multicultural campuses. The process is long and complex, and so many factors contribute to our successes and failures. It is not possible for any one book or model to completely transform higher education. We do hope, however, that the ideas and ideals shared in this book contribute to your own thinking about multicultural change in higher education and in that way make a difference.

ABOUT THE AUTHORS

Raechele L. Pope is an associate professor in the Higher Education program in the Department of Educational Leadership and Policy at the University of Buffalo. In the past several years she received the National Association of Student Personnel Administrators (NASPA) Robert H. Shaffer Award for Academic Excellence as a Graduate Faculty Member and was recently chosen to be a Senior Scholar for the American College Personnel Association (ACPA). With over 30 years of experience in college student affairs, she has written numerous journal articles and book chapters on multicultural competence, multicultural organization development in higher education, and student development. Along with two colleagues, Dr. Amy L. Reynolds, and Dr. John A. Mueller, Dr. Pope is a coauthor of the book *Multicultural Competence in Student Affairs*, a Jossey-Bass bestseller. She is highly regarded as a speaker and consultant on multicultural issues on campus.

Amy L. Reynolds is an associate professor in the Department of Counseling, School, and Educational Psychology at the University at Buffalo. She is also the director of training for the combined doctoral program in Counseling Psychology and School Psychology. Dr. Reynolds received her master's in student personnel work and her doctorate in counseling psychology from Ohio State University and has been working in higher education as both a staff psychologist and professor for 25 years. Her work as a scholar, teacher, and consultant focuses on multicultural competence in counseling and student affairs as well as college mental health issues. She has published more than 45 journal articles and book chapters and made over 40 presentations at regional or national conferences. She coauthored *Multicultural Competence in Student Affairs* with two colleagues, Dr. Raechele L. Pope and Dr. John A. Mueller, and also wrote *Helping College Students: Developing Essential Skills for Student Affairs Practice*.

John A. Mueller is a professor in the Department of Student Affairs in Higher Education at Indiana University of Pennsylvania. He has worked in higher education for over 25 years, with practitioner and teaching experience at five institutions. Mueller is an active member and leader in the American College Personnel Association (ACPA) and has received several association awards, including Annuit Coeptis, Emerging Scholar, and Diamond Honoree. His publications, presentations, and service activities have focused primarily on issues of diversity, multiculturalism, and inclusion. He is a coauthor, along with Dr. Amy L. Reynolds and Dr. Raechele L. Pope, of the Jossey-Bass publication *Multicultural Competence in Student Affairs.*

I

MULTICULTURAL COMPETENCE AND MULTICULTURAL CHANGE

CREATING MULTICULTURAL CAMPUSES HAS BECOME an aspirational goal for many colleges and universities today. However, moving beyond aspirations to actual concrete steps can be a rather challenging task. When asked, most campus administrators acknowledge this quest for diversity (Levine & Cureton, 1998), yet few have the awareness, knowledge, or skills to achieve this laudable goal (Pope, Reynolds, & Mueller, 2004). "In light of the reality that colleges and universities are becoming more racially, ethnically, and culturally diverse, extensive knowledge of diversity issues and topics related to multiculturalism are vital for higher education and student affairs professionals" (Flowers, 2004, p. 3). During the past four decades, multicultural initiatives and change efforts have become abundant in higher education. Many institutions have developed specific programs, hired uniquely qualified professionals, and made changes to the curriculum to address multicultural issues; however, many of those efforts have been inconsistent, fragmented, reactive, and based on trial and error rather than relying on well-developed scholarship, assessment data, and leadership within the institution (Kezar & Eckel, 2008; Krishnamurthi, 2003; Pope, 1992; Smith, 2009; Williams, 2013).

Williams (2013), in his extensive research study of senior diversity officers at more than 700 diverse academic institutions, provides a snapshot of the current status of many diversity efforts on college and university campuses. His research focuses on higher education diversity capabilities that he views as vital to the development of a multicultural vision and strategy. His study found that while most campuses embrace general diversity planning strategies in which diversity is part of the campus mission statement or mentioned within some strategic or academic plans, few colleges and universities have created the commitment and infrastructure of more robust, substantial, and concrete campus diversity plans. Additionally, most campuses are not engaged in intensive or extensive accountability efforts to ensure campus-wide investment in the multicultural change effort. Instead, what often happens is that particular individuals or offices are responsible for specific diversity goals. Almost half of all campuses studied by Williams have used diversity training and education programs to educate their employees; however, senior administrators and faculty members rarely participate in such training. Although engaging in campus-wide conversations on diversity is necessary, it is not sufficient without a broader effort toward accountability. Likewise, despite the emphasis on assessment at many colleges and universities (Pope, Reynolds, & Mueller, 2004), few campuses engage in meaningful and rigorous assessments or research studies to ensure that their multicultural change efforts are having the desired effect.

Remember that these multicultural initiatives are part of a longer trajectory toward diversity within higher education. "Contrary to popular belief, the deliberate, conscious effort to achieve greater student diversity on our campuses was not born in the 1960s. In fact, it reaches back to the mid-nineteenth century, when issues of racial, ethnic, and other forms of diversity were no less volatile in American life than they are today" (Rudenstine, 2001, p. 32). Fast-forward to the mid-twentieth century and the same issues of access and equity were still the centerpieces of diversity efforts on campus (Chang, 2005; Smith, 2009). Although legal battles ultimately shaped the outcome of many of these access and equity endeavors, the aftershocks of those fights remain and have evolved into ongoing conversations, sometimes debates, about curriculum, campus climate, student success, and institutional multicultural efforts (Smith, 2009). As the student body became more diverse in recent decades, many college administrators began to address issues of climate, which led to programmatic interventions and the creation of diversity-related offices (e.g., Office of Multicultural Affairs) whose task was to integrate underrepresented students into the overall student body. This dynamic also led to the growth of many student groups or organizations whose purpose was to provide support and educate the broader campus on diversity issues. Yet, even as the student body diversified, the overall culture of higher education often has not changed, frequently leading to high attrition and low satisfaction (Rankin & Reason, 2005). "While our campuses often look more diverse . . . that appearance is misleading and can camouflage the concerns that emerge as one looks deeper into the institution" (Smith, 2009, p. 254). Despite this apparent diversity, many students still sit with their own racial groups and rarely develop *deep* friendships with members of another race, attend cultural functions with other races, or meet other meaningful multicultural markers (Stearns, Buchmann, & Bonneau, 2009). Instead, many students of color, lesbian, gay, bisexual, and transgender (LGBT) students, and religious minorities continue to report feeling isolated, harassed, singled out, and unwelcome (Rankin & Reason, 2005).

This enduring reality led many campuses to create or expand retention efforts for underrepresented students and the recruitment of diverse faculty in hopes of halting the revolving door. Although many colleges and universities have focused on retention, with limited programmatic efforts and minimal institutional strategic planning focused on multicultural issues, extensive research evidence was generated that helped to build the case for admitting underrepresented students because of the educational value of a diverse student body (e.g., Antonio, Chang, Hakuta, Kenny, Levin, & Milem, 2004; Gurin, Dey, Hurtado, & Gurin, 2002; Hu & Kuh, 2003; Hurtado, Dey, Gurin, & Gurin, 2003; Milem, Chang, & Antonio, 2005; Orfield, 2001). This scholarly direction, which became the crux of the argument supporting affirmative action in college admission cases before the Supreme Court in 2003, moved the conversation away from the notion that campuses should embrace diversity because it was the right thing to do. Instead, the new diversity rationale began to focus on the educational, social, and economic benefits of a culturally diverse student body (Chang, 2005; Chang, Chang, & Ledesma, 2005; Gurin & Nagda, 2006).

History of Diversity Efforts in Higher Education

In her review of the past forty years of diversity efforts in higher education, Smith (2009) identified two important themes: "great change and great unfinished business" (p. 80). From her vantage point, great change included "changing demographics, the increasing calls for inclusiveness in higher education, the expanding accountability mandates, and the growing understanding of the multiplicity of perspectives concerning identity" (p. 132). Marchesani and Jackson (2005) offered a historical analysis of multicultural change efforts that highlighted four common response patterns. First, a crisis-driven social diversity and social justice agenda has often been the fulcrum of change efforts in higher education, leading to unresolved concerns and long-standing problems. Second, many change efforts have focused on increasing underrepresented student groups, with little attention paid to increasing underrepresented faculty and staff members or educating dominant members of the community about their privilege or contribution to the multicultural challenges facing the institution. The third response pattern is that most change efforts target individual behavior change rather than systemic structures that perpetuate monocultural values and practices. This has led to what Miller and Katz (2002) call "diversity in a box," in which "diversity activities are pre-packaged, one-size-fits-all training exercises strictly relating to differences between people" (p. 28). Finally, the reality is that for many institutions, the individuals personally committed to creating multicultural change often exist at the margins of power within the organization. They attempt to intervene and advocate, but with limited power and influence, their efforts are often short-lived and have limited effect.

Chang (2005) suggested that whereas early diversity efforts focused almost exclusively on race and ethnicity, current discussions and interventions incorporate a very dynamic and growing collection of identities and concerns, which create challenges for many institutions. Many campus leaders are hesitant and unsure of the complexity of all these changes and often are unable to fully substantiate that their diversity efforts have made an actual difference on their campuses. This reality has led to increased calls for assessment and accountability as well as a push for heightened institutional leadership (Aguirre & Martinez, 2002; Harper & Hurtado, 2007; Kezar & Eckel, 2008; Smith & Parker, 2005). This is part of the unfinished business identified as Smith's second theme: Diversity is no longer enough; rather, "creating the conditions under which diversity thrives will be critical to institutional success" (p. 132). Diversity as an end goal is shortsighted; instead, viewing diversity as a source of excellence within higher education has become the new direction (Williams, 2013).

How Campuses Deal with Multicultural Issues

Understanding how multicultural issues are conceptualized and addressed is essential to the process of creating multicultural campuses. First, campus leaders must undertake the task of grasping the reality of the multicultural enterprise, from recruitment to curricular changes to programmatic efforts, on their campuses on a daily basis. The need to increase the primacy of numerical or structural diversity in higher education is a well-established fact (Kezar & Eckel, 2007; Smith, 2009). The diversity of students continues to expand; more students of color, international students, older students, and first-generation college students attend college every year. In addition, other subgroups of students (e.g., students with disabilities, LGBT students) who were previously invisible are increasingly active and vocal on campus (Pope & Mueller, 2011; Pope, Mueller, & Reynolds, 2009). Research has demonstrated that increasing diversity on campus has both positive and negative consequences. Positive effects, such as enhanced student engagement, measurable educational outcomes, and comprehensive academic success, have been broadly reported (Antonio, Chang, Hakuta, Kenny, Levin, & Milem, 2004; Gurin, Dey, Hurtado, & Gurin, 2002; Harper, 2008; Hu & Kuh, 2003; Hurtado, Dey, Gurin, & Gurin, 2003; Milem, Chang, & Antonio, 2005); however, as suggested by Smith, increasing campus diversity alone is inadequate. According to Castellanos, Gloria, Mayorga, and Salas (2007), "increasing the numerical representation of diversity is insufficient to actualize substantive changes in the practice, policy, and even attitudes within university infrastructure" (p. 644). Without attention to the campus climate and campus-wide multicultural initiatives, positive effects may be unsustainable and sometimes even harmful to subgroups of students attending (Chang, 2007; Milem, Chang, & Antonio, 2005). Chang and others (e.g., Harper, 2008; Hu & Kuh, 2003; Hurtado, Dey, Gurin, & Gurin, 2003) have suggested that increased diversity without meaningful multicultural programs and initiatives in place can, in fact, reinforce or increase stereotyping, racial microaggressions, discrimination, self-segregation, toxic racial climate, and student resistance to diversity. Therefore, *how* higher education addresses the increasing diversity and manages the challenges and opportunities such diversity brings is likely more important than merely increasing the structural diversity; in fact, such efforts may determine a campus's ability to achieve success as an institution (Smith, 2009).

In addition to exploring how campuses engage with increased diversity, focusing on what effect the campus environment has on all college students and their ability to function and thrive in the increasingly interconnected and diverse world has become gradually more important in the rationale for diversity (Deardorff, 2011; Musil, 1996; Smith, 2009). Bok (2006) and others (Cox, 2001; Deardorff, 2011) strongly suggest that one of the essential roles of higher education in this global society is to matriculate students who have the sensitivity, knowledge, and skills to effectively work with and contribute to the ever-changing marketplace. According to Musil, "For higher education, then, diversity is, above all, a challenge that demands we rethink how we educate students and for what ends; how we define our scholarship, our disciplines, and our departments; and how we organize our educational communities, both within our institutions and in relation to the local and larger communities of which we are a part" (p. 222). Not only have corporations been addressing diversity issues and their impact on the bottom line for much longer than educational institutions, they have been pressuring colleges and universities for several decades to improve their efforts to educate a student body that is multiculturally competent, composed of effective critical thinkers, and motivated to work in an increasingly changing, expanding, and demanding global reality (Association of American Colleges and Universities, 1995; Bowser & Baker, 1995; Deardorff, 2011; King & Baxter Magolda, 2005). Such a task is well within the purview of higher education and, as Smith, Wolf, and Levitan (1994) suggest, "preparing students for the world in which they live and work has long been the role of the American colleges and universities" (p. 10).

This task of creating an effective learning environment where students can gain personal insight and gather knowledge about the world around them has fallen on the shoulders of higher education academics and administrators alike. Whether driven by faculty-designed curriculum or out-of-classroom experiences created by student affairs staff and other higher education administrators, every campus has the opportunity to assist students in the development of the essential awareness, knowledge, and skills to be successful in our increasingly complex and diverse world. Although it has often been the responsibility of student affairs professionals to specifically address multicultural issues on campus (Pope, Reynolds, & Mueller, 2004), the obligation is certainly not theirs alone (Howard-Hamilton, Cuyjet, & Cooper, 2011). In the past, multicultural experts whose job it was to ensure access and success of students of color and other underrepresented students on campus (e.g., educational opportunity programs [EOPs], multicultural affairs, women's centers) often led the multicultural efforts. However, Pope, Reynolds, and Mueller made the case that all professionals working in higher education need to develop multicultural competence to create and implement meaningful and efficacious multicultural initiatives. As long as only a few experts are responsible for addressing multicultural issues on campus, lasting and consequential multicultural change is unlikely to occur. Likewise, until a broader array of campus faculty, staff, and administrators, who directly serve the needs of students, take on the mantle of diversity, colleges and universities will continue to address multicultural issues in narrow, fragmented, and often crisis-driven ways (Smith, 2009; Williams, 2008). Because most multicultural student services units remain the responsibility of student affairs, many multicultural change efforts fail to cross that indiscernible barrier into academic affairs or spread throughout the entire campus (Pope, Reynolds, & Mueller, 2004; Williams, 2013).

Williams (2008) suggests, "Many institutional diversity initiatives are largely symbolic and fail to deeply influence organizational culture and institutional behavior" (pp. 27–28). According to Petitt and McIntosh (2011), Williams and Wade-Golden (2007), and Kezar and Eckel (2008), until college presidents get actively engaged with multicultural issues and demand accountability, multicultural campus efforts will flounder. In an effort to move beyond this piecemeal approach, "a new era has clearly begun with college campuses creating administrative positions— such as chief diversity officer—that assist with the promotion, creation, development, and assessment of diversity initiatives on campus" (Howard-Hamilton, Cuyjet, & Cooper, 2011, p. 18). Often tenured faculty members hold these positions, and their presence on the cabinets of many college presidents implies a level of institutional importance (Williams & Wade-Golden, 2007). Barcelo (2007) suggests that the increasing visibility of these new positions "indicates an acceptance of diversity as a reality of this century, and an acceptance of the opportunity to bring diversity from the margins to the center of campus" (p. 5). This "increased institutional commitment to diversity" (Petitt & McIntosh, 2011, p. 202) is essential for realigning the centrality of multicultural change efforts. Through accountability measures, campus-wide leadership, strategic planning, and institutionalized approaches to diversity, more opportunities exist than ever before for the development of campus climates that affirm all students.

Why Many Multicultural Change Efforts Fail

Before implementing campus diversity efforts or initiating multicultural programs, one must understand why many diversity plans either fail or stagnate. Williams (2008) suggested that most campuses initiate multicultural change efforts after a crisis, which may increase the likelihood that they will return to their old institutional practices and models twelve to eighteen months after such a watershed moment. "To advance the agenda of diversity, institutions that truly value diversity must move toward considering wholesale changes in their underlying structures and day to day activities" (Brayboy, 2003, p. 74); however, many institutions seem unable or unwilling to make the unwavering commitment that leads to true institutional change (Williams, 2013). Williams, Berger, and McClendon (2005) identified specific reasons for why many diversity efforts fail, including an inability to view diversity work as essential to excellence; minimal levels of consistent support from senior leadership; inadequate resources; and the absence of a unifying framework for conceptualizing diversity, tracking progress, and engaging all members of the campus community.

Part of the resistance to multicultural change is also based in the inherent power differences that exist in higher education. Reed and Peet (2005) suggest that "any change tends to surface unspoken and often unrecognized unexamined beliefs as well as culture and power-related issues within an organization and among participants that can either facilitate or impede desired changes and learning" (p. 476). If institutional resistance is not addressed and limited efforts are made to garner support for lasting institutional change, multicultural change efforts will likely fail.

Chang, Chang, and Ledesma (2005) provided additional caution about the challenges facing diversity efforts in higher education. When examining Justice Powell's reasoning for the Michigan affirmative action cases, they suggest, "the educational benefits of diversity seem to him [Powell] to just magically and organically occur if the right ingredients and environment are present" (p. 13). In particular, it has been assumed that cross-cultural contact and engagement would automatically create enhanced relationships and openness to diversity. However, much like in horticulture, planting different types of seeds in the same soil does not automatically make them all sprout. Each plant needs the proper environment and climate and must be continuously nurtured if it is to grow. The same is true for college students, and assuming that increasing structural diversity alone will be enough is overly simplistic. Many in positions of leadership easily succumb to this type of magical thinking, resulting in limited vision and a lack of appreciation of the herculean effort needed to create sustainable and meaningful multicultural change in higher education.

Contextual Realities of Multicultural Change Efforts

Attending to the realities and unique context of each institution is also essential to any diversity effort. One size does not fit all. Such attention to context must occur at both the micro and macro levels. Although increasing calls have been made for institution-wide diversity efforts rather than reliance on narrow and piecemeal attempts to address multicultural issues (e.g., Aguirre & Martinez, 2002; Harper & Antonio, 2008; Kezar & Eckel, 2008; Smith & Parker, 2005), some scholars stress the importance of attending to the specific and unique realities of environmental context. For example, Williams (2008) does not support a unified and universal approach to diversity on campus; rather, he advocates for a decentralized approach to diversity plans, suggesting that most campus-wide efforts are unable to adequately deal with the decentralized nature of higher education. Many campus-wide efforts "fail to burrow deep into the culture and overcome institutional resistance, to accrue sufficient buy-in for the change vision, to place accountability with the right people, or to develop strategies that match the environmental context in which campus change efforts must occur" (p. 30). However, rather than merely focusing on narrow domains within a campus, Williams also suggests that campuses combine centralized diversity planning with decentralized efforts that require individual divisions, colleges, and schools to develop and introduce their own plans that will supplement and enhance the campus-wide efforts. According to Williams, "The challenge is to develop an approach that will create strategic consistency and, at the same time, allow for freedom, individuality, and creativity in the planning and implementation process" (p. 30).

Using approaches that encourage individual campuses to apply lessons regarding multicultural change in higher education to their unique circumstances is also important. Different realities and environmental contexts exist in distinctive regions of the country as well as across various types of institutions. When contemplating diversity, often the campus setting (e.g., rural, urban, suburban) and region of the country shape the opportunities and challenges facing different institutions. Urban campuses often serve a very different student body than do rural or suburban campuses, and their goals and missions reflect those differences. For example, many rural and suburban areas are generally racially homogeneous and predominantly white. However, many inner city environments are equally homogeneous, with an abundance of people of color and fewer white individuals present in many urban neighborhoods. In fact, most college students arrive on campus having attended racially homogeneous high schools with limited experiences and opportunities to interact with and form meaningful relationships with individuals who represent different races and ethnicities (Moody, 2001; Orfield, Bachmeier, James, & Eitle, 1997; Quillian & Campbell, 2003). The different realities of these rural, urban, and suburban settings ultimately shape the culture of a campus. Similarly, in certain regions of the United States (e.g., Midwest), there is limited racial diversity; however, the types of racial diversity that exist on both coasts and in much of the southwest and southeast regions can differ significantly.

For example, there are higher concentrations of Latino/as on the west coast, southwest, southeast, and along the northeast coastal areas. However, in each of those areas there are different Latino/a subgroups (e.g., Cuban, Guatemalan, Puerto Rican, and Chicano/a), whose history and culture influence the region. Because the enrollment of many institutions of higher education is drawn from their surrounding region, attending to these issues is quite important. Additionally, certain areas of the country and different settings have more immigrants, openly LGBT individuals, and nontraditional students. Without knowledge of the unique circumstances of those who live in the surrounding community and who enroll at their institutions, these campuses will be less effective in their diversity efforts.

The type of institution (e.g., mission, primary populations served) likely has an impact on a campus and should be addressed when conceptualizing and implementing various diversity efforts. Historically black colleges and universities, tribal colleges, women's colleges, and institutions serving high numbers of Hispanic and Asian students all have unique missions based on the primary population they serve. However, they also serve other students on their campuses representing different races, ethnicities, and genders. Addressing the needs of white students on campuses whose charters focus on students of color creates unique challenges and issues. Additionally, within-group differences that exist for the predominant racial groups on these campuses also must receive consideration. Far too often we focus our efforts on differences between groups. Attending to issues of nationality, gender, ethnicity, religion, social class, sexuality, and other issues that exist within a particular group creates ongoing opportunities for powerful conversations that add depth and complexity to our understanding of diversity. Having a strategic multicultural plan that addresses how these campuses intend to address diversity on a structural and strategic level is no less vital than it is on a predominantly white coeducational campus. However, the specific goals and methods used likely will differ. Similarly, religiously based colleges and universities have values that shape their policies and practices and may affect how they relate to and accommodate LGBT students, for example. One size does not fit all; therefore, when discussing how to incorporate multicultural issues, campus leaders must attend to the unique context of their campus. If, as Hale (2004) purports and research supports, "students do best at institutions that mirror themselves, their culture, and their interests" (p. 18), then much work needs to be done.

These contextual realities can be illuminated by the Astin (1993) Inputs, Environments, and Outputs (IEO) model. Astin's model offers a framework for understanding the various inputs, environments, and outputs that shape and are shaped by the college experience. Inputs involve the diverse demographic background, knowledge, and life experiences that students bring to campus. Environment constitutes those experiences students have while in college that also affect them. Finally, outputs or outcomes are those results (e.g., knowledge, awareness, values, characteristics) that students exit with when they graduate from college. The unique environment where students attend college must be computed as part of the overall equation because it has a profound effect on the outcome of their college experience as well as the overall culture of the campus (Cuyjet, 2011; Strange & Banning, 2001), and administrators and leaders must focus on these issues if they want to create change.

Regardless of unique challenges and strengths resulting from the type of institution and its region of the country, many scholars have suggested that "leadership is perhaps the most important factor in ensuring institutional transformation and institutionalizing a diversity agenda" (Kezar & Eckel, 2008, p. 380). Yet, as suggested by Kezar and Carducci (2009), such leadership has to be carefully developed and actively nurtured. Leaders in higher education, both academic and administrative, need both informal experiences and explicit training opportunities to develop the essential multicultural competence to introduce, plan, and implement effective multicultural initiatives. As Pope, Reynolds, and Mueller (2004) have suggested, enhancing competence among leaders at all levels of higher education to include multicultural awareness, knowledge, and skills is crucial to creating educational environments that fully embrace diversity. Given that "professionals at every level of each position are faced daily with multicultural issues, concerns, and dynamics that affect their work" (Pope & Mueller, 2011, pp. 348–349), providing practitioners within higher education with the concrete insight, understanding, and tools to address these issues on both a personal and professional level must be a commitment made by all institutions. However, as Williams (2013) suggests, despite the abundance of multicultural efforts, few high-level administrators and faculty members receive multicultural training.

Connecting Multicultural Change and Multicultural Competence

Understanding what constitutes multicultural competence and how to achieve this fundamental collection of awareness, knowledge, and skills is essential to meaningful multicultural leadership on campus today. Multicultural competence, based on seminal works in the field of counseling psychology (e.g., Pedersen, 1988; Sue et al., 1982), has been defined as the specific "awareness, knowledge, and skills needed to work with others who are culturally different from self in meaningful, relevant, and productive ways" (Pope, Reynolds, & Mueller, 2004, p.13). Extending the tripartite model of multicultural competence in counseling, Pope and Reynolds (1997) specified a list of 33 competencies that would be useful for student affairs practitioners wanting to enhance their ability to serve the needs of all students and address multicultural issues on campus.

This characterization of multicultural competence has grown and developed over the past thirty years to incorporate a broader appreciation of what *multicultural* means (i.e., incorporating issues of social class, gender identity and expression, sexual orientation, and others into the initial conversations, which primarily focused on race) as well as the inclusion of additional components such as how multicultural issues and dynamics affect relationships (Sodowsky, Taffe, Gutkin, & Wise, 1994) and multicultural advocacy (Sue, 2001). Some scholars have further detailed what constitutes multicultural competence in a higher education context (e.g., Howard-Hamilton, Richardson, & Shuford, 1998; Iverson, 2012; King & Baxter-Magolda, 2005), whereas others have focused more on how to create multicultural competence among college students or staff (e.g., Cheng & Zhao, 2006; Einfeld & Collins, 2008; Kelly & Gayles, 2010).

Although a more thorough exploration of multicultural competence in student affairs and higher education has occurred elsewhere, having a basic understanding of the core constructs underlying multicultural competence is helpful in conceptualizing multicultural change efforts in higher education. Most commonly, multicultural competence has been described as consisting of three necessary components: awareness, knowledge, and skills. Multicultural awareness involves the essential attitudes, values, biases, and assumptions that each of us carries with us, whether we realize it or not, that influence our worldview. Our ability to be aware of diversity and our comfort with that awareness is shaped by our upbringing, education, and life experiences. Our worldview is fundamental to how we view the world around us, others, and ourselves. Of course, this lens cannot help but influence our assumptions, beliefs, and expectations for multicultural change on campus. Multicultural awareness is often viewed as personal and interpersonal in nature (Pope, Reynolds, & Mueller, 2004); however, some perceive their attitudes and values in a more intellectual manner. In addition to multicultural awareness, multicultural knowledge is another key component of multicultural competence.

Multicultural knowledge is our intellectual understanding or content knowledge about various cultural groups and specific multicultural constructs. This knowledge, which includes facts and information, can be obtained through books, media, relationships, and even life experiences. Unfortunately, for many of us the various sources of our knowledge may lack diversity and complexity, which diminishes our ability to know and understand others. Ironically, the self-segregation that often occurs in higher education and society as a whole can limit our knowledge rather than expand it (Chang, 2007). Multicultural knowledge also includes information about important constructs such as acculturation, oppression, identity, social justice, and privilege, which ultimately affect our understanding of others who are different from us. Without in-depth understanding of ourselves and an equally thorough appreciation of the realities of others, it is too easy to assume that our own experiences are the norm or the reality for others. This is especially true for individuals who have not examined the privileges they have as a result of their membership in various identity groups. This reality exists not only for those individuals who occupy places of privilege because of their race or gender (e.g., white men or women) but also for individuals who often view themselves as only having targeted identities (e.g., LGBT people of color or women with disabilities). None of us is completely privileged or completely targeted. Rather, we all occupy multiple locations and identities that have the potential to interfere with our ability to reflect on our reality or assumptions about the world.

Finally, multicultural skills include the ability to apply our multicultural awareness and knowledge to our interactions, interventions, and our daily lives. How do we relate to and interact with individuals whose culture and life experiences are so very different from our own? Rather than assuming all interventions have universal appeal, how do we determine which activities, programs, or opportunities resonate with which groups? First, we must recognize that we may need a broader array of skills and then we need to have diverse experiences so we can learn those skills.

When exploring multicultural competence, one must understand that all individuals—regardless of whether they are members of groups that are often the target of societal discrimination or microaggressions or groups that are born with privileges based on race, class, gender, and other social identities—need to evaluate and explore their level of multicultural awareness, knowledge, and skills. Multicultural competence is not just about understanding the other; it is also about working with issues of race, gender, and sexual orientation with people like ourselves and increasing our understanding of within-group differences. For example, white men need to explore their race and their gender by working with other white men; just as Native American women can further their self-understanding by digging deeper into their relationships with other Native American women. The multifaceted nature of the values, identity, and life experiences of most individuals means that expanding our multicultural awareness, knowledge, and skills is inherently a complex and dynamic process.

Understanding multicultural competence is important because it has become the foundation on which many training efforts and educational programming for students, staff, administrators, and even faculty have been based. A brief review of the scholarly work on multicultural competence in student affairs and higher education indicates that demographics as well as multicultural education and experience variables seem to influence multicultural competence levels. Demographic categories such as race as well as identification as a member of a socially marginalized cultural group have been shown to affect multicultural competence (Mueller & Pope, 2001, Weigand, 2005; Wilson, 2011). Additionally, multiculturally oriented education, supervision, and life experiences also have predicted multicultural competence across a variety of studies (King & Howard-Hamilton, 2003; Miklitsch, 2006; Mueller & Pope, 2001; Weigand, 2005). Although many of these scholars suggest that the multicultural competence of individual leaders within higher education is a necessary prerequisite to ethical, efficacious, and multiculturally relevant practices at colleges and universities, such competence may not be sufficient to create truly multicultural campuses (Pope, Reynolds, & Mueller, 2004).

Multicultural competence is not the panacea to all multicultural challenges facing campuses today, but it can serve as a transformational tool or vital construct used to reshape and change individuals, groups, and organizational units (e.g., programs, departments, divisions) within higher education. The development of multicultural competence can occur at the micro level, focusing on the individual or group, as well as the macro level, or institutional efforts to develop multicultural competence among the students, staff, administrators, and faculty members of an institution (Flash, 2010a). Within diverse fields such as psychology, education, organization development, and medicine, there are growing discussions on creating change on the individual, group, and organizational levels.

Discussions on changing the individual have received much attention within the medical field of health psychology, often when exploring health conditions such as obesity or diabetes or encouraging healthy behavior such as smoking cessation (e.g., Prochaska et al., 1994; Zimmerman, Olsen, & Bosworth, 2000) or in the broader counseling profession, where change is often viewed as central to the goals or desired outcomes of therapy (Good & Beitman, 2006; Prochaska & Norcross, 2009). For example, motivational interviewing, which is a directive counseling approach focused on creating behavioral change, has been successful in treating addictions, mood disorders, and other psychological concerns (Burke, 2011). Research has shown that the more individuals discuss their needs, desires, ability, and commitment to change, the more likely they are to actually change (Miller & Rose, 2009; Prochaska, Norcross, & DiClemente, 2007). The transtheoretical model of behavior change, first introduced by DiClemente and Prochaska (1998), describes the stages that individuals traverse as they consider change (Passmore, 2011). The insights provided by these models and related research have meaningful implications for creating multicultural change on the individual level and will be explored in more depth later in this book. Creating such personal changes not only will alter how individuals view the world, themselves, and others, but also will likely profoundly influence how they relate to and interact with others on both personal and professional levels. Additionally, further discussion is needed to explore how this information and insight can be applied to program planning (e.g., workshops, programs, trainings) and curriculum across campus.

In addition to individual change, focusing on groups and how change occurs in that context has received much attention within the counseling and organization development fields. Yalom and Corey are just two of the group theorists who have offered models for understanding how change or action occurs on the group level. Yalom and Leszcz (2005) identify therapeutic factors that influence the change process at the group level. Although some of these factors may not seem immediately relevant to creating and sustaining change on a group level within a higher education context, some factors, such as group cohesion, universality, or interpersonal learning, are very applicable. Given that the change process is inherently complex and often complicated, having an understanding of the factors influencing groups is highly important and meaningful. Other theorists, such as Tuckman (1965) or Corey (2011), have focused more specifically on the developmental stages experienced by groups. Whether it is Tuckman's model (forming, storming, norming, performing, adjourning) or Corey's exploration of how the various phases of the group (forming, initial stage, transition stage, working stage, ending stage) influence group dynamics, their work has been applied to both counseling and organization development work. Research exploring group dynamics in a multicultural context within higher education has been expanding in recent years through exploration of the factors influencing change and group climate within intergroup dialogue programs and other group interventions in higher education (Miles & Kivlighan, 2012; Sorensen, Nagda, Gurin, & Maxwell, 2009).

Although exploring individual and group change has often been found in counseling-related literature, addressing issues of organizational or institutional change has typically occurred within the fields of management, business, or industrial or organizational psychology. The theories used for such work have been roundly criticized for being overly conceptual and lacking empirical evidence (Prochaska, Prochaska, & Levesque, 2001). Given the complex nature of organizational and institutional change, it is vital that such efforts move beyond theorizing to proposing and evaluating the theoretical constructs underlying such change. Whether the goal is developing a multicultural organization (Cox, 2001) or a multiculturally competent organization (Wilcox & McCray, 2005), growing literature is available on the tools, strategies, and models for multicultural change in organizations and institutions. Specifically, when focusing on creating multicultural change on the institutional level within higher education, Pope (1993) and others such as Grieger (1996) and Flash (2010a) have argued for the use of multicultural organization development (MCOD) theory as the mechanism and strategy for change. According to Wilcox and McCray, "to move an organization toward multicultural competence, the organization may need to create new policies, practices, and internal structures that support and advance cultural diversity" (p. 83). MCOD practices include targeting mission, leadership, policies, recruitment and retention, multicultural competence expectations and training, student activities and services, and physical environment and ensuring that multicultural issues are being adequately addressed at all levels of the organization or institution (Grieger, 1996).

The purpose of this book is to provide higher education professionals with the awareness, knowledge, and skills they need to help create multicultural change on college and university campuses. To achieve such a goal, it is essential to understand the available and viable theories, tools, and strategies. Learning from, enhancing, and extending existing theories and models, such as multicultural competence or multicultural organization development, is an important first step in the process. Previously we have written about multicultural competence as essential to creating multicultural campuses. Flash (2010a) suggested viewing multicultural competence as needed on both individual and organizational levels. From her perspective, organizational multicultural competence uses assessment/evaluation, strategic planning, and training/education programing to expand talent, awareness, knowledge, and skills to build a capacity for multiculturalism within organizations. The goal of this book is to create a deeper understanding of the strategies and practices that are essential for creating campus environments that are inclusive, welcoming, and affirming for all who work, teach, and learn in colleges and universities.

2

MULTICULTURAL ORGANIZATION DEVELOPMENT (MCOD)

OUR UNDERSTANDING OF DIVERSITY AS well as our approaches and strategies for addressing multicultural issues in higher education have evolved significantly during the past fifty years. Most colleges and universities began to diversify, in many cases reluctantly, in the late 1960s and 1970s (e.g., women were not admitted to Princeton and Yale until the late 1960s; Williams College, Johns Hopkins, and Duke, in early 1970; and Amherst, Columbia, and Harvard in the late 1970s). In the 1980s, they continued to diversify, motivated primarily by compliance and affirmative action. In the 1990s, campuses began to tentatively embrace multiculturalism as the right thing to do, and since then they have been grappling with how to best create truly multicultural campuses amidst resistant institutional structures, dwindling popular and political support, and mounting legal battles. The evolution has been spurred, at least in part, by changing demographics, campus discontent, public scrutiny, globalization, fiscal pressure, and most often, public furor over campus incidents or crises.

In addition to these evolving environmental influences, research has provided compelling reasons to diversify the college campus. During the last several decades, research has suggested that increased structural diversity (campus population) and enhanced multicultural understanding reduce prejudice and have a positive effect on the academic, cognitive, and interpersonal skills of college students (c.f., Chang, 2001; Gurin, Dey, Hurtado, & Gurin, 2002; Hurtado, Dey, Gurin, & Gurin, 2003; King & Shuford, 1996; Williams, 2013).

Despite the evidence supporting the educative value of creating multicultural campuses, efforts to create such campuses are sporadic, fragmented, and uncoordinated, and the results are, at best, uneven (Cheatham, 1991; Pope, 1993; Pope, Reynolds, & Mueller, 2004; Smith & Parker, 2005). Williams (2013) suggested, "Academic institutions are recognizing that diversity success should no longer reflect a mix of good will and haphazard, disconnected efforts" (p. 13). Acknowledging the need for cohesive diversity efforts, Pope, Reynolds, and Mueller (2004) advocated for systemic approaches and innovative constructs and tools to create multicultural campuses. They suggested that despite decades of diversity programs and individuals hired to manage these programs, campuses remain essentially monocultural, offering an illusion of progress with little substantial movement. As Heath and Heath (2010) masterfully demonstrated, change is difficult, and resistance to change is nearly universal. To lessen resistance and move beyond the artifice of change or repetitive and perhaps ineffective efforts, it is vital that we fully understand the available systemic multicultural change constructs and models that are well suited to higher education.

Scholars such as Aguirre and Martinez (2002), Kezar (2007), Pope, Reynolds, and Mueller (2004), Smith and Parker (2005), Williams (2013), and others have identified intentional diversity leadership as crucial to the successful creation of multicultural campuses and have outlined specific practices to keep in mind as colleges and universities contemplate multicultural strategies. For example, for Williams, these principles include

> (1) Refine issues of diversity, equity, and inclusion as fundamental to the organizational bottom line of mission fulfillment and institutional excellence; (2) Focus on creating systems that enable all students, faculty, and staff to thrive and achieve their maximum potential; (3) Achieve a more robust and integrated diversity approach that builds on prior diversity models and operates in a strategic, evidence-based, and data-driven manner, where accountability is paramount; (4) Focus diversity-related efforts to intentionally transform the institutional culture, not just to make tactical moves that lead to poorly integrated efforts and symbolic implementation alone; and (5) Lead with a high degree of cultural intelligence and awareness of different identities and their significance in higher education. (p. 14)

The principles outlined by Williams highlight the necessity of relying on methods and approaches that are evidence based and data driven; however, many multicultural change efforts have used diversity-related strategies and tools that are not based in research and are atheoretical (Marshak & Grant, 2008; Pope, Reynolds, & Mueller 2004; Williams, 2013). Increasingly, however, multicultural scholars have been exploring various theories from the evolving field of organization development as a basis for understanding current multicultural change strategies and proposing fresh approaches to creating meaningful and lasting multicultural change (Aguirre & Martinez, 2002; Pope, 1993; Smith & Parker, 2005; Williams, 2013).

Historically, organization development (OD) techniques and theories were used to help organizations become more effective and efficient by focusing on planned systemic change (Chesler, 1994; Coyne, 1991). In fact, OD approaches were used "as a means for transforming the structure of [college] student affairs divisions to infuse theories of student development into the mainstream of the profession" (Pope, 1995, p. 237). With its emphasis on addressing fundamental organizational structures and processes as part of a strategic, system-wide effort to create organizational change, OD seems well suited for multicultural change efforts. However, consultants and scholars soon discovered that although OD theory and practice is invested in creating a more humane and affirming workplace, it remains "embedded in the dominant culture and retains the organizational values, goals, and practices which that culture produces" (Pope, p. 238). Even those organizations that embraced social justice or attempted to eradicate racism, sexism, or other inequities within the traditional organizational structure would not evolve without new tools, theories, and insights (Chesler, 1994; Jackson & Holvino, 1988; Pope, 1993, 1995). In reality, "traditional OD has fallen short in meeting the challenges of addressing diversity issues in organizations" (Flash, 2010a, p. 9).

In an effort to be more relevant and provide tools to create more diverse and responsive organizations, newer OD practices, often shaped by constructionist and postmodern theories, are altering how organizational change is viewed (Marshak & Grant, 2008). Chaos theory, self-organizing systems, organizational discourse, and other theories have been reshaping OD and have led to "increased emphasis on socially constructed realities, transforming mindset and consciousness, operating from multicultural realities, exploring different images and assumptions about change, and forging common social agreements from the multiple realities held by key constituencies" (Marshak & Grant, p. S10). Additionally, some empirically based theories, such as the transtheoretical model of change, which were historically focused on individual change, are now being applied as new ways to conceptualize and enact organizational change (Prochaska, Prochaska, & Levesque, 2001). Multicultural scholars, who embrace diverse theories and perspectives to conceptualize and develop multicultural change such as organizational learning or multicultural organization development (MCOD) (Jackson & Holvino, 1988; Pope, 1993, 1995; Smith & Parker, 2005), have also helped to shape and transform the OD field.

MCOD Theory

Jackson, Hardiman, and Holvino first proposed MCOD as a concept and theory for planned, systemic, and systematic multicultural change in the 1980s (Pope, 1993) and as a way to merge OD, social justice, and diversity (Jackson, 2005; Jackson & Hardiman, 1994). Because of the inability of OD to assist in the creation of a socially just workplace, they focused on expanding the assumptions, tools, and strategies of OD to assist organizations in becoming more multicultural. Jackson and Holvino (1988) highlighted the necessity of moving beyond the individual consciousness–raising strategy that was often the basis of "diversity training" within organizations. They suggested that MCOD could be used to create a comprehensive change effort that focused on the organization as a system rather than merely targeting the individuals within the system. Because MCOD "questions the underlying cultural assumptions and structures of organizations, as opposed to assuming that system change will be accompanied or followed by themes of social justice" (Pope, p. 203), it is better suited to eradicate or diminish the adverse nature of most monocultural organizations. This questioning leads to moving beyond celebration of diversity and explores any underlying patterns of discrimination, inequality, or oppression within the organizational structure (Chesler, 1994). According to Reynolds and Pope (2003), "MCOD encourages organizations and institutions to reexamine their beliefs, assess their practices, and transform how they work" (p. 374). Not only did Jackson and Holvino believe that organizations could not be effective and productive without embracing multicultural values and becoming more inclusive in their practices, they suggested that the true success of an organization was not possible without fully addressing multicultural issues.

MCOD theory, strategies, and practices have been suggested as the basis for multicultural change efforts within colleges and universities (Pope, 1993, 1995). Initially met with skepticism because of corporate roots and failure to acknowledge the environmental realities and structures in higher education, OD and MCOD strategies have evolved to more directly address the unique needs, systems, and structures within higher education (Jackson, 2005). Pope (1993) introduced a conceptual framework that extended the application of MCOD concepts to higher education and specifically to student affairs. Grieger (1996), Flash (2010a),

Pope (1995), Reynolds (1997), and Reynolds and Pope (2003) provide specific examples of how MCOD theory can be applied to curricular, programmatic, or assessment change efforts in higher education. According to Grieger, "multicultural organizational development (MOD) has been posited as a useful model for facilitating comprehensive long-term change for divisions of student affairs committed to transforming themselves into multicultural organizations" (p. 561). Further understanding of the principles of MCOD is needed to fully understand its potential as a mechanism of multicultural change within both student affairs and the broader higher education community.

What Is a Multicultural Organization?

Before attempting to create a multicultural organization, one must have an understanding of what that entails. Varied scholars have proposed a definition of a multicultural organization, which is the end goal of the MCOD process, but Grieger (1996) provides a thorough and meaningful definition that provides important insight:

> A multicultural organization: (a) is inclusive in composition of staff and constituencies served; (b) is diversity-positive in its commitment, vision, mission, values, processes, structure, policies, service delivery, and allocation of resources; (c) is permeated by a philosophy of social justice with decisions informed by consideration of ensuring fairness, ending oppression, and guaranteeing equal access to resources and opportunities for all groups; (d) regards diversity as an asset and values the contributions of all members; (e) values and rewards multicultural competencies, including diversity-positive attitudes, knowledge about salient aspects of diverse groups, and skills in interacting with and serving diverse groups effectively, sensitively, and respectfully; and (f) is fluid and responsive in adapting to ongoing diversity-related change. (pp. 563–564)

By articulating the end goal or multicultural organization vision, it becomes easier to plan and move forward. Jackson (2005) suggests it is important to fully embrace social justice *before* focusing on the structural diversity or numerical diversity of an organization. He further cautions, "Many have tried to move directly to social diversity objectives by building a climate of inclusion in the workplace without adequately attending to the absence of social justice (e.g., the existence of sexism, racism, classism, anti-Semitism, heterosexism, and other manifestations of social justice). The goal of becoming a [multicultural organization] MCO involves the achievement of both social justice, or an anti-exclusionary objective, and social diversity or an inclusion objective" (Jackson, p. 8).

MCOD Stages

Organizations and campuses are not simply monocultural or multicultural; instead, they exist on a continuum from one to the other (Jackson & Holvino, 1988). An effective diagnosis allows one to identify appropriate and meaningful goals and interventions for multicultural change. Several multicultural scholars have proposed or extended models of multicultural development that portray the process of transformation that moves an organization from monocultural to multicultural (e.g., Holvino, 2008; Jackson, 2005; Jackson & Hardiman, 1981; Jackson & Holvino, 1988; Katz, 1989; Katz & Miller, 1996; Loden, 1995; Sue, 1995). Although each model is somewhat unique, the underlying assumptions are similar. Jackson and Hardiman (1981) first developed the MCOD developmental stage model as an extension of their work on social identity development. The MCOD model (see Figure 2.1), more recently depicted in Jackson (2005), is developmental in nature, with three levels and six stages that progress sequentially, depending on the commitment of the organization and the environmental context. An organization is unlikely to occupy only one particular stage at a time, because change and growth are rarely linear. "In fact, in most large systems, it is typical to find divisions, departments, groups, or other single units in different places from each other and/or from the larger system with respect to their affinity for, or against, MCO goals for the educational system or campus" (Jackson, 2005, p. 8). The three stages are described as monocultural, nondiscriminating, and multicultural. The monocultural stage affirms and endorses the values and point of view of the dominant group (e.g., men, whites, Christians). The nondiscriminating stage involves making initial efforts to integrate others into the system or organization that is based on the dominant values. Finally, the multicultural stage is focused on embracing the perspectives of diverse individuals, cultures, and groups into a re-envisioned organization.

Jackson (2005) describes the six stages of the MCOD model focus in more depth. Within the monocultural stage or level, there are two distinct phases: exclusionary and passive club. The first phase (*the exclusionary system*) is intentionally and openly exclusive in the underlying values and norms of the organization. These organizations are less visible and more rare today, and this is especially true in higher education, which has a long history of institutions that excluded women and

Figure 2.1 The Multicultural Organization Development Model

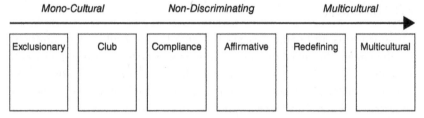

Source: *Jackson (2005). Used by permission.*

people of color. Today some colleges still exclude lesbian, gay, bisexual, or transgender (LGBT) students or at least make them sign a pledge that they will not participate in same-sex sexual behavior. Overt exclusion based on race or gender is pretty rare in higher education today. The second phase (*the club*) is much more passive in its acceptance and implementation of a monocultural perspective, but these organizations still actively rely on monocultural values, traditions, informal rules, and ways of doing things through the missions, policies, and procedures that are used. A small contingency of the underrepresented groups is allowed, but they need to be willing to adapt to the rules and norms of the organization. One example of this type of higher education institution is military institutions that now accept women and openly LGBT members but often make them feel unwelcome and unsafe (Drake, 2006; Swarns, 2012).

Two phases constitute the nondiscriminating stage of the MCOD model. *The compliance system*, the first phase of this stage, makes an effort to comply with federal law and community pressure by providing access to previously denied groups. No effort is made to change the organization in any way, so there is often a revolving door with token members, and retention of these individuals is often poor. The second phase (*the affirming system*) involves moving beyond compliance and toward eliminating any discriminatory practices. More of an effort is made to retain underrepresented individuals who have been brought into the organization; however, the underlying values, norms, and practices of the organization rarely change. Both of these phases that constitute the nondiscriminating stage likely include a large percentage of higher education institutions that do the minimum in terms of multicultural interventions and typically focus their efforts on increasing structural or numerical diversity, especially of underrepresented students.

The final multicultural stage of the MCOD model has two phases. First is *the redefining system*, which involves transitioning from being nondiscriminatory to embracing inclusion, diversity, and equity. This transition entails moving beyond accepting diversity as an organization because it *should* to embracing and valuing diversity as essential to the success of the organization. Within this phase are many colleges and universities that have moved beyond affirmative action and are actively seeking to remove barriers to inclusion. They have made some important steps toward becoming more multicultural by infusing multiculturalism into the mission of the institution and implementing important programmatic changes (e.g., creating a diversity office). Although the investment in multiculturalism is there, underrepresented individuals are often not fully included at all levels of the organization. The latter phase (*the multicultural system*) depicts an organization that strives to place multiculturalism at the core of its mission and strategic planning process. Such organizations actively seek to eliminate oppression and embrace social justice as the core of the institution. According to Holvino (2008), a multicultural organization is one in which "(1) the diversity of knowledge and perspectives that different groups bring to the organization shapes its strategy, work, management and operating systems, and its core values and norms for success; and (2) members of all groups are treated fairly, feel included, have equal opportunities, and are represented at all organizational levels and functions" (p. 3). Given the complex organizational structure of most higher education institutions, it is challenging at this time for any colleges and universities as an entire unit to be at this stage of development. In fact, some (e.g., Pope, Reynolds, and Mueller, 2004) suggest that multiculturalism not be viewed as an endpoint but rather as a process that requires commitment, passion, self-reflection, and continual effort.

MCOD Change Process

In addition to the MCOD stage model as a diagnostic tool to help assess the campus's or organization's current challenges and opportunities, the model has additional heuristic value. The MCOD stage model provides organizations with the possibilities for the type of multiculturalism it desires and the ability to select appropriate goals, strategies, and interventions to reach its desired vision (Holvino, 2008). Moving beyond assessment and goal setting, Jackson (2005) identified four components central to the MCOD change process: (1) identifying change agents; (2) determining how ready the system is for a multicultural change effort; (3) providing assessment or benchmarking of the system; and (4) planning and implementing change. Typically multiple change agents are present in the process, including internal change agents, external consultants, and a leadership team. All of these partners or members of the change team must be invested and actively involved in the change process to ensure the success of the MCOD effort. System readiness is a crucial component of any MCOD effort. An MCOD readiness tool to assist organizations in evaluating their ability to move forward must be developed and given to members of the internal and external change groups and the leadership team. To be successful, the MCOD process should be driven by data from multiple sources, including surveys, interviews, and audits. This assessment process must be thorough and assess perspectives and practices across all levels of the organization or institution. All points of view must be included. Once the data are collected, members of the organization or community must be invited to explore and evaluate the accuracy and validity of the data. "Once the data [are] owned, or the group has indicated that, 'Yes, the data represent our system,' the next step is to identify those things that must be changed so that the system can become an MCO" (Jackson, 2005, p. 18). Finally, after that vetting has occurred, the change team becomes involved in working with subunits and the larger unit to identify goals and create a change plan for the organization. Despite the desire of many organizations that this be an immediate and short-term process, creating a multicultural organization takes significant time (Jackson & Hardiman, 1994; Pope, Reynolds, & Mueller, 2004). Once the change plans have been developed and evaluated, the feedback process continues, and then it is time for the organization to renew its commitment to the multicultural change process.

Whether one uses the previously discussed MCOD model or other approaches as a basis for assessing or understanding of where one's organization or institution exists on the continuum toward multiculturalism, few tools are actually available to assist in that assessment process. Williams (2013), Flash (2010a), and others have expressed concern about the lack of empirical evidence for multicultural change models and the dearth of empirically derived assessment tools that can be used to aid multicultural change leaders in their efforts. Williams states that diversity issues "are often addressed by uninformed or politically expedient solutions rather than by analysis, evidence, and proven best practices" (p. 180).

MCOD Models in Higher Education

Several examples of efforts to implement and even evaluate the effectiveness of MCOD frameworks or assessment tools are available within higher education. These illustrations are briefly described to provide understanding of the potential for developing models sensitive to the unique features of the higher education setting, such as decentralization and other contextual constraints that provide challenges to multicultural change agents on college and university campuses. First was Pope (1993, 1995), who used MCOD theory to develop the multicultural change intervention matrix (MCIM). Reynolds (1997) applied the MCIM model to curriculum development, and Pope, Reynolds, and Mueller (2004) then expanded this model. Based on Pope's early work on MCOD, Grieger (1996) proposed the multicultural organizational development checklist (MODC), which is an effort to "translate the theoretical model of MOD into the specifics of everyday pragmatic professional practice, while building ongoing diagnosis and evaluation into its methodology" (p. 564). The MODC was created using qualitative procedures and theme analysis and then was validated and evaluated by three independent student affairs practitioners. The result was a checklist with 12 categories (mission, leadership and advocacy, policies, recruitment and retention, expectations for multicultural competency, multicultural competency training, scholarly activities, student activities and services, internships and field placements, physical environment, diagnosis, and evaluation). According to Grieger, "the MODC is meant to serve as a model, road map, or guide for the implementation of holistic multicultural change within a division of student affairs" (p. 565). Reynolds and Pope (2003) later adapted Grieger's model into a 10-category template that could be used for strategic planning purposes in a college counseling center or other student affairs units. The 10 categories proposed by Reynolds and Pope include (1) comprehensive definition and inclusive use of the term *multicultural*; (2) mission statement; (3) leadership and advocacy; (4) policy review; (5) recruitment and retention of diverse staff; (6) multicultural competencies in expectations and training; (7) scholarly activities; (8) programs and services; (9) physical environment; and (10) assessment. The goals, structure, and desired outcomes introduced by this template provide multicultural advocates with a practical framework to guide the multicultural change process.

Although the work of Grieger (1996) and Reynolds and Pope (2003) is conceptual in nature, it creates essential tools that can be used to create multicultural campuses. Flash (2010a) took it one step further in her call for empirically derived multicultural assessment tools to drive the multicultural change efforts. In her research, she developed the multicultural competence in student affairs organizations (MCSAO) questionnaire, which was adapted from the work of Reynolds and Pope and Grieger. The result of this adaption was a 189-item questionnaire designed to:

> (1) assist student affairs' organizations in assessing their multicultural competence along multiple organizational dimensions/components and across organizational units; (2) provide data to support student affairs administrators and practitioners in strategic planning around multicultural and diversity efforts to create an inclusive and affirming climate; (3) provide an instrument to help scholars and researchers explore questions pertaining to multicultural competence, diversity, and multicultural organizational development in higher education; (4) push climate-related research beyond the constituency of students and faculty to include staff at multiple roles and functioning responsibilities within higher education institutions; (5) expand the conversation on multicultural competence to shift from assessing and developing individual multicultural competence to examining organizational multicultural competence on an organizational-systems level; (6) expand on the work of Grieger (1996) and Pope et al (2004) by broadening and reconfiguring their conceptual frameworks; and (7) potentially serve as the basis of an instrument that can be adapted for fields with similar human resource, foundational, and organizational products dimensions. (p. 33)

Although this questionnaire is still in its early stages of development, it may be the beginning of a new phase of development within MCOD whereby higher education institutions will begin using psychometrically validated instruments as part of their MCOD assessment process. Such assessment tools will provide rigor and reliability to an often-haphazard data collection process (Williams, 2013). Given the complex and idiosyncratic nature of higher education, the need remains for institution-specific assessment tools, which can provide specific information about the multicultural change efforts at a particular college or university. Rejecting the cookie cutter approach in assessment and intervention that is often used in higher education is essential to the success of multicultural change efforts (Miller & Katz, 2002; Williams, 2013).

Multicultural Change Intervention Matrix (MCIM)

One way to move beyond the "diversity in a box" approach discussed previously (Miller & Katz, 2002, p. 28) is to embrace specific theories or models that can be used as a basis for the multicultural change effort. Because of the complicated and multifaceted nature of higher education, one can easily get lost in the complexity and create frameworks that are overly complex and sometimes overwhelming to the multicultural change agents who are responsible for creating and implementing the multicultural change process. Instead, it is often helpful to rely on frameworks that are theoretical in nature and parsimonious in their representation. Pope (1992), to depict her conceptualization of MCOD within the higher education context, created one such model, the MCIM. The MCIM was initially designed to assist student affairs practitioners in conceptualizing and planning their multicultural interventions. Pope surveyed 126 vice presidents of student affairs to gather information on the type of multiracial interventions being implemented on their campuses. The MCIM was used to codify and understand the type and range of multiracial activities occurring in higher education. The 2 × 3 matrix used to schematically represent the MCIM (Table 2.1) is based on two different dimensions. The first dimension identifies three possible targets of multicultural interventions: (1) individual (e.g., individual students, staff members, faculty, administrators); (2) group (e.g., paraprofessional or professional staff, student organizations); and (3) institutional (e.g., entire college or university, student affairs division). The second dimension of the MCIM categorizes two levels of intervention: first- and second-order change.

Lyddon (1990) explored the notion of first- and second-order change based on work from the family systems literature by Watzlawick, Weakland, and Fisch (1974) to understand the therapeutic change process across different theoretical orientations. Scholars in higher education (Pope, 1993, 1995; Reynolds, 1997; Williams, 2013), leadership development and education (Waters, Marzano, & McNulty, 2003), and medical informatics (Lorenzi & Riley, 2000) have explored the notion of first- and second-order change. Pope (1993) described "first-order change as a change within the system that does not create change in the structure of the system. Second-order change is any change that fundamentally alters

Table 2.1   Multicultural change intervention matrix (MCIM)

Target of change	Type of change	
	First-order change	Second-order change
Individual	A. Awareness	B. Paradigm shift
Group	C. Membership	D. Restructuring
Institutional	E. Programmatic	F. Systemic

© Raechele L. Pope (1993)

the structure of a system" (p. 241). Williams (2013), in his discussion of first and second order as part of strategic diversity leadership, states, "Whereas *first-order changes* refer to minor adjustments such as developing a new diversity office or establishing a new diversity requirement, *transformative changes* [or second-order changes] by contrast often create new patterns of behavior and assumptions governing organizational life" (p. 16). Conceptualizing change in new and different ways requires a paradigm shift (Hunt, Bell, Wei, & Ingle, 1992; Pope, 1993) that is essential to creating genuine multicultural change in higher education. Understanding the distinctions between first- and second-order change requires such a change in worldview or perspective.

Lyddon (1990) used mathematical concepts to help describe the difference between first- and second-order changes. Numbers can be combined in a variety of ways using the same mathematical operation, such as addition, without changing the actual numbers or what constitutes that particular number set. For example, $(5 + 2) + 4 = 11$ and $(2 + 5) + 4 = 11$ reach the same sum even though the same numbers are added in different ways. Lyddon suggests that these changes within this numerical set do not create any true change in the group. This first-order change, although it is change, does not alter the structure of the group or create a different outcome. However, changing the mathematical operation from addition to multiplication, such as $(5 \times 2) + 4 = 14$, does lead to a different result. Such a second-order change does create "a radical transformation in the way in which the group is viewed and defined, a change in processes which transforms outcomes" (Pope, 1993, p. 242).

One can change the diversity of a group or institution by simply adding new "diverse" members or creating a new diversity program or office. However, such efforts typically maintain the original system or status quo and do little to create truly multicultural campuses. These efforts are examples of first-order changes. Changes that lead to a transformation in the actual structure of a group or institution are second-order changes. For example, when new "diverse" members are added to a group and the entire group reexamines mission, objectives, policies, procedures, and practices in an effort to integrate diverse perspectives from voices that have been traditionally underrepresented, this is the beginning of second-order change (Pope, 1993, 1995; Reynolds, 1997). Creating multicultural campuses is a deeper, more complex, and qualitatively different process than simply adding women, people of color, and other traditionally underrepresented people and stirring. Lyddon (1990) viewed first-order change as "change without change" and second-order change as "change of change." Lorenzi and Riley (2000) suggest that first-order change means improving what we already do, and second-order change involves altering how we do things in meaningful and profound ways. Workman (2009) suggests that when the policies, practices, and approaches contribute to the problem then it is time for second-order change. This type of change, called *transformative change* by Eckel, Hill, and Green (1998), "(1) alters the culture of the institution by changing select underlying assumptions and institutional behaviors, processes, and products; (2) is deep and pervasive, affecting the whole institution; (3) is intentional; and (4) occurs over time" (p. 3).

From their efforts to manage change within a medical informatics context, Lorenzi and Riley advise that such a transformation is necessary to address the resistance to change that naturally occurs within systems. Waters, Marzano, and McNulty (2003), in their exploration of leadership and change, suggest that not all changes are of the same magnitude or significance. Their notion, which is particularly powerful when attempting to introduce multicultural change, is that all individuals do not perceive changes in the same way. They suggest that "To the degree that individuals and/or stakeholder groups in the school or school system hold conflicting values, seek different norms, have different knowledge, or operate with varying mental models of schooling, a proposed change might represent a first order change for some and a second order change for others" (p. 7). Their description of characteristics of first- and second-order changes, as depicted in Table 2.2, is very helpful in understanding the distinctions across types of change.

Table 2.2   Characteristics of first- and second-order changes

First-order change	Second-order change
An extension of the past	A break with the past
Within existing paradigms	Outside of existing paradigms
Consistent with prevailing values and norms	Conflicted with prevailing values and norms
Focused	Emergent
Bounded	Unbounded
Incremental	Complex
Linear	Nonlinear
Marginal	A disturbance to every element of a system
Implemented with existing knowledge and skills	Requires new knowledge and skills to implement
Problem- and solution-oriented	Neither problem- nor system-oriented
Implemented by experts	Implemented by stakeholders

Used with permission from Waters, Marzano, and McNulty (2003). Copyright 2003, McREL. Used by permission of McREL.

The multicultural change intervention matrix (MCIM) provides a practical rubric for understanding how first- and second-order multicultural change efforts, interventions, and activities occur across the individual, group, and institutional levels within higher education. As shown in Table 2.1, MCIM specifies six ways to codify existing efforts and envision new interventions or programs. This detailed figure provides multicultural change agents with a deeper understanding of the various types of activities, strategies, and tools that can be used to create multicultural campuses. Brief descriptions of the six cells are shared here, and more specifics regarding change at the individual, group, and institutional levels are explored later in this book.

In cell A (first-order change, individual level), interventions are typically focused on sharing content and may involve sharing information about various racial and cultural groups. Pope (1993) and Williams (2013), despite 20 years between their works, suggest that most multicultural interventions are targeted at this level. Often these interventions target increasing knowledge or cultural sensitivity and include examples such as National Coming Out Day programming, a presentation on Japanese internment camps in the United States, a poster series on famous people of color, or an international cultural food festival.

Cell B (second-order change, individual level) shows interventions that are typically longer in duration and aimed at deeper education or understanding that ultimately may lead to cognitive restructuring or an "ah ha" moment in which individuals achieve a transformation in their worldview regarding oppression or the life experiences of other groups. Such worldview or paradigm shifts require more intensive, interactive, or experiential emphasis beyond sharing of information on content on various groups. Often these interventions are more process oriented and challenge an individual's underlying assumptions. By focusing on process and interpersonal interaction, much like what occurs in many intergroup dialogue programs, participants are able to challenge their assumptions and beliefs about the world, themselves, and other individuals. Examples might include more extended consciousness-raising workshops or ongoing staff training that requires introspection and self-examination.

A cell C (first-order change, group level) change effort is a change in the composition, not in the structure, of the group (i.e., add people and stir) in which members of previously not-represented groups are added, but there are no changes in structure, mission, norms, or practices of the group. This cell focuses on diversity without examining the interpersonal and structural dynamics of a group. Numerical diversity will not automatically change the interpersonal and structural dynamics of a campus or even a group. In fact, research has shown that changing the composition of a campus does not necessarily change the experience of those students who traditionally have been underrepresented on campus (Rankin & Reason, 2005). Traditional recruitment efforts are good examples of this type of first-order change, in which a campus may attempt to increase the number of students of color or when a predominantly male academic program such as engineering admits more female students. If the climate or environment is not altered and if the underlying mission of the institution or academic program does not evolve, it is likely that many of these new group members will leave or feel unwelcome.

In cell D (second-order change, group level), interventions are typically focused on restructuring groups with new goals, missions, and members. This type of change dictates examination of group makeup, values, and goals before changing the group. For example, before actually adding new members, the group takes the time to examine what has prevented diversification from occurring and what changes are needed to ensure that new individuals brought into the system will be invested and will stay. When new members join or are hired, they are then involved in this examination process and in creating new norms, policies, and practices rather than creating new norms and then inviting new people to join. A retreat in which a specific group, department, or unit re-examines and reformulates its mission and goals and infuses multicultural values and practices with input and participation from new members would be an excellent example of this type of change.

Cell E (first-order, institution level) typically focuses on multicultural programmatic interventions targeting the college or university or a particular division or school within an institution. Creating a new position on campus or developing a new multicultural office or developing a multicultural sensitivity in-service for staff members are important multicultural interventions, but they do not necessarily alter the underlying institutional dynamics, values, or priorities of the entire campus. For example, hiring individuals to address multicultural issues (e.g., vice-provost for diversity, senior diversity officer, affirmative action officer, director of the campus diversity center) frequently makes them responsible for the diversity work on campus and fails to also make others accountable. Another example is adding a diversity section to a mission statement of a department or academic unit without changing evaluation or budgetary criteria. If criteria for evaluating work performance or distributing discretionary funds are not tied to diversity issues (as they are with other goals or expectations, e.g., class size or enrollment issues), then the paradigm shift needed for second-order change is less likely to occur.

For cell F (second-order, institutional level) interventions to occur, a strategic and systematic exploration of the underlying mission, values, goals, and practices of the campus is needed that then links them to multicultural values and initiatives throughout the institution or unit. These interventions are typically more intrusive and lead to more extensive dialogue and changes within the organization. Instituting a campus-wide multicultural strategic planning process would be one example of this type of change. Examples include requiring goal-directed multicultural initiatives within all units that directly link the outcomes of those initiatives to budget allocation, salary, evaluation, and promotion decisions. Although top leadership must be involved, true second-order change at the institutional level cannot occur unless individuals at all levels are involved and invested in the process.

Understanding each of these six cells is helpful, but it is important to view this matrix as a systemic model that incorporates all types of change. There is no assumption that one type of change (first order vs. second order) is better than another or that change efforts should be more focused on one level than on another. For lasting multicultural change to occur, interventions that target all six cells are needed. These cells each suggest unique approaches or interventions for multicultural change; however, they also provide a rubric for conceptualizing and developing a multicultural strategic plan. There is no hierarchy, so campuses that discover that they are overemphasizing first-order changes should not turn around and then only focus on second-order changes. There needs to be balance. Without some work on the awareness level, paradigm shifts may not be possible. Without active recruitment, there is no need to attend to issues of retention. The dynamic and fluid nature of the MCIM is depicted by the dotted lines between the six cells. Pope (1995) viewed those lines as evidence of the interconnections among and between the various types and targets of change. In addition to diversifying interventions across types of change, this framework reinforces the importance of targeting at all levels. The long-standing overreliance on individual educational interventions has made it difficult for many multicultural change efforts to succeed. According to Reynolds (1997), using systemic planned change efforts such as the MCIM to "create multicultural change may not only assist with the necessary goal setting but also will identify methods of implementation" (p. 220).

Even a parsimonious theoretical framework such as the MCIM has limited value unless the model is applied to practice. This model has numerous strengths that are not present in some other theoretical approaches to creating multicultural change.

Many approaches to creating multicultural campuses have focused more on strategy and tactics than on theory (Williams, 2013). The MCIM provides a comprehensive yet elegant conceptualization of multicultural interventions that will allow change agents to be more purposeful and thorough in their efforts. Emphasizing the need for multicultural efforts to occur at all three levels (individual, group, institutional) will provide campus leaders with the framework that they need to ensure the broadest approach possible. The MCIM is a user-friendly and portable model that can be used by change agents all over campus, from a paraprofessional staff member in the residence hall, to a director of a student affairs unit, to a chair of an academic department, to the chief diversity officer on a campus. In addition to these strengths, there are some limitations to the MCIM as well. By far, the primary limitation is a lack of research to support the validity and utility of the MCIM. Beyond the initial work of Pope (1993), there is no research on the MCIM and no effort to further validate or test the psychometric features of the initial instrument used in Pope's early research. Although there is anecdotal support for the MCIM based on consultation and campus interventions, more research is needed. In addition, there needs to be more exploration of what truly distinguishes first- and second-order change and which mechanisms allow one to create more transformational interventions.

In moving toward a more thorough application of the MCIM framework, one should identify possible areas for use of the MCIM. Pope (1995) suggested three significant uses of the MCIM: assessment/evaluation, strategic planning, and curricular transformation. As previously discussed, it is difficult to create a multicultural campus without a model or framework that can be used to evaluate and understand what has been done and what has been successful. Through use of the MCIM, campus leaders can assess and discern the types of interventions currently being used on their campus and where there are shortcomings in the multicultural change efforts. The MCIM is quite versatile and can be used as part of a benchmark approach to assessment as well as part of quantitative, qualitative, and case study research designs. Once the assessment is completed so that institutions understand where they are, they can use this same framework to guide a strategic planning approach. Given that strategic planning is viewed as essential to the multicultural change process (Pope, Reynolds, & Mueller, 2004; Williams, 2013), the MCIM can assist in setting goals and priorities for the campus or one small unit within the campus. Ensuring that the strategic plan embraces both first- and second-order change and targets individual, group, and institutional levels will help to ensure the success of the strategic planning process. Finally, the

MCIM can be used as part of a curricular transformation effort. Faculty members attempting to infuse multicultural issues into the curriculum are often at a loss for how to proceed. The framework provided by the MCIM, as evidenced by Reynolds (1997), can be used to design the goals, objectives, and activities of an individual course or restructure an entire curriculum to ensure that students leave with changes at both the first- and second-order levels. The MCIM can be used to evaluate the class-room strategies and activities and gain a deeper understanding of what needs to be done to be successful.

Serious evolution has occurred in the approaches to creating multicultural campuses over the past fifty years. Multicultural organization development has become an increasingly consequential theory that has been used to conceptualize and drive multicultural change on college and university campuses. Important characteristics and features make MCOD unique and provide new strategies, interventions, and tools to multicultural change agents in higher education. MCOD suggests the importance of systemic and systematic change at all levels of an organization and provides a roadmap for achieving important diversity benchmarks. Systemic change efforts target the larger system or structure that exists on college campuses, and systematic change focuses on methodical and organized approaches to creating change. Both are important, and both are necessary. In particular, the MCIM offers a meaningful framework to codify, evaluate, and understand the various multicultural change efforts on campus. The exploration of first- and second-order change provides vital conceptual tools to assist in creating rigorous and long-lasting multicultural change that can happen at the individual, group, and institutional levels.

3

MULTICULTURAL INTERVENTION AT THE INDIVIDUAL LEVEL

Paul was a first-year student at Dakota Lake College and was concerned about the ongoing debate on campus about whether to remove the Native American symbol as the mascot for the school. Paul was adamantly against removing or changing the school mascot and believed that pressure from the National Collegiate Athletic Association and the state legislature was insensitive to the history and tradition of the college. Despite growing up in the area, as a white man, Paul had little interaction with local Native people. Both of his older brothers attended Dakota Lake, so he had been around campus for years and had strong feelings about the mascot issue. However, because he was curious he decided to attend an open meeting on campus in which elders and youth from the nearby Lakota Sioux tribe spoke about the effect of mascots on them as individuals and as a people. Paul sat there quietly listening and absorbing the feelings expressed by the Sioux people. As he listened, it dawned on Paul that the Sioux had traditions that were so much older than Dakota Lake College and that maybe the issue was more complicated than he had previously considered.

———o———

As the coordinator of staff training for the student affairs division, I organize a lot of diversity training programs. In those training interventions we often focus on multicultural competence and use

(continued)

a variety of activities such as small group work, journaling, panels, and group excursions. I enjoy planning the training, and the staff members generally seem to enjoy the experience. I don't get near as many complaints as I expected I would. However, I really don't know how to help them translate what they learn about multicultural competence to the real world and their work in higher education.

Creating multicultural awareness or sensitivity has been the cornerstone of many multicultural educational efforts in higher education. According to Pope (1995); Pope, Reynolds, and Mueller (2004); and Williams (2013), many campuses have used programmatic responses to address multicultural concerns, with particular attention to individual awareness or consciousness-raising activities. In fact, in her assessment of multiracial change efforts in student affairs, Pope (1992) discovered that regardless of the size and location of the college or university, most multiracial interventions targeted individuals or groups rather than focus on the student affairs division or institutions as a whole.

Creating transformation on the individual level is essential to helping individuals determine how to move from wanting to be culturally aware to knowing how to make that change happen. Whether it was during sit-ins in the 1960s, when white people were challenged by black people to think differently about race, to a Day of Silence to raise awareness of homophobia at a high school, to a staff development training on multicultural competence at a small Midwestern liberal arts college; all of these events have in common the goal of raising sensitivity to multicultural issues. Increased understanding of WHAT constitutes multicultural awareness for all individuals as well as appreciation of HOW to achieve such deeper learning and insight is essential to larger multicultural change efforts on campus.

This chapter explores the multicultural change strategy of creating individual change. In this chapter, the term *individual* refers to any individual student, staff member, administrator, or faculty member who is affiliated with the college or university. Using the framework of the multicultural change intervention matrix (MCIM), this chapter focuses on the principles, activities, and strategies for creating multicultural change at the individual level, using both first- and second-order change methods. At the individual level, first-order change involves developing multicultural awareness within individuals; second-order change involves creating paradigm shifts in how individuals understand and relate to diversity.

First, this chapter explores what is meant by the concepts of multicultural awareness and paradigm shift. Additionally, we discuss benefits of both types of individual change as well as exploration of what some of the barriers and challenges are that make it difficult for campuses to instill multicultural awareness among its varied members. This is followed by a brief exploration of some of the core competencies that are needed to create individual change in others. Finally, exemplars of multicultural change at the individual level are provided to encourage and expand how the readers think about multicultural interventions targeting the individual level and ultimately influence how their own efforts and practice within their divisions and institutions can be altered and expanded to create lasting multicultural change on campus.

Individual Change: Theoretical Frameworks

When exploring multicultural change efforts targeting the individual, it is important to comprehend the end goal or outcome one is seeking. Chavez, Guido-DiBrito, and Mallory (2003) described individual diversity development as "cognitive, affective, and behavioral growth processes toward consciously valuing complex and integrated differences in others and ourselves" (p. 453). To better understand how these growth processes occur, one must rely on theories to provide "an important and necessary lens through which to engage our roles and responsibilities and make decisions" (Jones & Abes, 2011, p. 161). Theories have long informed and benefited student affairs practice, whether contemplating college student development, student engagement, organizational planning, or campus environments. Ultimately, theories and the ability to translate them into practice should be one of the core competencies of effective student affairs practice and "should help inform why we choose particular practices, assessments, and interventions" (Pope, Reynolds, & Mueller, 2004, p. 30). And "because of the complexity of much of our work, it is rare that one theory will carry enough explanatory power for a particular phenomenon so that when applying theory to practice, theories often are used in combination" (Jones & Abes, p. 162).

For the purpose of this chapter, three theories will be used as a backdrop to better understand *how* change occurs on an individual basis and what mechanisms are important to consider when exploring this change process. First, several developmental models or frameworks that address multicultural change and development (e.g., Chavez, Guido-DiBrito, & Mallory, 2003; King & Baxter Magolda, 2005; Ortiz & Rhoads, 2000) are briefly explored as a foundation for comprehending multicultural change on the individual level. The second theory, trans-theoretical model of behavior change, which has been used extensively in the fields of medicine, health psychology, counseling, and even organization development (Prochaska & Norcross, 2009; Prochaska, Prochaska, & Levesque, 2001; Prochaska et al., 1994; Zimmerman, Olsen, & Bosworth, 2000), offers a deeper exploration of the individual change process. Finally, intergroup contact theory (Pettigrew, 1998), which serves as a basis for the intergroup dialogue programs that help many college students understand social diversity and social justice, is considered. The writings and research connected to all three of these theoretical frameworks are quite extensive, so it is not possible to explore them in any depth. However, the basic framework and major tenets of these theories have great heuristic value in helping multicultural advocates grasp how individual change occurs and how those principles can be applied to multicultural change efforts at both the first-order and second-order levels of change.

Developmental Frameworks

To fully understand individual diversity development, one must grasp the range of individual differences in personality, comfort, life experiences, and readiness to learn about multicultural issues. Chavez, Guido-DiBrito, and Mallory (2003) articulate the importance of appreciating how many internal and external factors (e.g., parental values, diversity exposure) can shape how one's multicultural awareness, knowledge, and skills are able to develop. Although various developmental models address the transformational process that many individuals experience as they expand their openness to diversity and their ability to interact with others who are culturally different from themselves, most acknowledge the importance of identity, affect, cognition, and behavior in that developmental journey (e.g., Bowman, 2010; Chavez, Guido-DiBrito, & Mallory, 2003; King & Baxter Magolda, 2005; Ortiz & Rhoads, 2000).

Chavez, Guido-DiBrito, and Mallory (2003) proposed a nonlinear and multidimensional diversity development framework that describes how individuals process and make sense of others who are different from them. Their model can be used to explore multiple identities of importance to an individual. Within each of those identities, individuals will transverse periods of exploration that depict varying levels of comfort and related thoughts, feelings, and actions regarding diversity. Specifically, they depict the five developmental periods as (1) unawareness or lack of exposure to the other; (2) dualistic awareness; (3) questioning or self-exploration; (4) risk taking or active exploration of the other; and (5) integration and validation of self and others. Ortiz and Rhoads (2000) offer a parallel framework that helps to explain specifically how white individuals come to explore and understand themselves and others as cultural beings. They describe their model as encompassing five steps that once understood can be used to enhance multicultural education. Their five steps are (1) understanding culture; (2) learning about other cultures; (3) recognizing and deconstructing white culture; (4) recognizing the legitimacy of other cultures; and (5) developing a multicultural outlook. As such, "elements of each step may be incorporated in one educational intervention, used separately in individually designed educational programs, or the framework as a whole may be used to guide the development of curricula addressing multicultural issues" (p. 86).

Although some multicultural scholars conceptualize this process of learning to embrace multiculturalism as a developmental journey with various phases or steps, other researchers have focused on how as various cognitive developmental changes occur, individual attitudes toward and comfort with diversity evolve (e.g., Bowman, 2010; King & Baxter Magolda, 2005; King & Shuford, 1996). King and Baxter Magolda "propose a multidimensional framework that describes how people become increasingly capable of understanding and acting in ways that are interculturally aware and appropriate" (p. 573). Their multidimensional intercultural framework involves three primary developmental domains: cognitive, intrapersonal, and interpersonal, and is based on college student and adult developmental theories. Commonalities among these various developmental frameworks exist and help explain how individual changes occur; however, the most important takeaway is that individual differences must be taken into consideration. One-size-fits-all diversity interventions cannot succeed because important individual differences and developmental trajectories must be considered when designing and implementing diversity training and programming. Present at any multicultural workshop or staff training on a campus are a collection of individuals who each exist in a different spot on the developmental road toward multicultural awareness and transformation. No one intervention can possibly target each person equally and effectively, providing the spark that is needed to create change. Given the complex and multifaceted nature of individual diversity development, "educating for this outcome requires a broader, more comprehensive approach than that suggested by training for knowledge or skills alone" (King & Baxter Magolda, 2005, p. 572).

Stages of Change Model

With that important lesson in mind, it is helpful to briefly consider the transtheoretical or stages of change model developed by Prochaska and colleagues to help explain the stages or processes of change that can be used to create effective interventions. This theory is very well researched and supported, forms the foundation of motivational interviewing, and is used extensively in the medical, health, and counseling fields (Burke, 2011; Passmore, 2011). Above and beyond the developmental models previously discussed, the stages of change model can help multicultural advocates better understand why certain multicultural interventions may not work with certain individuals. By "tailoring interventions to meet an individual's stage of change" (Passmore, p. 38), one can prevent or lessen the likelihood of relapse or resistance to the change effort. This does not mean that there is a right way to create change and that if we can determine an individual's stage of change, then we can develop multicultural interventions that will always be successful. Rather, it highlights the significance of seeing change as a process that can be understood but not controlled.

The transtheoretical model conceptualizes behavioral change as a developmental process involving a series of five stages: precontemplation, contemplation, preparation, action, and maintenance (Norcross, Krebs, & Prochaska, 2011). Zimmerman, Olsen, and Bosworth (2000), when discussing how physicians can use the stages of change model to help patients change, provided an excellent snapshot of this change process, in which, for most individuals,

> a change in behavior occurs gradually, with the patient moving from being uninterested, unaware, or unwilling to make a change (precontemplation), to considering a change (contemplation), to deciding and preparing to make a change. Genuine, determined action is then taken and, over time, attempts to maintain the new behavior occur. Relapses are almost inevitable and become part of the process of working toward lifelong change. (p. 1410)

The stages of change model suggests that resistance is a result of professionals not being properly aligned or in sync with those they are trying to help. This is different from the common assumption that the individuals participating in training are likely resistant to change. So, for example, if interventions are targeting individuals who are fully invested in change but the individuals are at precontemplation, then resistance is likely. This mismatch mirrors the Sanford (1967) notion of challenge and support, which can help professionals to identify and implement appropriate multicultural interventions. If our interventions are too challenging and not based on where students, administrators, or staff members are in their own development or stages of change, those individuals are likely to resist those interventions, become overwhelmed, or possibly withdraw or retreat. If the interventions are not challenging enough and if there is more support and empathy than warranted given where the students, administrators, or staff members are, then they are also likely to disengage and not challenge their own attitudes, values, or thoughts around multicultural issues.

Using these developmental frameworks can be invaluable to multicultural change agents; however, it also becomes very challenging to implement effective interventions, because within a given classroom, department, workshop, or administrative unit, each individual will be at a different developmental level. That is why attention to the process of change through human interaction as suggested by intergroup contact theory is an excellent way to apply theory and determine ways to use human contact as a means of reducing prejudice and enhancing multiculturalism (Zuniga, Nagda, & Sevig, 2002).

Intergroup Contact Theory

Intergroup contact theory, based on the work of Allport (1954), and offered and supported by Pettigrew (1998) and Pettigrew and Tropp (2006), suggests that under certain conditions articulated by Allport (e.g., equal status, shared goals, interdependence, support from authority, and potential for friendship), intergroup contact is likely to weaken or lessen prejudice. In other words, the more contact we have with others who are different from us and about whom we may have certain prejudices learned from our families, communities, and society, the less likely we are to retain and advance those prejudices or biases. The amount of literature supporting these claims has grown exponentially in the past decade, varying from broader scholarly work that has significantly influenced educational policy (e.g., Chang, Astin, & Kim, 2004; Gurin, Dey, Hurtado, & Gurin, 2002; Gurin, Nagda, & Lopez, 2004) to work explicitly researching the effectiveness of intergroup dialogue programs currently in place in campuses across the country (e.g., Hurtado, 2005; Miles & Kivlighan, 2012; Nagda & Zuniga, 2003; Sorensen, Nagda, Gurin, & Maxwell, 2009).

Zuniga, Nagda, and Sevig (2002) suggested that focusing attention on opportunities for interactional engagement with diversity was an underutilized area for multicultural intervention. Intergroup dialogues provide "students with opportunities for sustained and meaningful engagement across race and other social group boundaries" (p. 7). Although intergroup dialogue is not the only dialogue-based program currently being used (e.g., study circles, sustained dialogue, difficult dialogues, privileged identity exploration [PIE] model), its roots in higher education, emphasis on more intensive multicultural interactions, and the fact that it has been more researched than any of the other campus dialogue programs make it well suited to the academy (Zuniga, Nagda, Chesler, & Cytron-Walker, 2007).

Intergroup dialogue is a distinct and innovative approach to interpersonal engagement that can be described as "a face-to-face facilitated learning experience that brings together students from different social identity groups over a sustained period of time to understand their commonalities and differences, examine the nature and impact of societal inequalities, and explore ways of working together toward greater equality and justice" (Zuniga, Nagda, Chesler, & Cytron-Walker, 2007, p. 2). The pedagogical foundations of intergroup dialogue include sustained communication, consciousness raising, and bridging of differences (Zuniga, Nagda, & Sevig, 2002). Intergroup dialogue often occurs in the context of an academic course that joins at least two different social identity groups such as people of color and whites or men and women and then provides structured and guided opportunities with trained facilitators. Then, "using both identity and structural inequality as a framework for understanding diverse perspectives, students explore controversial 'hot topics' (e.g., affirmative action in race dialogues, media and body image concerns in gender dialogues), reconsidering their own assumptions and perspectives in light of listening to their peers and the emergent differences and similarities" (Sorensen, Nagda, Gurin, & Maxwell, 2009, p. 14).

Zuniga, Nagda, and Sevig describe a four-stage developmental model that is the basis of intergroup dialogue: (1) group beginnings: forming and building relationships; (2) exploring differences and commonalities of experiences; (3) exploring and dialoguing about hot topics; and (4) action planning and alliance building. These small group discussions, typically lasting for several hours per week for 12 to 15 weeks, build sustained engagement that has been shown to have significant effects on participants' attitudes. Further strengthening the developmental model are several practice principles that reinforce core beliefs that are embedded in intergroup dialogues (Zuniga, Nagda, & Sevig). The first principle is maintaining a social justice perspective, which ensures that the interactions within these dialogue groups are not just about creating civil discourse but are essentially about using interaction to better understand the structural inequalities that exist in society and affect relationships. Balancing process and content is the second principle, which is essential to creating change. By attending to both how we talk (process) and what we discuss (content), individuals are more likely to develop effective and meaningful dialogue and relationships. The final practice principle is relying on reflection and action in an ongoing and interactive way. Reflection without action and action without reflection are unlikely to create lasting multicultural change. By relying on theories such as intergroup dialogue, multicultural interventions are better situated to create meaningful multicultural change within the individual.

The three foundational theories shared here are meant to provide a way to conceptualize some of the influences and factors affecting multicultural change efforts focused on individuals. By acknowledging the importance of development, especially within a higher education context, change efforts are less likely to be focused on one-size-fits-all. The brief exploration of the stages of change demonstrates how many individuals have been able to make important behavioral changes, especially in health- and mental health–related areas (e.g., smoking cessation, recovery from addiction), which can be used as a model for creating multicultural change within individuals. Finally, the inclusion of intergroup dialogue theory and practice provides an example of a successful multicultural intervention, which is theoretically based and empirically supported and creates intrapersonal and interpersonal change within individuals. These three theories can be used to increase understanding of how the MCIM can be best used when examining multicultural change efforts targeting individual students, staff members, faculty members, and administrators.

MCIM: Change on the Individual Level

The individual level of the MCIM (Table 3.1) is concerned with creating multicultural awareness within the individual, using both first- and second-order change methods. This chapter focuses on the individual as the target of the intervention, which may consist of individual students, staff members, faculty, and administrators. The two types of change targeted at the individual level result in two different cells of interest: first-order change or *awareness* (multicultural attitudes, beliefs, knowledge, or skill) and second-order change or *paradigm shift* (core changes in how individuals perceive diversity). Each of these is described in greater detail in the following sections.

Table 3.1   Multicultural change intervention matrix (MCIM)

Target of change	Type of change	
	First-order change	Second-order change
Individual	A. Awareness	B. Paradigm shift
Group	C. Membership	D. Restructuring
Institutional	E. Programmatic	F. Systemic

© Raechele L. Pope (1993)

First-Order Change: Multicultural Awareness

This cell of MCIM (cell A) is focused on increasing the multicultural awareness and sensitivity of individuals. Although most multicultural change efforts in higher education focus on the multicultural awareness of students (Pope, 1992; Williams, 2013), it is quite feasible to conceptualize this cell of multicultural awareness as being relevant and necessary for any individual member of a college or university community.

Multicultural awareness is often conceptualized as one aspect of the tripartite model of multicultural competence, which is defined as "the awareness, knowledge, and skills needed to work with others who are culturally different from self" (Pope, Reynolds, & Mueller, 2004, p. 13). Reynolds (1997) states that when examining cell A of the MCIM, it is important to consider any educational efforts focused on awareness, knowledge, and skills rather than awareness alone. Gayles and Kelly (2007) describe these three components as follows:

> Multicultural awareness involves openness to learning about differences associated with various cultures and being conscious of biases and assumptions we hold and the impact they have on individuals different from ourselves. Multicultural knowledge involves obtaining accurate and complete information about people from various cultural groups, and an understanding of within group differences and the intersection of multiple identities. The multicultural skills component involves the capacity to work effectively with individuals from various cultural backgrounds by translating awareness and knowledge, as defined above, into good practice. (p. 194)

Reynolds (1997) suggested that cell A change efforts (first-order change at the individual level) are typically content oriented and include information on various cultural groups as a way to enhance the awareness and knowledge of others. When such interventions and programming target students, they seem to focus on building cultural sensitivity, reducing prejudice and bias, increasing cultural knowledge, and building harmony and community. When such interventions and training are for staff, faculty, or administrators, they often target multicultural competence and work-related skills.

Regardless of whether the focus is on multicultural awareness, knowledge, or skills, Pope, Reynolds, and Mueller (2004) suggest that the values, attitudes, assumptions, and knowledge that individuals hold shape how they view themselves and others. Whereas many first-order interventions encourage participants to learn new information and insights about themselves and others who are culturally different from them, they are less likely to challenge their core beliefs, leading to an "aha moment" that transforms their view of the world. Rather, they often expand their worldview, building on what they already know and believe. Such change efforts typically involve diversity training in classrooms, student union, residence halls, and other places around campus, such as black history or safe zone workshops, cultural speakers on campus, cultural festivals and performances, and book readings, among others. These interventions may be more focused on creating cultural harmony or a "we are the world" mentality than challenging how the participants view privilege, power, and the underlying inequities that exist in society.

BENEFITS OF MULTICULTURAL AWARENESS As described through the work of Gurin, Chang, Hurtado, and others, many social and academic benefits are gained by enhancing the multicultural awareness of all students on campus. Celebrating differences can help underrepresented and underserved students (e.g., students of color; lesbian, gay, bisexual, and transgender [LGBT] students) feel like they matter and can make those students who represent the majority (e.g., whites, males) feel a connection to others who are different. By focusing on celebrating and understanding differences rather than critically examining social inequalities and individual biases, there may be less tension and initially more unification. Such togetherness is important and can build a foundation for later interventions and change efforts that are more challenging to the status quo.

The developmental models previously discussed demonstrate that not all individuals are ready to be challenged or examine themselves or the world in new and different ways. Likewise, not all campuses are prepared to stir the pot and invest time, resources, and energy into increasing the capacity that individuals have to create radical change within themselves or on campus. Cell A interventions that focus more on increasing multicultural awareness and knowledge are necessary and can contribute to forward movement toward creating a culture of acceptance and inclusion on campus. Building openness to transformation takes time and repeated effort. Enhancing multicultural awareness is not a singular or isolated goal but rather a process or path toward ongoing growth and development, as suggested by Ortiz and Rhoads (2000) and Chavez, Guido-DiBrito, & Mallory (2003). First-order change is vital, and often, second-order change cannot occur unless first-order change is already in place.

CHALLENGES TO MULTICULTURAL AWARENESS   In addition to benefits to creating multicultural awareness, there are also challenges. With any type of multicultural change effort, the issue of social desirability can become a problem. We live in an age in which most individuals, once aware that there are differences and inequities, desire to be accepting and open to others, so much so that they may hesitate to dig deeper and find any biases and prejudices that they may actually have. This is especially true for interventions that focus on enhancing the multicultural awareness of faculty, staff, and administrators. When it is work-related, presenting oneself as multiculturally sensitive and competent may very well be seen as necessary for employment and advancement. This means there is an incentive to possibly appear more open, aware, and knowledgeable than one truly is. In the language of statistical analysis, this can lead to a "false positive," where it is assumed that a given condition (in this case multicultural awareness) has been fulfilled when it actually has not. This false representation may cause administrators to assume that their department, office, or campus is more evolved multiculturally than it really is. When this happens, it is not uncommon to move on to other areas of interest within the institution. Under those conditions, it becomes increasingly difficult for individuals to acknowledge discomfort with multicultural issues or normalize being vulnerable and open to recognizing what they do not know or understand.

Finally, "awareness—critical or not—does not necessarily translate into different ways of being and acting in the world" (Iverson, 2012, p. 70). Multicultural awareness that is more superficial and does not challenge core beliefs can easily wear off and become less important, thus allowing individuals to easily return to their previous lives, in which they did not examine themselves or society in critical ways. This tendency is especially common for those individuals from dominant social groups (e.g., whites, men, heterosexuals), who have privilege and benefit from societal inequalities whether they want to or not. Such challenges must be openly addressed and discussed within the context of multicultural training to counter their negative effects.

Second-Order Change: Paradigm Shifts

Whereas cell A of MCIM or first-order change efforts focus on increasing the multicultural awareness and sensitivity of individuals, cell B change efforts are focused on creating second-order change within students, staff, faculty, and administrators in terms of how they view themselves, others, and the world around them. Such interventions are typically focused on the cognitive restructuring or paradigm shift level. Although Kuhn (1970) was discussing the nature of change within science when he introduced the notion of a paradigm shift, such a concept is highly meaningful when trying to explain the distinction between first-order and second-order multicultural change on the individual level. Kuhn suggested that when scientific methods and theories no longer effectively explain or describe what is happening or are able to solve new problems, it is natural for a shift in worldview or paradigm to occur that allows for innovation and new perspectives. According to Pope (1993), "paradigmatic shifts are essential for student affairs practitioners to create genuine and lasting multicultural campus environments" (p. 233). Reynolds (1997) suggested that for such shifts in worldview to occur, multicultural interventions must be more intensive, experiential, interactive, and affective in nature. This may require that change efforts focus less on content and more on multicultural insight, often "challenging an individuals' underlying cultural assumptions or beliefs" (p. 217). Ortiz and Patton (2012) suggest that "self-awareness is quite a complex process and requires individuals to engage in metathinking regarding how they see themselves as well as how they are perceived by others" (p. 12). They further identify three key steps to developing awareness of self: (1) set agenda for self-exploration; (2) establish a safe space for yourself and others; and (3) courageously engage in risk taking.

Moving beyond multicultural awareness and toward a paradigm shift often requires active self-exploration so that individuals become aware of their underlying values, attitudes, and assumptions. According to Pope, Reynolds, and Mueller (2004), "Without such self-evaluation, individuals may not realize that they hold inaccurate or inappropriate views of a particular culture in the form of stereotypes, biases, or culturally based assumptions. For multicultural development to continue, individuals must be able to challenge their misinformation and correct their erroneous assumptions and beliefs" (p. 15). Iverson (2012) views this "self-reflexive work through which individuals (might) unpack their identities, reveal their blind spots, and interrogate the givenness of what they know" (p. 69) as being essential to developing true multicultural competence.

Viewing learning as a process can be useful in making the distinction between first-order change (awareness) and second-order change (paradigm shift). Transformative learning, introduced by Mezirow in 1978, offers one such lens through which we can learn to "recognize and reassess the structure of assumptions and expectations which frame our thinking, feeling, and acting" (Mezirow, 2009, p. 91). This model is particularly relevant for multicultural work because its goal is to understand the process by which individuals take their everyday mindsets (that are often unexamined and taken for granted) and "make them more inclusive, discriminating, open, emotionally capable of change, and reflective" (p. 92).

Daloz (2000) identified four conditions necessary for this type of transformative learning, specifically, the presence of the other, reflective discourse, a mentoring community, and opportunities for committed action. These conditions are parallel to much of what has been discussed as necessary conditions for multicultural change on the individual level as evidenced by intergroup contact theory previously discussed in this chapter. Mezirow suggests that reflective discourse is probably the most important element necessary for transformative learning. It is not enough to attend multicultural workshops or attend diversity events without opportunities for reflection and dialogue. Such experiences create opportunities to expand one's worldview and engage in the internal process necessary to create and maintain such changes.

To create a shift in worldview and achieve such transformative learning, educational programs or interventions typically require more prolonged and extensive activities that can occur as a segment of a workshop series, on a retreat, or as part of an ongoing group experience focused on creating multicultural awareness and social justice insight, such as intergroup dialogues (Reynolds, 1997). Through these more intensive change efforts, as "individuals engage in critical self-reflection and difficult dialogues, and experience cognitive dissonance, cognitive restructuring or shifts in one's belief structure can occur" (Iverson, 2012, p. 70). This transformation increases the likelihood that individuals may become social change agents, and once they develop the essential skills, will be able to maintain this shift in their view of themselves and the world.

BENEFITS OF PARADIGM SHIFT   As stated previously, all multicultural change efforts have merit and value. However, interventions focused on creating awareness alone at the first-order level are typically necessary but not sufficient for creating lasting multicultural change within individuals and thus organizations. One of the key benefits of targeting second-order change at the individual level is that such efforts may be more likely to be self-sustaining. Once individuals shift their perspective, they may take more risks within their social circle, challenging others and the status quo, leading to rippling effects of change. One of the biggest challenges in any ongoing multicultural education or training effort is that many individuals believe that they already know all they need to know. Therefore, one of the primary benefits of a paradigm shift is that it creates critical consciousness that values self-exploration and allows individuals to move beyond "talking the talk" to "walking the walk." That level of awareness may make individuals more malleable and open to both personal and societal change. For example, awareness may help some individuals understand why *African American* may be the preferred term for some but then get easily frustrated or confused when other people use different terms such as *black* or *people of color*. However, someone who has made that paradigm shift can understand how identity is very individual and often variable and will use these terms more fluidly without feeling frustrated.

CHALLENGES TO PARADIGM SHIFT   Two primary challenges to developing multicultural change efforts target individual paradigm shifts. The first challenge is that no research has explored what distinguishes multicultural awareness (first-order change) from a paradigm shift (second-order change), and if we don't know what differentiates these two types of change then it will be difficult to achieve and sustain such efforts. Although a few scholars have more recently explored multicultural stages of change (e.g., Caban, 2010; O'Neil, 2010), more research and exploration is needed so that we can understand what our goals are and what activities, interventions, and training can create and sustain deeper learning. Part of the answer may come with more examination of meaningful theories such as transformative learning and applying such constructs to the process of multicultural self-awareness.

Second, creating a paradigm shift that ultimately may challenge the status quo requires a leap of faith and some risk taking. The PIE model offered by Watt (2007) identified eight defensive reactions that naturally occur when individuals reflect on multicultural issues, especially their power and privilege in the world. These reactions include denial, deflection, rationalization, intellectualization, principium (meaning to avoid examination based on a core personal or religious principle), false envy, benevolence, and minimization and are often the result of exposing individuals to dissonance-provoking awareness, which occurs more frequently at the second-order level of change. Such resistance is especially true for staff, faculty, and administrators who may face negative feedback or repercussions when they question current practices and worldviews of those surrounding them. It is often difficult to maintain a paradigm shift. There can be push back from family, friends, colleagues, and supervisors when individuals change their worldview, and not all individuals are ready or willing to take such risks (Iverson, 2012). Unfortunately, it is difficult to rock the boat without making yourself and others a little seasick. That is why such change cannot occur in a vacuum, and individuals need a support system of other like-minded individuals who are also engaged in self-exploration.

Relevant Competencies for Change on the Individual Level

Creating multicultural awareness or, even more broadly, multicultural competence among students, staff, administrators, and faculty members can be a challenging task. Of the student affairs competencies identified by Pope, Reynolds, and Mueller (2004), the competencies that are most relevant (in addition to the integrated multicultural awareness, knowledge, and skills) are the competencies of teaching and training, ethics and professional standards, and theory and translation.

Multicultural competence within the teaching and training area, as described by Pope et al. (2004), primarily focused on curricular transformation, multicultural issues in student affairs preparation programs, and multicultural issues in outreach and training efforts. Relying on theories to build effective classroom interventions or workshop activities to build or enhance multicultural awareness is essential to creating efforts that have a lasting impact on individuals. Finally, the competency of ethics and professional standards not only requires multicultural issues being infused into all educational efforts but suggests the importance of creating interventions that assist in the exploration of values, build important and effective dialogue skills, and do not cause harm.

Those who teach multicultural issues, whether they do so in the classroom or through stand-alone workshops on campus, often face unique educational challenges (Baxter Magolda, 1997; Jackson, 1999; Kelly & Gayles, 2010; Pope, Reynolds, & Mueller, 2004). Given that multicultural interventions can lead to emotionally charged dialogues and challenge the core beliefs and identities of individuals (Johnson & Longerbeam, 2007; Kelly & Gayles, 2010; Reynolds, 2011; Watt, 2007), individuals who are involved in designing and implementing such interventions must have essential competencies. Kelly and Gayles (2010) strongly suggest that facilitators who design and guide multicultural discussions need to be experienced and skilled; however, very few faculty members, student affairs practitioners, or university administrators have been taught how to manage intergroup dialogues or develop multicultural workshops. Although bringing in outside facilitators or contributors to assist with multicultural training on campus is valuable, it is not a viable long-term strategy. Colleges and universities need to invest more resources into the training of their staff so that individuals are present on campus with the appropriate level of skill and expertise to organize, create, and marshal multicultural efforts.

In preparation for facilitating multicultural workshops, whether targeting first- or second-order change, some basic competencies must be identified. First, designing multicultural workshops or interventions to match a student's level of awareness, knowledge, and skills can be difficult, given the varied multicultural competence levels among students (Sammons & Speight, 2008). Being trained in workshop design and having insight into the developmental differences around multicultural issues previously discussed is essential in the creation of an effective educational intervention. Additionally, facilitators must have the ability to handle the emotionally charged dialogues and resistance that may occur when individuals are afraid to directly face emotional content around controversial topics (Gloria, Rieckmann, & Rush, 2000; Mildred & Zúñiga, 2004; Steward et al., 1998). Likewise, studies have found that members of different racial groups have different expectations and responses to multicultural content, and facilitators need to be prepared for that reality (Steward et al., 1998). Accounting for differences in life experiences, identity, and overall views must be taken into consideration in the planning and implementing of multicultural interventions. Relying on Sanford's (1967) notion of challenge and support is a basic competency that should be embraced by all who are involved in multicultural change efforts.

Exemplars of Creating Individual Change

Exemplars of creating individual change at both the first- and second-order levels are beneficial in increasing our cohesive and tangible understanding of these important change efforts. These exemplars are not meant to be all-inclusive or provide a cookbook for how to design and implement multicultural change interventions at the individual level; however, they do capture the insight and skills that must be incorporated in our individual change interventions across diverse settings and roles in higher education.

A higher education professional is well read and has a thorough under-standing of the various theories and research that help to explain how multicultural change happens. Many individuals who develop and imple-ment multicultural interventions do so because they are personally com-mitted to multicultural issues. However, commitment and passion are not enough when creating educational interventions. Professionals must rely on the many theories and practices available on how to create effective programming or training. Such understanding can help a professional make a distinction between designs that create important multicultural awareness or celebrations, such as cultural festivals, diverse films, or lec-tures, and those that encourage deeper shifts in beliefs, such as retreats or intergroup dialogues. For example, an athletic director might choose to bring in a panel of LGBT athletes to speak to coaches from a very personal level rather than a one-hour lecture on homophobia in sports in hopes of achieving a deeper level of insight and change.

A higher education professional appreciates that multicultural aware-ness is a process and occurs on a continuum that is shaped by individ-ual and group identity and experiences and cannot be forced to change through any specific intervention or change effort. Given that multicul-tural awareness occurs over time, one must not become overly fixated on moving along that continuum of growth. Such efforts are often misguided and do not allow individuals to make sense of what they are learning at their own pace and in their own time. We cannot institute change efforts and expect all individuals to change just because they participated. It is vital, especially when occurring within the context of an institution-wide multicultural change effort, that we are patient and focused on the pro-cess rather than some predetermined outcome. Otherwise, administra-tors, staff members, and faculty are likely to get discouraged when there continues to be multicultural insensitivity on campus even after exten-sive multicultural training efforts and initiatives. That type of frustration often short-circuits multicultural strategic plans because naysayers use such realities as reasons to not bother with multicultural interventions. If we realize that we can learn as much from our mistakes as we do from our successes, then we will be better prepared to accept the up and down nature of multicultural change.

A higher education professional has done enough of her/his own per-sonal work around multicultural issues, such as identity and privilege, to be able to empathize with various points of view and diverse life experi-ences. To be an effective facilitator of multicultural interventions, indi-viduals must participate in an exploration of their values, biases, identity, privilege, and life experiences. This means that professionals must commit time and resources to their own multicultural education at work, professional conferences, and even in their personal lives. Without addressing one's own defensiveness, dissonance, or emotional reactions, it is not easy to truly empathize or understand the reactions of others. For example, just because a staff member is an effective facilitator around issues of race does not mean they have the awareness, knowledge, or skills to implement workshops on issues of disability or religion. Such awareness may seem less essential on interventions focused more on awareness than on paradigm shift, but that depends on the identity, expectations, and experiences of those in attendance.

A higher education professional is aware of the various challenges that result from multicultural interventions, such as conflict, raw emotion, or resistance, and has the necessary skills to work through and effectively address such reactions. Given that many multicultural educators and scholars have documented the challenging nature of multicultural change efforts, professionals must be prepared for a variety of strong reactions to multicultural training and education. Facilitators need to be comfortable with conflict and tolerant of raw emotion, directly and indirectly expressed. Direct expression often involves anger or tears, and indirect emotion might be expressed as silence or withholding thoughts and feelings. Having specific interpersonal and group skills is essential to implementing multicultural interventions. This can be especially challenging when it is occurring within a work group. For example, if financial aid officers were all required to attend sensitivity training, there could be fallout from that training that simmers over time. That is less likely to happen with a facilitator who can effectively anticipate and manage the diverse expectations and reactions of participants. One also must understand that sometimes things have to become tense and complicated as diverse experiences and views are expressed and examined. This is especially true when interventions are focused on deeper interventions that create dissonance and target paradigm shift.

A higher education professional understands that not all individuals respond to multicultural interventions in the same way and are able to take such divergent reactions into account in both the design and implementation of such interventions. Being aware of group differences across race, gender, or sexual orientation in terms of diverse beliefs, identity, and life experiences can assist facilitators in their efforts to design and implement multicultural programming or training. For example, when creating staff training on racial awareness, a director of residence life needs to understand that individuals from different racial groups may have different expectations and reactions to that training. It is not uncommon in such trainings for white individuals to get very silent and uncomfortable and people of color to feel frustrated that the conversation is one-way. Without such awareness, an effective design will not be created, and the opportunity for meaningful dialogue might be lost. With the proper skills, an effective facilitator will notice what is happening and will be able to make a process comment about the group dynamic that would allow for deeper and more substantial conversation to occur in the moment.

A higher education professional is aware that multicultural interventions, when done poorly, have the ability to harm individuals and reinforce negative stereotypes and biases. Well-intentioned individuals who are committed to multicultural issues yet do not have proper training on multicultural issues can do more harm than good. Through being unprepared to handle one's own personal reactions to others, difficult dialogues, or intense emotional reactions of others, an unprepared facilitator can create an atmosphere that has a negative impact on the participants. Although all higher education professionals must obtain multicultural competence to effectively do their work, not all of those individuals will have sufficient awareness, knowledge, and skills to be efficacious multicultural facilitators. In the area of designing and facilitating multicultural change efforts, especially those interventions targeting second-order change, some expertise is needed to create meaningful and lasting change.

Conclusion

Most college campuses have focused their multicultural change efforts on individuals through the provision of campus activities, workshops, and training opportunities. Such efforts have sometimes been ongoing but often were the result of campus crises or the specific values or goals of a particular administrator. In addition, most programs or interventions target students, with some attention to staff training within student affairs. Even fewer efforts are focused on increasing multicultural awareness, knowledge, or skills of campus administrators, staff members, or faculty. Although such change efforts are valuable and important, these interventions have rarely been based in theory, relied on campus assessment data, or were the result of empirical investigations into their efficacy or effectiveness. The commitment to creating multicultural change at either the first- or second-order change level is essential to a larger multicultural strategy on campus; however, it is also vital that such efforts be grounded in both theory and data.

Understanding how to create multicultural change at the individual level requires forethought and planning. This chapter shared several theories that can provide a meaningful foundation to any change efforts. Theories provide insight into the mechanisms of change, which is the first step in developing an effective, intentional, and broad-based collection of interventions to instill multicultural awareness, knowledge, and skills. Rather than gravitating toward programs that have historically been implemented on campus or using the consultant or training du jour, one rather should understand how individuals vary in their levels of sensitivity, comfort, and knowledge about multicultural issues. As discussed throughout this chapter, basic multicultural awareness is valuable and essential; however, it is not enough. To effect multicultural change on campus through interventions on the individual level, we must develop and implement multicultural interventions that intentionally target a deeper level of understanding. Such second-order changes can ensure the presence of individuals on campus who are equipped and motivated to address multicultural issues at the broader institutional level. Focusing on creating and maintaining multicultural awareness that is transformative in nature will ensure that individuals who are participating in various group efforts targeting diversity and multicultural strategic planning across the college and university will have the competencies they need to be successful.

4

MULTICULTURAL INTERVENTION AT THE GROUP LEVEL

The Lesbian, Gay, Bisexual, and Transgender (LGBT) Faculty/Staff Consortium at a large university was holding its monthly steering committee meeting when the seven members reached the final agenda item about the membership in and diversity of their group. The steering committee, comprising four white men, two white women, and a Latino man, quickly commenced a lively conversation about strategies to recruit more people of color to the consortium and to the steering committee. Reuben, the only person of color, was uncharacteristically silent throughout the conversation. When a pregnant pause suspended the conversation, Reuben asked, "Why do we want more people of color in the group? And are we prepared for more diversity?" The other members of the consortium fell silent and looked blankly and uncomfortably at one another.

---o---

The Associate Dean of the College of Education has, for almost six years, chaired his college's undergraduate curriculum committee. When he first arrived, one of his goals was to increase the racial and gender composition of the committee's membership. For two years, he had the most diverse curriculum committee among all the colleges at the university. In the past two years, he has seen a steady decline in that diversity, and as he starts a new year, he sees that he is essentially back to where he started. He's wondering why he and the committee have not been able to sustain the diversity it enjoyed for those two years.

Situations like these take place at many colleges and universities. They are particularly common during search processes and discussions about the composition and processes of task groups and committees. They tend to focus immediately on strategies, assuming the rationale and readiness for group diversity is understood and appreciated by all. However, this assumption can undermine genuine and successful attempts to enhance and benefit from diversity in organizational units in higher education. These conversations can gain much from an honest, open, and (sometimes) challenging dialogue about why diversity in the group is important and how to maximize the benefits of that diversity.

Krumboltz (1966) observed, "The way we think about problems determines to a large degree what we will do about them" (p. 4). Yet, as Pope and Mueller (2011) observe, because of the applied nature of our field, student affairs practitioners (and, by extension, other higher education professionals) are often eager to find solutions and to act on problems before fully understanding them. This can lead to frustration, inaction, or premature or poorly guided strategies.

This chapter examines multicultural change strategies of diversifying and restructuring the membership within a group. In this chapter, the term *group* refers to any organizational unit of a college or university, whether a staff, a committee, a task group, or a student club or organization. Although groups may range in size from 2 to 40 members, the average size group tends to be approximately seven members (Forsythe, 2006). Multiple groups will constitute an organization and, in some instances, the literature will use the terms interchangeably, because an organizational unit is, by definition, a group. For example, an interfraternity council at a college may comprise multiple fraternities and sororities. The network of members in each sorority or fraternity constitute a group, as does the network of members within the council.

Using the framework of the multicultural change intervention matrix (MCIM), this chapter focuses on the principles, considerations, and approaches to multicultural change at the group level, both first-order and second-order change. At the group level, first-order change involves diversifying membership within groups; second-order change involves maximizing the benefits of that diversity. First, this chapter explores what is meant by the concepts of diversifying and restructuring group membership. Additionally, a discussion of the benefits of both types of group change is presented, as well as exploration of some of the barriers and challenges that make it difficult for groups on campus to fully embrace multicultural change. This is followed by a brief exploration of some of the core competencies needed to create group change. Finally, exemplars of multicultural change at the group level are provided to stimulate readers' thinking about group interventions and enhance their understanding of how these key issues can reshape their own multicultural change efforts.

Group Change: Theoretical Frameworks

Any discussion on multicultural interventions at the group level benefits from defining the term *group*. Forsythe (2006) defined a group as "two or more interdependent individuals who influence one another through social interaction" (p. 3). Key to this definition are the notions of interdependence and interaction. *Interdependence* refers to the mutual influence members have on one another's actions, feelings, behaviors, and experiences (Wageman, 2001). *Interactions* are the behaviors among members in the group that focus on task accomplishment (e.g., deciding, generating a product, achieving a goal) and the socio-emotional life of the group (supporting, disagreeing, collaborating) (Bales, 1999). To illustrate the significance of interdependence and interaction, consider two buses: on one bus there are 30 individuals who constitute a basketball team traveling to a tournament, and on a different bus the same number of passengers traveling along a busy city street. Though there are 30 individuals on each bus, the collection of individuals alone does not mean there is a "group" on each bus. The first bus contains a group of 30 individuals who must interact in interdependent ways to achieve a mutually agreed upon goal (i.e., winning the tournament), whereas the other bus contains individuals who have no commonalities except that they all happen to be passengers on the same bus.

This is not to say that interaction and interdependence are the only characteristics that help us understand groups. Forsythe (2006) suggests that in addition to interaction and interdependence, other characteristics are essential to studying and understanding groups. *Size*, for example, can indirectly affect many other characteristics of the group such as interdependence and structure. The *structure* of the group describes the organization and the stable patterns of roles and relationships among the group members. These are often determined by status (rank, power, prestige), attraction (likability, affection), and communication networks. Groups often exist in pursuit of *goals*. The goal of a group is a key characteristic and will, in large part, determine the activities of the group, which may fall into one or more of four primary activities identified by McGrath (1984): generating, choosing, negotiating, and executing. Another important characteristic of groups is *cohesiveness,* or the strength of the bonds among the members (Forsythe, 2006). Cohesiveness—based on the degree to which there is liking, respect, or trust—helps to keep the group unified.

Group Development and Change

A particularly important characteristic of groups is how they change and develop over time. One of the most long-standing, referenced, and influential models of group development was proposed many years ago by educational psychologist and researcher Bruce Tuckman (Miller, 2003). Tuckman (1965) examined 55 research articles on therapy groups, human relations training groups, and natural and laboratory groups. He focused, in particular, on the interpersonal stage of group development and the corresponding task behaviors exhibited by members within the group. The four stages of the interpersonal realm were ordered as testing and dependence, intragroup conflict, development of group cohesion, and functional role relatedness. The corresponding tasks for each of these stages were labeled orientation to the task, emotional response to task demands, open exchange of relevant interpretations, and emergence of solutions. The sequential interpersonal stages and their corresponding tasks were summarized in a model of four stages more widely referred to as forming, storming, norming, and performing. Interestingly, Tuckman did not coin these four labels until the discussion section of the article, yet they became the naming scheme that would describe group development for decades and would account, in large measure, for the popularity of Tuckman's work (Bonebright, 2010). Based on a review of additional research since he first proposed the four-stage model, a fifth stage—adjourning—was later added (Tuckman & Jensen, 1977). Each of these stages is detailed below.

FORMING. In the forming stage, group members become oriented to one another, to the leaders, and to the group. It is a stage characterized by uncertainty as members of the group attempt to define the group's objectives and to test interpersonal boundaries. During this stage, there is a tendency to be dependent on the authority figure or established procedures to provide direction. Maples (1988), cleverly using alliteration to characterize this stage, uses terms such as *courtesy, confusion, caution,* and *commonality.* With time, this caution gives way to budding trust and openness (Forsythe, 2006).

STORMING. As the name suggests, this stage is characterized by intergroup conflict and confrontation. This conflict arises from an exchange of viewpoints on the goals, tasks, and functioning of the group and differences of opinion on these. Tuckman (1965) noted that in this stage typically one sees resistance to the task at hand and to the influence of the group. Much time and energy is devoted to working through and working out conflicts and disagreements. Maples (1988) used terms such as *conflict, concern, confrontation,* and *criticism* to describe this stage.

NORMING. This stage is characterized by greater cohesiveness and consensus as attention is directed toward establishing ground rules and agreed-on roles for group members. Mutual understanding of these rules and roles helps members evaluate the appropriateness of behavior within the group. The norms established in this stage are both procedural (e.g., how decisions are made) and relational (e.g., how information is exchanged) (Dose & Klimoski, 1999). Unlike the forming stage, there is less dependence in this stage on authority figures and preestablished standards to establish the group's norms. Maples (1988) described this stage with the terms *cooperation, collaboration, cohesion,* and *commitment.*

PERFORMING. In this final stage of the original model, the group becomes more flexible and fully functional, and its attention and activity (e.g., problem-solving, decision-making, implementing) are directed toward delivery of the group's goals and objectives. Also, although conflict may surface during this stage, it is worked through promptly and constructively. Forsythe (1990) proposed that even those groups that reach this stage must mature within the stage before becoming fully productive. Terms such as *challenge, creativity, consciousness,* and *consideration,* according to Maples (1988), characterize this stage.

ADJOURNING. Tuckman and Jensen (1977) added this fifth stage to the model after years of research on the original model. Key to this modification was acknowledging the significance of separation, termination, and dissolution as part of a group's "life cycle." As such, groups, particularly those that are short-term or temporary, will end when they have reached their prescribed goals. In other instances, groups may adjourn when they exhaust their resources or when an unanticipated problem occurs that makes continued interaction impossible. Maples (1988) used terms such as *compromise, communication, consensus,* and *closure* to describe this stage.

Critique of Tuckman's Model

As with many stage-sequence models, there are strengths and weaknesses (Bonebright, 2010). Among the strengths of this model are (1) it is accessible and easy to understand; (2) it is flexible enough to apply to many groups in many different settings; (3) it is the most commonly identified group development model mentioned by practitioners and researchers. Among the limitations are (1) it may be overgeneralized beyond therapy-group settings; (2) the linearity of the stages suggests that all groups must go through all the stages in sequential order. Finally, though less a criticism of the validity of the model, is the rhyming scheme, which may make the model vulnerable to oversimplification or misapplication.

Still, the model has applicability in student affairs and in higher education. First, the terminology and the key concepts of the model have heuristic value even if the linear nature of the stage is not embraced. Indeed, groups may go through many of the stages multiple times and not necessarily in order (Shaw & Barrett-Power, 1998), and even as Tuckman (1965) noted, groups may experience aspects of multiple stages at a given time, but one stage will still be more predominant. Similarly, groups may focus on relationship issues at one stage of the model while focusing on task issues at another stage of the model (Jones & Bearly, 2001). Also, Tuckman acknowledged that groups may foreclose at a stage, or they may revert back, or (as leadership, membership, or purpose changes) a group may cycle back to an earlier stage. Second, the flexibility of the model makes it applicable to the wide range of groups that exist in student affairs and higher education organizations from student groups (e.g., clubs, fraternities, sororities, intramural teams), to departmental staff teams, to therapy groups, to short-term task groups.

Multicultural Groups: Theoretical Framework

Having provided a theoretical framework for groups (i.e., characteristics and stages of development), we now turn our attention to a theoretical framework for addressing multicultural interventions at the group level. Critical to this discussion, first, is a dissection of the term *diversity* and a definition of the term for the purposes of this chapter. Following this, we present the MCIM conceptualization of change on the group level: both first-order change (membership) and second-order change (restructuring).

Defining Diversity

Fundamental to a discussion on diversity in groups is an examination of the term *diversity*, because it is central to the notion of diversifying and restructuring the group. Arredondo (1996) observed that the common use of *diversity* is (perhaps unconsciously) erroneously associated with affirmative action policies and procedures and, consequently, connected to issues affecting white women and people of color only. This represents a limited understanding of the scope and complexity of diversity.

From Arredondo's (1996) perspective, diversity refers to a greater range of "individual human differences" (p. 15) and can be understood across three dimensions—A, B, and C—of personal identity (Arredondo & Perez, 2006). The A dimension includes those characteristics we are born with or into and, consequently, are least likely to change. These include age, biological sex, assigned gender, culture, ethnicity, race, language, physical/mental well-being, sexual orientation, and social class. Clearly, some may dispute the unchangeability of some of these characteristics, including gender, ability, and social class. The B dimension includes those characteristics that may be (but not always) a consequence of the A characteristics and may vary because of a wide range of historical, societal, economic, and political circumstances. The B characteristics include educational background, geographic location, language, hobbies, recreational activities, health care practices/beliefs, relationship status, religion and spirituality, work experience, and military experience. The C dimension includes generational status marked by the era one is born into. Arredondo argued that the B dimension characteristics are, in large part, a result of the A characteristics in the context of the socio-historical characteristics of the C dimension.

El-Khawas (2003) conceptualized dimensions of diversity very similar to those of Arredondo (1996) and, further, described a dimension she called "situational differences" (p. 46). These include demographic differences that are unique to the college student, including enrollment status, work status, degree objective, residential status, on-line learners, transfer students, and so forth. Overall, this functional approach to diversity illustrates the variability and complexity of the term.

Ely and Thomas (2001) observed that common across all demographic variables is the important dimension of cultural identity. In their discussion, they note that cultural identity (rooted in sociocultural differences such as race, gender, sexual orientation, ability, and so on) emphasizes shared worldviews, meanings, values, priorities, norms, and communication styles of members within a cultural identity. As such, there may be differences among cultural identities across groups and within groups, depending on the degree to which the individual or the group identifies with the cultural identity. There may also be variance within the individual, depending on the salience of their identity given the environment or situation (Jones & McEwen, 2000). As Reynolds and Baluch (2001) noted, sometimes the differences within cultural/identity groups are as compelling as the differences between cultural/identity groups.

Ely and Roberts (2008) further complicate the concept of diversity by suggesting that there is more to diversity than how group members differ on any given dimension such as race, gender, age, or sexual orientation. First, they suggest, we need to acknowledge the different social and historical meanings attached to each demographic. Race, for example, has been marked by a history of disparities and conflict, whereas the same cannot be said for age. Therefore, they note, we would not expect racial diversity to yield the same group dynamics and resources as age diversity. Second, each demographic identity cannot be viewed in a silo because of "simultaneity" (p. 177). This refers to the fact that people hold multiple identities, some dominant (e.g., men, white, heterosexual, Christian) and others marginalized (e.g., women, people of color, gay and lesbians), that interact with and affect the other. For example, the authors note, a gay white man and a straight Latino man may have different experiences of their "maleness" based on different cultural meanings and power associated with sexual orientation. Finally, when the focus is on the differences between groups, the intragroup dynamics are overlooked or assumed not to exist. A black woman, for example, within a group may monitor the behavior of her black co-worker to assess whether her own behavior is "black enough" or "too black," to manage others' perception of her. Ely and Roberts state, "sameness is more than just the absence of difference; it has its own dynamics that influence how diversity plays out in teams" (p. 178).

Rodriguez (1998) challenges the use of traditional demographic variables as a way to define diversity within a group, particularly with respect to the effect group diversity can have on creativity, effectiveness, and member satisfaction. Rodriguez argued, for example, that diversity of values is as strong an explanatory variable as demographic characteristics.

A thorough discussion of diversity (and all its dimensions) is useful and serves as a reminder that, as Frey (2000) observed, "The traditional, taken-for-granted ways of dividing the diversity pie may no longer be fulfilling" (p. 4). Still, Smith (2009) acknowledges that the challenge in defining diversity is often a balancing act between being inclusive and being meaningful. Sometimes, a long list of all possible identities and characteristics can become so exhaustive that it can start to lose meaning and focus when discussing matters of diversity. Linnehan and Konrad (1999) refer to this as the "dilution of the concept of diversity" (p. 410) and assert that viewing diversity as any or all differences between members within the organization distracts attention from the aspects of diversity that are most critical to an organization's effectiveness (i.e., race, gender, sexual orientation, and so forth).

Therefore, for the purposes of this chapter, we adopt a more conventional definition of diversity, one commonly used by higher education professionals and found in reports from the American Association of State Colleges and Universities and the National Association of Land-Grant Colleges (cited in McClellan & Larimore, 2009, p. 227): "all aspects of human difference, including but not limited to race, gender, age, sexual orientation, religion, socio-economic status, and status as a veteran." Sandeen and Barr (2006) remind us that because diversity comes in many forms, all must be considered in our efforts to diversify work groups and to make meaningful change within diverse groups.

MCIM: Change on the Group Level

The group level of the MCIM is concerned with diversifying groups in terms of membership and practice, using both first- and second-order change methods (Table 4.1). This chapter focuses on the group that is the target of the intervention, which may consist of professionals (faculty, administrators, and staff), paraprofessionals, or students and who may form one of many types of groups such as a staff team, a committee, or a club. The two types of change targeted at the group level result in two different cells of interest: first-order change or *membership* (the diversity of group composition) and second-order change or *restructuring* (how the group operates given its diversity). Each of these is described in greater detail in the following sections.

Table 4.1   Multicultural change intervention matrix (MCIM)

Target of change	Type of change	
	First-order change	Second-order change
Individual	A. Awareness	B. Paradigm shift
Group	C. Membership	D. Restructuring
Institutional	E. Programmatic	F. Systemic

© Raechele L. Pope (1993)

First-Order Change: Membership

This cell of MCIM (cell C) is concerned with the membership of the group. It addresses two important elements. First is the composition of the group in terms of its diversity. Hurtado, Milem, Clayton-Pedersen, and Allen (1999) refer to this as the "structural diversity" of the group or the numerical and proportional representation of various identities (typically race, ethnicity, and gender). The second element involves those efforts to increase or expand the structural diversity of the group. This goal is accomplished, according to Pope (1995), by adding underrepresented individuals to the group, usually through "traditional recruitment efforts" (p. 243).

The group development theory proposed by Tuckman (1965) and Tuckman and Jensen (1977) has limited applicability when discussing first-order change, because it assumes that development of the group starts once, or shortly after, the group has already formed. It does not address the conditions that precede the formation of the group or efforts to change the structural diversity of the group. For this, we must turn to a conceptualization that provides insight on efforts, which address structural diversity of the group.

As discussed previously in the book, several authors, such as Katz, Jackson, and Holvino, have depicted the developmental process by which organizations come to embrace multiculturalism. Katz (1989) and, later, Katz and Miller (1996), extended the developmental model originally created by Jackson and Hardiman (1981), describing the process as a continuum from monoculturalism to multiculturalism (or from status quo to change) that can assist a group, department, or organization in conceptualizing its goals of diversity and inclusion. The model can be a useful tool in helping a group assess its location along this continuum and to design interventions to move the group (or organization) forward toward embracing diversity. The first points along the continuum describe the process of diversifying the composition of the group (first-order change). The later points describe necessary structural changes within the group (second-order change), which are discussed in the next section of this chapter.

The monocultural extreme, or "*the club*" (p. 9) as Katz (1989) called it, is that initial point on the continuum characterized by attempts to exclude any diversity. Examples of this are rare and include such groups as Nazis, the Ku Klux Klan, or all-male country clubs. In higher education such exclusivity is typically not an issue. However, there may be elements of this in more passive ways, in which members of homogeneous groups are unaware of or avoid procedures, practices, and policies that might make the group more heterogeneous. The next point along the continuum is called *"symbolic difference"* (Katz, 1989, p. 10; Katz & Miller, 1996, p. 108). Here the group ensures that there is symbolic representation of diversity, usually to remain in compliance with policies or to avoid perceptions of being "the club." For example, a search committee for a new vice president of enrollment management may actively recruit the one African American college dean to serve on the committee. The next point on the continuum is referred to as "critical mass" (Katz & Miller, 1996, p. 108). Here the group becomes more conscientious about structural diversity and emphasis moves from the numbers only (recruitment) and to maintenance of diversity (retention). Katz (1989) noted that this is crucial point in moving a group from monoculturalism to multiculturalism, because the group has begun to accomplish its goal of creating structural diversity and is beginning to examine important questions about norms, power, and structure. For example, a summer orientation staff may have realized its goal of greater racial diversity but is beginning to question why the staff seems to be fragmenting into smaller subgroups along race lines. Katz and Miller (1996) described this stage as a pivotal point in which "the old rules no longer work, but the new rules have not all been created" (p. 108). This stage will be further discussed in the next section on second-order change.

BENEFITS OF DIVERSIFYING MEMBERSHIP In the scenario at the beginning of the chapter, when the members of the consortium were asked, in effect, "why diversify?," they fell silent. Many in higher education seem to agree that diversity in the group is important, but few can articulate why. Adapting the insights of Smith and Wolf-Wendel (2005) and Smith (2009), we present several benefits of diverse organizational units (i.e., groups) within higher education.

First, and most commonly identified, diversity in any group brings the richness of different and sometimes new ideas and perspectives on how to think about and respond to the group's goals, objectives, problems, and solutions. Second, diversity breeds diversity. Diversity within a group can create a more comfortable and welcoming environment for those from underrepresented groups who seek access to peers and colleagues whom they perceive, based on shared identity, will understand their experience and issues. This, in turn, can expand and increase the number of connections and networks of diverse communities and, in turn, positively impact the social and cultural capital on campus. For example, a faculty scholarship support group over the years may have gained a reputation for consistently having a diverse representation of members, which, through its established networks, perpetuates itself and attracts more diversity, not only for the group itself but for the institution. Third, and in a related way, greater diversity within groups conveys, to those outside the group, a genuine commitment to inclusion. Smith (2009) asserts, "The absence of any diversity, especially, sends signals about possibilities and lack of recognition and appreciations of talent in people from diverse backgrounds. The presence of diversity, on the other hand, creates a sense of possibility" (p. 69). Finally, diversity within a group and across multiple groups at an institution may reflect institutional achievement with respect to espoused values and goals of pluralism and inclusion. Smith proposed that when there is diversity within multiple subgroups on campus (e.g., academic departments, staff teams, student groups), which more closely reflects the student population as well as the community outside the institution, there is more validity placed in decision-making that is informed and enriched by the diversity of the decision-makers.

CHALLENGES OF DIVERSIFYING MEMBERSHIP Whereas diversity within the group presents numerous advantages and opportunities, it also can present some challenges. Foldy (2004) identified four dynamics that undergird some of the inherent challenges of diversity within the group. First, she argues that individuals tend to be more comfortable when surrounded by people like themselves. When individuals find themselves in a more heterogeneous group, they are more likely to "feel strange or to perceive others as strange" (p. 531). This, in turn, may result in group members feeling less safety and less trust. Second, although differences of opinions and perspectives are regarded as one of the benefits of group diversity, differences regarding how to define a problem, proceed with a discussion, view possible solutions, and decide on a solution can lead to irresolvable conflicts if not handled appropriately. Third, no matter how diverse the group, some members may perceive themselves as the minority, thus as different, less comfortable, and perhaps not welcome. Those in the majority, whether they are aware of it or not, may end up creating an environment that makes feelings of inclusion difficult for others.

A response—sometimes a threat—to diversifying a group can be resistance. As Maurer (2006) argued, resistance is an important consideration in change, and it is often the primary reason change fails. Resistance may manifest itself as "direct confrontation, disagreement or denial, questioning, lack of trust, lack of commitment or follow-through, helplessness, confusion, excuses or blaming" (Gallant & Rios, 2006, p. 188). Kayes

(2006), in an analysis of recruitment and hiring practices in higher education, presents three myths (and related assumptions) that undermine a group's best efforts to enhance diversity. Though they are specific to hiring faculty and staff, they have implications for a variety of groups in that they all underscore the role that resistance plays in harming efforts to diversify.

The first myth is that if the leadership embraces diversity, then it will be realized by those engaged in the process of recruitment and selection. The assumption is that those on search committees have discussed and have agreed on this as a priority, when in fact the institutional culture may be resistant to diversity and a multiculturalism. This can result in "a backlash that plays out behind closed doors of search committee deliberations" (Kayes, 2006, p. 65). The second myth is that expanding the diversity pool and will result in hiring a more diverse staff. The assumption here is that the only reason there is less diversity on the staff is because there is less diversity in the candidate pool. However, as Kayes argues, "diverse candidate pools do not necessarily result in diverse hires" (p. 65), because the organizational culture may unconsciously sabotage efforts to increase diversity. Finally, recruitment and retention are two very different things. Any initiative to diversify staff that does not also address institutional and departmental cultures that are indifferent or hostile to staff of color will end up with a revolving door. In sum, Kayes argues that institutional and individual resistance to diversity and multiculturalism must be rooted out if organizations are to realize their goals of faculty and staff diversity.

Second-Order Change: Restructuring

This particular cell of the MCIM (cell D) goes beyond the group membership in terms of diversity (first-order change); it addresses restructuring the group (second-order change). Restructuring the group, according to Pope (1995), involves an examination of the group's membership, mission, values, and norms; involvement of all group members in determining the planning process for change within the group in terms of its goals and objectives; and incorporation of multicultural principles in how the group operates and achieves its goals. This intervention, then, is not only concerned with who is participating in the group, but in how those individuals go about conducting their business in a way that values all and effectively negotiates the diversity of ideas, customs, identities, worldviews, and behaviors. Manning and Coleman-Boatwright (1991) refer to these cultural, structural, and systematic changes as an overall change to the status quo of the organization or group. Without thoughtful and systemic ways to leverage diversity within organizations, we may be operating under the assumption that once there is diversity within the organization, the benefits will accumulate as if by magic—what Chang, Chang, and Ledesma (2005) called "magical thinking" (p. 9). In sum, successful second-order change interventions are critical in helping a group become truly multicultural, beyond the numbers.

Here we return, momentarily, to the continuum proposed by Katz (1989) and Katz and Miller (1996) at the pivotal point where emphasis on numbers and structural diversity (first-order change) gives way to an emphasis on group dynamics within the diversity of the group (second-order change). This point of the continuum, termed *acceptance* (p. 108), is the location where the group acknowledges procedures and norms that need to be changed and begins to effectively incorporate and empower its diverse membership. This, however, is also where the very challenging work of second-order change (restructuring) begins.

Group Development Implications

Halverson (2008) provides a compelling look at Tuckman's model (Tuckman, 1965; Tuckman & Jensen, 1977) through a multicultural lens. In doing so, she examines the implications of each stage of development in terms of how multicultural or diverse the group (or team) is. She uses the term *one-up* to describe members of privileged cultural and identity groups, and *one-down* to describe targeted and marginalized group members. Halverson's analysis of the Tuckman model has significant applicability for second-order change interventions of groups and is described in detail in the following sections. The first stage of this conceptualization (forming) captures the overlap between the diversification of the group (first-order change) and restructuring within the group (second-order change).

Forming

The forming stage has a "complex fabric of issues" (Halverson, 2008, p. 87) that multicultural groups must face. Norms for the group that are usually taken for granted in more homogenous groups—pacing of speech, use of silence, nonverbal cues, emotional expression—take on greater significance for multicultural groups. For example, members from more individualistic cultures may be oriented to individual or personal achievement, making them more cautious about the joining-up process. Members of more collectivistic cultures, however, may more readily emphasize interdependence, group identity, and understanding and meeting the expectations of others.

The role of privilege (i.e., power) associated with different group identities also needs to be considered (Halverson, 2008). One-up group members may make a number of assumptions about the formation of the group. They may assume that all members of the group feel the same comfort and assurance they feel as a new member of the group. They may assume leadership, automatically initiate, and do much of the talking. They may make assumptions about hidden identities of group members, assuming that all are heterosexual, native speakers, Christian, or without a disability. Conversely, one-down group members may "wonder what the price of membership is" (p. 88) and question the degree to which they must abandon (or conceal) their identity to become part of the group as it forms. During this stage, in diverse groups, there is a high degree of politeness among group members as they size up interpersonal and task relationships; this politeness may even become exaggerated to the point of being awkward or disingenuous.

Storming

At this stage, the politeness gives way to open disagreement. The assumed ways of operating (e.g., communication, work styles, and so forth) that emerged in the forming stage are now challenged as the group faces their differences in identity, culture, and levels of power. Depending on culture and identity, members may vary in their preferred approach to this storming: avoidance, indirect communication, or direct communication. Regardless of approach, most will adopt language that is "I/me" more than "we/us." Complications in understanding others' expression of emotions, often culturally driven, may also arise in this stage.

Members of the one-down group may express anxiety with having to conform to the one-up group members' modes of communication, social habits, or work styles. Likewise, they may express frustration with any exclusion they experience for not conforming. They may be aware that they are being accused of not participating in the group or of subgrouping with other one-down group members. At this stage, the one-up group members may struggle with being confronted by the perceptions, tensions, and emotions of their one-down group member counterparts. They may, as Katz and Miller (1996) suggest, pine for "the good old days" (p. 108), when there was less upheaval of the group culture. The challenge in this stage is to work through these conflicts and find constructive and productive ways of working with differences.

Norming

By this stage, many of the interpersonal issues have been negotiated and there is greater acceptance of differences and greater mutual understanding. Although tentative, this sets the foundation for how to proceed as the emphasis shifts from "I/me" to "we/us." The challenge in this stage is to establish and commit to norms that reflect and incorporate the diversity of its members. This is usually most successful when implicit norms (usually the norms of the up-group) become explicit through open conversation, negotiation, and commitment. Also, this is the stage in which greater time and attention is paid to including the perspectives and views of everyone in the group. During this stage, diversity becomes viewed not as a source for conflict but as an opportunity for richness, deepened relationships, and higher productivity.

Performing

At this stage, interpersonal relationships are genuine and supportive, and task accomplishment is high. The group has reached a point of synergy in which the whole is greater than the sum of its parts. For the multicultural group, a number of important skills and strategies support and maintain this synergy. There is active and genuine listening to all members of the group, there is risk-taking and support, there is openness to probing and challenging ideas. In addition, the multiple identity dimensions of a person become appreciated. The gay member is appreciated not only for being gay, but for all of her or his other group identities. In sum, the multicultural group in this stage benefits from increased creativity, unique insights, and a range of observations that all come to bear on expanded ways of understanding and responding to the task. Finally, regarding interpersonal relationships, the multicultural group is better able to adjust to changes as members leave and new members join the group. Adler (2008) argues that multicultural groups that reach this stage will—because of better observations, greater insights, and more creativity—outperform monocultural groups.

Adjourning

All groups come to an end whether because of an end to the academic year, a high turnover in membership, or the completion of a specific task. For the multicultural group, adjournment is another stage in which cultural implications need to be addressed. For example, the level and expression of emotions may differ based on gender and cultural identity. Some experience joy or relief at the dissolution of the group; others may mourn the loss of relationships. Some may want to end the group unceremoniously; others may want to recognize, ritualize, or celebrate this stage of the group. Some may want to put the group behind them and move on to the next project; others may want to redefine and repurpose the group for a new project. All of these ways of terminating the group may be influenced by culture and identity and may need to be addressed as part of the adjourning process.

Benefits of Restructuring

Returning to the insights from Katz and Miller (1996), Miller (1998), Smith and Wolf-Wendel (2005), and Smith (2009), benefits of restructuring the group emerge. First, although diversity allows for a greater range of insights and perspectives, restructuring allows for a shared and mutually respectful understanding of goals, roles, and procedures. This can enhance buy-in among all of the group members and can help groups to be more unified and nimble in their responses to the challenges and opportunities and better able to adapt, evolve, and learn as they encounter new issues. Bunker and Alban (2006) referred to this as finding "common ground" (p. 300), a position from which the group members do not focus on their differences as much as on what they agree. A second benefit is that the group effectively incorporates and empowers the diversity of group members. Multicultural norms and values then become fundamental to the group's mission, values, norms, and ways of operating, including how decisions are made, how resources are allocated, and how conflict is addressed. Group members recognize that multiculturalism is more than the right thing; it is value-added and essential to the group's ability to reach its goals. In short, multiculturalism becomes part of the DNA of the group, as monoculturalism once was.

Challenges of Restructuring

One the biggest challenges that accompanies the second-order change of restructuring is the inevitability of conflict. This conflict, if not handled appropriately, can cause a group to revert back to the old ways of conducting business, discontinue the change process, or avoid and move on to other priorities (Katz & Miller, 1996). Conflict, however, from the multicultural perspective is not viewed negatively as much as it is viewed as essential for growth to occur and for the goals of multiculturalism to be realized (Manning & Coleman-Boatwright, 1991). Manning and Coleman-Boatwright observed, "Power relationships, role definitions, and priorities shift, both in a revolutionary and evolutionary sense, as multiple cultural perspectives become prevalent, recognized, and valued" (p. 371). A second challenge, identified by Katz (1989), is the discomfort a group will experience and endure because it realizes that it wants to eliminate firmly entrenched racism, sexism, and other forms of oppression, but it does not know how to. Those within the organization who wish to move forward in spite of the discomfort may find themselves "in unchartered waters" (p. 12). This discomfort may cause the organization to stop its efforts and return to its old norms and patterns of behaviors. Third, similar to changes in diversifying the group is the possibility of resistance among group members who either want to keep the norms and roles as they are or are immobilized by the challenge of making changes. This may put the group through some painful discussions as they decide how to handle resistance and the resistors.

Relevant Competencies for Change on the Group Level

Designing and implementing multicultural interventions at the group level is a complex task that requires a great deal of thought, skill, and patience. Of the student affairs competencies identified by Pope, Reynolds, and Mueller (2004), the competencies that are most relevant (in addition to integrated multicultural awareness, knowledge, and skills) are the competencies of management and administration as well as ethics and standards.

Pope, Reynolds, and Mueller (2004) described multicultural competence in management and administration as implementation of organizational models, practices, and policies that challenge and alter a single (typically white male) dominant perspective. As a result, essential aspects of supervision, goal setting, and resource allocation reflect multiple approaches that are appropriate to the conditions, problems, and needed solutions that practitioners are addressing on a daily basis. The competency of ethics and professional practice involves the acts of clarifying and communicating values, negotiating competing needs, role modeling, and decision making.

Interventions at the group level involve these competencies in that making important decisions about the process of creating, maintaining, and maximizing the benefits of a diverse group involves thoughtful allocations of resources (time, staff, and money) as well as clearly communicated policies and practices that reflect shared vision of inclusion and equity. Reynolds, Pope, and Wells (2002), in their multicultural organization development (MCOD) template, address the competencies relevant to diversifying the group when they discuss the importance of a comprehensive and inclusive definition of diversity, the incorporation of diversity in mission statements, the participation of all in carrying out the mission, and recruiting and nurturing a diverse staff. Each of these is undergirded not only by management practices but by a principled commitment to the goal of diversity.

Exemplars of Creating Group Change

Exemplars of interventions at the group level are helpful in creating a more integrated, concrete, and meaningful understanding of this intervention. These exemplars are not intended to provide how-to solutions or to be all-inclusive; instead, they illustrate the important considerations and skills in both first- and second-order change interventions.

A university search committee has a thorough understanding of the term diversity, *the dimensions of the diversity, and how some dimensions may be more relevant across different contexts and situations.* An open discussion about what diversity means can be instrumental to any group's efforts to diversify. Without a shared understanding and vision, efforts to promote diversity may end up being confusing, conflicting, or constrained. *Diversity* is a term that is best understood in context. How diversity is conceptualized, for example, at a community college in a city on the East Coast may be very different from how it is conceptualized at a private, highly selective college in the Midwest. More specifically, what constitutes diversity at a predominantly white university may be very different from what diversity means at a historically black college or university. For example, at a Hispanic-serving institution, the professional staff advisor to the International Honor Society challenges the group's leadership to consider recruiting a more diverse group of students; he is met with confusion. Although the group is diverse in terms of ethnicity and culture, there are other forms of diversity that he urges them to consider. These might include commonly understood diversity characteristics such as ability, gender, sexual orientation, and language. They might also include less-conventional characteristics such as working styles, work histories, thinking and learning styles, and motivational sources.

A professional association entity group has considered, is aware of, and can articulate the benefits and challenges of diversifying membership. All too often, efforts to begin the process of diversifying group membership start with the assumption that all who have a stake in the group agree on the purpose and the task at hand. For example, a search committee convened to hire two entry-level academic advisors at a community college might find it beneficial to use the first meeting to discuss why diversity on the staff is important. Although members may be aware that there is a mandate (legal or otherwise) to foster diversity, they may be unable to articulate among themselves the importance of this goal. An honest and open discussion on the benefits of diversifying can help the individual committee members to clarify the goal, root out any resistance, and get on the same page with respect to the goal. This conversation can be framed by discussions about the benefits of diversity to an advising center as well as some of the challenges inherent in a diverse office setting. Rather than jump immediately into the very important tasks of the search committee (i.e., recruitment, interviews, evaluations, etc.), a thoughtful discussion on "why diversify?" may be the best starting point.

A student affairs division senior staff assesses the level of diversity within the group and is able to design long-term and sustained strategies to maximize diversity in the group. Diversifying the group (whether a staff or a division) is most successful when it is developed from a carefully constructed plan. Part of that plan includes a self-assessment of where the group is on the continuum of monoculturalism to multiculturalism (Katz, 1989). Several considerations and strategies are necessary in designing interventions to move the organization along this continuum and include an assessment of threats to the organization (legal or reputational); the readiness of the group for diversity; the courage to conduct an honest assessment of the level of discrimination, marginalization, and resistance that is present in the organization; and the ability to set reasonable goals and build in accountability measures for achieving goals (Katz, 1989). A newly hired director of alumni affairs at a historically black university, for example, may spend her first semester assessing the diversity of her clerical, professional, and administrative staff before she designs a long-term plan (perhaps three to five years) to increase the diversity in her department, and furthermore, develop strategies to examine the culture of the group to ensure that staff dynamics embrace, capitalize, and sustain that diversity.

Senior staff members of a student affairs division acknowledge that to diversify group membership they have to cultivate diversity. One of the key principles of diversifying a group is that diversity attracts diversity. Settling for the minimum or "the pioneers" (Katz, 1989, p. 10), in terms of diversity, may mean that diversity on staff is always a fragile condition. However, if a staff is diverse and continues to grow in its diversity, it may reach a tipping point where it continues to attract diversity and sustain itself. Many higher education professionals are aware of institutions, divisions, departments, and programs that have a strong reputation for growing and valuing diversity; these become places to work because others like themselves are in the environment. Just as Tatum (2000) observes about student diversity at higher education institutions, people need to see themselves reflected in the images, culture, individuals, and curriculum of the institution. This same principle can be applied to students, faculty, staff, and administrators in their respective groupings. An example of this phenomenon takes place at a graduate school program fair for higher education administration degree programs. A program coordinator may notice that certain institutions or programs attract more racially diverse cohorts than others. Indeed, it may be the location, the curriculum, the prestige of the faculty, or the opportunities for graduate assistantships. However, it may also be the reputation of the institution given the current demographic of its student body, where these prospective students can more readily see themselves fitting in, being affirmed, and feeling engaged.

Leaders of a professional association constituency group recognize that as their group membership becomes more diversified, open conversations about how the group will operate are key to making substantial and long-standing change within the group. Creating diversity in a group can be a challenging task and once achieved should not be viewed as an arrival point. An essential aspect of the group's ability to perform and make the most of this diversity is to have a shared understanding of the group's goals, decision-making processes, conflict management, and assignment of individual roles and responsibilities. Group members should not assume that the change in the composition of the group will automatically result in changes in how it operates. In fact, changes in membership may create tension and confusion, which can cause the group to retreat to more familiar (i.e., monocultural) ways of operating. It takes leadership, from the positional leader or members within the group, to ensure that there are open conversations about the implications of diversity within the group and equal sharing of ideas on how the group can operate, given its diversity.

Conclusion

Diversifying and maximizing the benefits of membership in groups that constitute a college or university campus has been a priority in higher education for decades. There are many reasons for this: complying with federal mandates; honoring democratic principles of equality and egalitarianism; or recognizing the value and benefits of living, learning, and working in heterogeneous settings. Whatever the reason or reasons, it is a worthy but challenging objective. Perhaps it is a worthy objective *because* it is challenging.

Realizing this objective can be enhanced, we believe, by unpacking the concept of multicultural interventions at the group level. To that end, this chapter has posed and answered the following questions: What do we mean by diversity? What does it mean to go beyond diversifying a group to restructuring the group? What are the benefits? What are the challenges? And, what are some practical considerations, recommendations, and examples? Although these are important questions to ask and answer, they are not enough. To effect multicultural change on campus, through interventions on the group level, we must not only attend to the composition and demographics of the group; we must look at the norms, values, communication, and culture of the group. In short, and echoing what has been stated elsewhere in this book: when striving for multicultural change on campus, diversifying membership in the group is necessary but not sufficient. As Marquis et al. (2007) maintain, diversity in numbers alone will not contribute to effective practice and harmony in a group; it must be viewed as "value added" and baked into the structure of the group. Similarly, we contend that effective multicultural change on campus at the organizational level is a process and not an arrival point.

5

MULTICULTURAL INTERVENTION AT THE INSTITUTIONAL LEVEL

The director of multicultural affairs at a large Midwestern university had an active and well-developed program of undergraduate diversity advocates who provided diversity programs all over campus. Her advocates were committed to their work and truly invested in creating change, but they were currently feeling rather demoralized because of a recent biased incident on campus. They were beginning to wonder whether any of their efforts made a difference. She believes in the importance of this campus program but is beginning to wonder if this is the right approach to changing hearts and minds toward diversity.

○

As the director of multicultural affairs at a small liberal arts college on the West Coast, Dr. Johnson often touted the abundant student-oriented diversity programming they did on his campus every year. He was quite proud of this work. Recently, after attending a national conference on diversity issues, he began to think about the lack of diversity initiatives on the academic side of the campus and how overall the campus lacked any campus-wide diversity goals or expectations. Once back on campus, Dr. Johnson met with both the president and the provost and suggested that the campus create a vice-provost for diversity position to ensure that multicultural issues were integrated throughout the campus, not only through his office. Both the president and provost listened carefully but were clearly resistant to the idea. Dr. Johnson left the meeting discouraged and began to question the administration's actual commitment to diversity.

Evidence clearly demonstrates that more and more colleges and universities are exploring campus-wide approaches to addressing multicultural issues; however, many of those efforts lack depth and breadth (Williams, 2013). Educational efforts that do not focus on faculty and administrative initiatives can be superficial (Pope, Reynolds, & Mueller, 2004; Williams, 2013). Simply including "diversity language" in the campus mission and values statement is not enough. Instead, both systemic and systematic strategies are necessary to incorporate multicultural issues throughout the fabric of the institution in self-sustaining ways.

Creating multicultural campuses requires transforming underlying values, mission, policies, and practices in ways that weave multiculturalism into every aspect of the campus fabric. This level of change cannot occur without new approaches, strategies, and tools that have been explored in much depth previously in this book and in other publications. Relying on a cafeteria-style approach to multicultural interventions will not achieve the stated goal of creating campuses that value diversity, support all students, and create a citizenry committed to social justice and equality.

This chapter focuses on creating institutional change. In this chapter, the term *institution* can refer to a specific unit or department on campus, a division of student or academic affairs, or the entire college or university. Hence, *institution,* in this case, refers to a sphere of influence or a unit of control. For the purposes of this discussion, such units, divisions, or campuses typically have their own mission, strategic goals, and operations and often interact with other areas of campus in interdependent ways. Using the framework of the multicultural change intervention matrix (MCIM), this chapter focuses on the various strategies and approaches to creating multicultural change at the institutional level, using both first- and second-order change methods. At the institutional level, first-order change involves developing more programmatic approaches to diversity within the institution; second-order change involves generating a more systematic and systemic diversity plan. First, this chapter explores what is meant by the concepts of programmatic and systemic change. Additionally, the benefits of both types of institutional change are discussed as well as exploration of what some of the barriers and challenges are that make it difficult to create campuses that fully embrace multicultural issues in every aspect of the institution. This is followed by a brief exploration of some of the core competencies that are needed to create institutional change. Finally, exemplars of multicultural change at the institutional level are provided to encourage and expand how the readers think about multicultural interventions targeting the institutional level and ultimately to influence how their own efforts and practice within their divisions and institutions can be altered and expanded to create more successful multicultural change efforts.

Institutional Change: Theoretical Framework

Williams (2013) describes creating multicultural change as being both an art and a science. The art portion is intuitive and responsive, whereas the science part is likely grounded in theory and empiricism. Unfortunately, in the area of diversity, not enough empirical research has guided practice. However, a growing number of theories and models explore multicultural change. "Having a multidimensional philosophy toward change is a fundamental theme in the organizational literature, a key aspect of becoming a strategic diversity leader and vital to navigating the turbulent cultural, political, and administrative contexts of colleges and universities" (Williams, p. 209). Reliance on theory in the service of creating organizational change has long been the purview of the field of organization development (Chesler, 1994; Marshak & Grant, 2008); however, one must remember that although "there is a certain neatness to theories and models that seek to explain human interaction and organizational behavior" (Ramos & Chesler, 2010, p. 4), practice and reality are rarely neat.

Previously in this book we have focused on multicultural organization development (MCOD) as the primary theory being used to explain the multicultural change process; however, other organizational theories can supplement this theoretical knowledge and add significantly to our foundational understanding and, therefore, our ability to act in well-informed ways. Although having theories that guide practice is valuable and necessary, Prochaska and Norcross (2009) suggest that integrating multiple theories to create deeper understanding has great possibility. To that end, for the purpose of this chapter, three theories are used to extend our understanding of organizational change. First, the theory of organizational learning, which has a long history of explaining how organizations learn and adapt (Argyris & Schon, 1978; Senge, 1990), is briefly explored. The second theory that is explored is the transtheoretical model of change, which has a long history of being applied to individual behavior change as discussed earlier in this book. Prochaska, Prochaska, and Levesque (2001) decided to turn their theory to help deal with some of the fragmented and unscientific approaches available for creating organizational change. Finally, the social change model of leadership development (Komives & Wagner, 2009) is shared as a global approach to creating social change on campus through a powerful leadership model. These three theories can add to our appreciation of how to instill multicultural change at both the first-order and second-order levels of change.

Organizational Learning

Smith and Parker (2005) suggest that organizational learning has promise as an approach to increase institutional capacity for diversity. Part of this recommendation is based on the unique structure of higher education (e.g., decentralized, nonhierarchical, collective decisions). According to Kezar (2007), organizational learning is a "powerful and successful approach to changing individual belief systems that shape institutional policies and practices to create an inclusive campus environment" (p. 579). Williams (2013) agrees and views organizational learning as a method well suited to "break the cycle of flawed diversity implementation efforts" (p. 209).

We cannot fully explore the underlying theory and mechanisms of organizational learning; however, some of its key constructs and their relevance to changing organizations, specifically colleges and universities, are briefly explored here. To create change, "organizations need knowledge/information as well as systems for processing this knowledge/information in order to learn. Systems help to translate information into learning, which shapes beliefs and resultant behaviors" (Kezar, 2007, p. 581). Organizational learning is a process-oriented approach to change, which fits well with the view that multicultural change should be focused on process more than outcome. By creating opportunities for members of a campus community to reflect on their multicultural efforts and examine what has succeed or failed and why, the prospect of change is enhanced (Smith & Parker, 2005). Those discussions can grow out of a campus assessment in which important and relevant information is gathered from all aspects of the organization. To be effective, the sources of information must be diverse and include quantitative surveys, focus groups, narratives, and other methods (Kezar). The process that follows must be intentional, focused, and structured. Although many campuses are engaged in gathering this information on diversity efforts, it can sometimes be viewed as a task of compliance rather than a learning opportunity (Smith & Parker).

Different approaches have been suggested in applying organizational learning to the multicultural change process. Williams (2013) offers a diversity-focused variation of the triple-loop model offered by Argyris and Schon (1974) that encourages reflection on the goals and tasks ahead, reframing what is happening, and understanding and translating the institutional context. Smith and Parker (2005) developed the Campus Diversity Initiative Project to increase institutional capacity for diversity and learning. Their three-step approach emphasized gathering baseline data, creating a plan for monitoring progress, and developing a process for reflection and discussion of the data and what changes need to be made. All of these authors suggested that engaging fully in an organizational learning process is not easy because it typically requires changes in the organizational culture. Kezar (2007) states that strong leadership is essential; in particular, "leaders can role model the learning by being open and visible in the ways that they learn from others on campus" (p. 601).

In many ways, organizational learning seems akin to the process of moving from first-order to second-order change at the institutional level. Through active evaluation and examination of the information gathered from diverse participants on campus and multicultural change efforts (e.g., programmatic), opportunity arises for a shift in perspective and campus culture that can reinforce more systemic change efforts, such as multicultural strategic planning. Using the theory and tools of organizational learning can reinforce the lessons of MCOD.

Transtheoretical Model of Change

The transtheoretical model of change or stages of change (Prochaska & DiClemente (1984) was first introduced 30 years ago to explain how individuals change their behavior and was later applied to organizational change behavior (Prochaska, Prochaska, & Levesque, 2001). Research has shown that individuals progress through five stages in their efforts to change, and interventions that are matched to the appropriate level of change for an individual are much more likely to be successful than cookie cutter, one-size-fits-all interventions. Prochaska, Prochaska, and Levesque, in their extension of stages of change to organizations, suggest that the same rule is true for organizations as well. They cite a study by Deloitte and Touche that reports that resistance to change was one of the most common reasons that organizational change efforts do not succeed. The stages of change model focuses more on readiness than resistance. According to the theory, if individuals or employees within an organization are in an earlier stage of change (e.g., precontemplation or contemplation), they are not ready for change. With regard to multicultural change, many authors have discussed the importance of readiness (Aguirre & Martinez, 2002; Jackson, 2005; Williams, 2013). Whereas support from top leadership is essential to creating multicultural campuses, systemic change emphasizes the importance of engaging and involving all members of the community. Prochaska, Prochaska, and Levesque quote an advertisement by Deloitte and Touche that speaks to this point: "Imposed change is opposed change" (p. 253).

The corporate world, with its top-down mentality, has often emphasized an action-oriented model of change. However, wanting someone or an organization to change is not enough. We can have a family member who smokes, and just because we are worried and want them to stop that destructive behavior does not mean that they are ready. We could try to force them, but that will not be successful. They may want to change as well, but that does not mean they are ready yet. The same is true for organizations. If faculty, staff, and administrators at a college have doubts about a multicultural strategic plan and worry that it will not be worth the effort, they are likely to resist such efforts in either subtle or open ways. By assessing the readiness of an organization using the stages of change model, choosing the type of interventions that are more appropriate for their stage of change will be easier. According to Prochaska, Prochaska, and Levesque (2001), "a more promising approach is social influence in which leaders scientifically and sensitively assess the stages of change in individual employees. Planned interventions and interactions are then matched to the employee's stage. A predictable consequence is greater participation, less resistance, and more progress (or change) toward the desired goal" (p. 255). This commitment to social influence, through some of the tools suggested by Prochaska (1979) such as consciousness raising, self-reevaluation, environmental reevaluation, reinforcement management, and social liberation, is a vital component of the multicultural change process and fits well with the tenets of MCOD.

Social Change Model of Leadership Development

In keeping with the focus on social influence is the social change model of leadership (SCM). First developed over 20 years ago (HERI, 1996; Komives, 2007), the SCM offers a new approach to leadership that emphasizes social justice and social change. Although it is primarily focused on undergraduate leadership, the seven dimensions or values of SCM are useful to consider when developing a multicultural campus. Those dimensions are citizenship, collaboration, common purpose, controversy with civility, consciousness of self, congruence, and commitment. These seven values are grouped into three dimensions: individual, group, and community or society, which are similar to the three targets of the MCIM. The creation of multicultural change is completely dependent on leadership, both at the top and throughout the institution (e.g., Aguirre & Martinez, 2002; Kezar & Carducci, 2009; Kezar & Eckel, 2008; Pope, Reynolds, & Mueller, 2004; Williams, 2013), so the leadership focus of the SCM is quite relevant.

Wagner (2009) describes social change as a response to social problems that is based on identifying and addressing the root causes of these problems through the use of a collaborative process. Although commonly individuals become involved in social change because the problems affect them personally, given that many community problems are intertwined, there is reason for all to get involved. This is certainly true when addressing multicultural issues on campus. Not all students may face discrimination or bias, and not all staff, based on their job responsibilities, are required to address multicultural issues, but no doubt the multicultural issues on campus touch everyone. Similar to MCOD, the tenets of the SCM are designed to improve the quality of all organizations or campuses by their emphasis on positive values, collaboration, and commitment to the social good. According to Cilente (2009), the SCM is a "framework for continual exploration of personal values in working with others to attempt change. This approach to leadership requires continuous reflection, active learning, involvement, and action" (p. 72). Like the MCIM, the SCM is not a checklist approach to creating multicultural change but rather emphasizes a process in which individuals, groups, and institutions can engage.

Socially responsible leadership is dependent on the development of change agents, who are individuals committed to change and serve as catalysts within a group or institution (Drechsler & Jones, 2009). A change agent, as discussed elsewhere in this book, helps to create conditions necessary for change. Such individuals can exist at every level of an organization, such as a financial aid officer, student organization advisor, provost, faculty member, dean, athletic director, or vice president for student affairs. Multicultural change cannot happen on campus without individuals who are involved, invested, committed, and actively working to create a multicultural campus. Through empowering others and nurturing a campus that emphasizes the seven Cs of the SCM, a change agent can make a difference. These lessons, as well as the values and approaches to leadership offered by the SCM (Komives & Wagner, 2009), can be easily incorporated into a systemic approach to multicultural change.

MCIM: Change on the Institutional Level

The institutional level of the MCIM (Table 5.1) is focused on creating broader, system-wide change using both first- and second-order change

Table 5.1   Multicultural change intervention matrix (MCIM)

Target of change	Type of change	
	First-order change	Second-order change
Individual	A. Awareness	B. Paradigm shift
Group	C. Membership	D. Restructuring
Institutional	E. Programmatic	F. Systemic

© Raechele L. Pope (1993)

strategies. This chapter focuses on the institution as the target of the intervention, which may consist of specific units or departments, divisions of academic or student affairs, or the entire college or university. The two types of change targeted at the institutional level result in two different cells of interest: first-order change or *programmatic* (e.g., creation of new positions, programs, or multicultural initiatives) and second-order change or *systemic* (e.g., deeper structural changes beginning with examining institutional values, goals, and practices and then linking them to diversity outcomes). Each of these is described in greater detail in the following sections.

First-Order Change: Programmatic

This cell of the MCIM (cell E) is primarily focused on programmatic interventions targeting the entire college or university or perhaps a particular division, school, or department within an institution. Such efforts have included highly visible changes, such as the development or expansion of programs that address multicultural student services. These offices may be broad in their mission (e.g., Office of Multicultural Affairs) or more specialized (e.g., lesbian, gay, bisexual, and transgender [LGBT] services, Native American cultural house). Developing a multicultural in-service to train all tutors within academic support services would be another type of programmatic change. Creating new positions on campus, whether it is the vice provost for campus diversity or a multicultural advocate within a specific office, is another way to make programmatic changes around multicultural issues. Although these efforts are important and can create an important and observable commitment to multicultural issues on campus, these interventions may not ultimately alter the underlying values or structure of an office, division, or overall institution. Hiring individuals or creating offices to address multicultural issues tends to make those individuals and programs responsible for diversity on campus but fails to make other individuals understand their responsibility or be held accountable. Such an approach is akin to simply relying on multicultural experts rather than the broader expectation of multicultural competence for all. If criteria for evaluating work performance or distributing discretionary funds are not tied to diversity issues, then the paradigm shift needed for second-order change is not likely to occur. Understanding programmatic interventions is essential to creating a foundation for broad and lasting multicultural change.

Benefits of Programmatic Interventions

The importance of increasing visibility of multicultural issues on campus cannot be understated. "Multicultural student services (MSS) offices have played a significant role in supporting underrepresented populations on campus and in developing systemic change around multicultural issues within institutions" (Shuford, 2011, p. 29). Given the history of exclusion within higher education, understanding the history of these programmatic efforts at specific institutions and within higher education as a whole is paramount to the development of future multicultural change efforts (Kupo, 2011). Without such programs and individuals, which typically have provided essential support to underrepresented and underserved students on campus, likely retention and satisfaction of underrepresented students would be greatly diminished. Manning and Munoz (2011) suggested that although MSS was expected to become obsolete once multiculturalism was truly embraced in higher education, such transformation has not yet occurred. Despite increasing structural diversity, incorporating of diversity in college mission statements, and more multicultural programming, true multicultural change has not yet arrived on campus (Pope & Mueller, 2011; Pope, Mueller, & Reynolds, 2009; Williams, 2013).

The presence of multicultural student services and other programmatic multicultural interventions in higher education is vital to the multicultural change process. As long as individuals on campus are committed to multicultural issues, opportunities exist to generate interest, build coalitions, and otherwise take advantage of a critical mass of students, staff, faculty, and administrators who can develop and participate in broader multicultural change efforts. Programmatic training efforts within specific offices or departments increase the number of individuals on campus who are invested in multicultural competence as a viable approach to ensuring that multicultural issues are relevant to everyone. Campuses in which limited programmatic efforts are made to address multicultural issues likely have more difficulty sustaining any multicultural interventions.

Challenges of Programmatic Interventions

In addition to the benefits of multicultural programmatic efforts on campuses, there are also several challenges. First and foremost, as long as individuals or offices exist at any college or university whose job it is to address multicultural issues, many other students, staff, faculty, and administrators will use that presence as a rationale for why they are not responsible for actively contributing to the creation of a multicultural campus. Given that such interventions do not necessarily increase the expectations or job responsibilities around multicultural issues or underrepresented students, other professionals on campus have little reason to change what they do.

Almost contradictory to the previous challenge are the detractors who claim that multicultural offices or multicultural programming or training are no longer needed or are themselves exclusionary. In a survey of over 130 professionals who view MSS as their primary job responsibility, Stewart and Bridges (2011) found evidence that many MSS offices experience lukewarm support on campus from a variety of sources, including students, faculty, and even senior leadership. Ironically, some in higher education use the evidence of increasing structural diversity as a rationale for why such specialized services are no longer needed. According to Stewart and Bridges, "the effectiveness of multicultural centers is hindered, in part, by perceptions that they serve a limited population based on race or that they are solely programming offices and by a lack of visibility with faculty" (p. 56).

One final challenge to programmatic change efforts on campus is the increasing complexity of student diversity. Initially MSS and multicultural training focused on racial differences, but as awareness has grown about exclusionary practices across other differences such as sexual orientation and religion, more of a call has been made to expand the populations served (Stewart & Bridges, 2011). In addition to developing more services for emerging underserved groups, increased attention has been paid to subgroups needing additional support (e.g., men of color). The multicultural services and training that exist on college and university campuses must accurately meet the needs of the students, staff, faculty, and administrators on campus. With increased attention on assessment around multicultural issues (Pope, Reynolds, & Mueller, 2004), such offices should easily have a more precise understanding of who needs what services. This challenge is an example of how the role of MSS can expand to include building coalitions and facilitating dialogue across differences and continue to make themselves relevant on campus (Patton & Hannon, 2008).

Second-Order Change: Systemic

This cell of the MCIM (cell F) specifically targets interventions within the college or university or a particular division or school within an institution that are more systematic and systemic in nature. Rather than relying solely on the creation of new positions or training programs, cell F change efforts ensure that multicultural issues are at the core of mission statements, goals, policies, and practices. These interventions are not meant to be merely additive, but instead involve, at their core, structural changes to how the institution, division, or department operates. Although they are more intrusive, if such change efforts are to be meaningful and successful, they must be more than simply edicts. They must involve a system-wide discussion of current policies and practices and what changes must be made to create a multicultural organization. The commitment to multiculturalism must be encouraged, supported, and formally included in the reward and accountability systems within the unit. Examples include requiring goal-directed multicultural initiatives within the unit of observation that directly link the outcomes of those initiatives to budget allocations or basing hiring, salary, performance evaluation, and promotion decisions on individual multicultural competence.

Benefits of Systemic Interventions

On campuses across the country, efforts are being made to address multicultural issues in broad systemic ways. The impact is beginning to be felt. As Manning and Munoz (2011) indicate, in addition to expansion of structural or numerical diversity, "power and authority are shifting, language use is expanding, leadership styles are diversifying, and cultural competence is increasing" (p. 283). They further suggest that new organizational changes are being brought about by these structural shifts, leading to reduced hierarchy, increased consensus and participation, and a reorientation toward inclusion, democracy, and social justice.

One of the most significant benefits to systemic approaches to multicultural change is the increased accountability for multicultural efforts. Once all members of the community share responsibility and investment for creating multicultural campuses, through linking multicultural criteria to staff training, policy revision, budget allocation, and performance appraisals, such efforts are more likely to persist and endure. No longer are diversity issues just the responsibility of the few with specific interest or expertise in multicultural issues on campus. Instead, everyone has an obligation to attend to these important concerns and become invested in how to integrate them into their job description and departmental responsibilities.

Additionally, systemic efforts are more likely over time to create a common voice and commitment to change so that those individuals who are resistant will have less support and influence. Then multicultural competence and the commitment to introduce a variety of multicultural interventions becomes the norm rather than the topic du jour. Once a change becomes embedded into the infrastructure of an organization and in the expectations of all who work and learn there, it is much more difficult to negate or eradicate those changes. As MCOD has suggested, as an organization or campus becomes invested in structural diversity and social justice, members of those organizations will come to care about those issues. With that shift in priority, student, staff, administrators, and faculty members, who live and work side by side, have more opportunities to become invested in each other, thus improving the quality of interpersonal relationships and overall campus climate.

Challenges of Systemic Interventions

Multicultural scholars and practitioners alike have long lamented the inevitable resistance, sabotage, and obstacles that exist whenever systemic change is attempted (Howard-Hamilton, Cuyjet, & Cooper, 2011; Maurer, 2006; Pope, Reynolds, & Mueller, 2004; Williams, 2013). Howard-Hamilton, Cuyjet, and Cooper suggested that "there are personal, political, educational, and legal methods of blocking the multicultural movement and perpetuating a sense of fear and mistrust among those who have not been part of the dominant group in our society" (p. 11). Although such resistance is not always public or openly expressed, it often exists at all levels of the institution. Arredondo (1996) said it well: "Barriers come in many forms and present themselves at different stages of a diversity initiative. Some are readily identifiable before the initiative gets under way; others emerge en route. The challenge is to recognize, not avoid them, and be prepared to keep a clear head to deal with them" (p. 178). Arredondo further suggested that barriers tend to target the initiative itself, organizational culture, and the people involved in the change process. Multicultural initiatives cannot fix other institutional challenges facing a campus, division, or department, such as low morale, poor communication, or lack of transparency. However, that does not stop such change efforts from being blamed for larger structural concerns. Without attention to the larger institutional issues, likely multicultural initiatives will inevitably fail. Attention must be focused on the underlying organizational culture and structure itself to be successful. Finally, individuals involved at all levels of an institution, including external stakeholders or consultants, can create barriers to systemic change because of either their general fear of change or their specific anxiety or discomfort around multicultural issues (Miller & Katz, 2002). Whether faculty members who resent being told to infuse multicultural content into their courses, the students with diverse friends who believe that they already know all they need to know about diversity, or the administrators who are intimidated by their new responsibilities, many reasons exist for individuals to resist. Resistance to change can happen at all types of campuses, including predominantly white universities, women's colleges, or minority-serving institutions, and from all types of individuals, including those who represent the traditionally targeted groups such as women or people of color. Change, even when it is desired, can be challenging and difficult.

Change is difficult in higher education because of the conservative and structural nature of colleges and universities (Aguirre & Martinez, 2002). Miller and Katz (2002), in their discussion of the barriers to inclusion within organizations, indicate, "expressed in conscious and unconscious behaviors, as well as routine practices, procedures, and bylaws, these barriers are typically rooted in the very culture of an organization" (p. 7). Williams (2013) further suggests that, unlike most corporations with clear reporting structures and systems, higher education is typically complex, decentralized, and has vague goals and highly differentiated functions. In the corporate world, top-down approaches have helped infuse diversity; however, higher education, which is often more democratic in nature, relies on participation and open exchange of ideas to create change. What can be even more challenging, according to Williams, is that barriers to change in higher education, especially multicultural change, are often invisible, subtle, and fortified by negative assumptions about diversity.

Finally, challenges inherent in every change process need to be faced and addressed. Heath and Heath (2010) identify some common problems that need to be overcome. Some of the most compelling are that people:

(1) do not see the need to change; (2) resist trying new things that they have never tried before; (3) may not be motivated to change; (4) procrastinate change; (5) doubt that change will work or will make a difference; (6) become overwhelmed; and (7) are initially excited about change but then lose enthusiasm. Acknowledging and addressing these challenges head on, as a natural part of the change process, will make it easier to not be sidetracked and disheartened when the challenges occur.

Relevant Competencies for Change at the Institutional Level

Introducing meaningful, effective, and rewarding multicultural change at the institutional level involves long-term commitment and planning that can be challenging to implement in a dynamic and externally influenced setting in higher education. Of the student affair competencies described by Pope, Reynolds, and Mueller (2004), the competencies that are most relevant (in addition to integrated multicultural awareness, knowledge, and skills) are the competencies of theory and translation, ethics and professional standards, administration and management, and assessment and research.

The importance of relying on theories as the foundation for multicultural change has been reiterated throughout this book. Pope et al. (2004) emphasize the importance of theory as a guiding force, in particular, MCOD, in efforts to create multicultural campuses. As suggested earlier, ethics and professional standards as suggested by a variety of professional organizations such as the American College Personnel Association (ACPA), the American Association of Colleges and Universities (AAC&U), and the National Association of Student Personnel Administrators (NASPA) implore higher education to prioritize multiculturalism as a matter of ethics and principles of good practice (e.g., ACPA & NASPA, 1997; Blimling & Whitt, 1999; Smith, 1997).

Having the ability to incorporate multicultural issues through the use of standard organization development tools and the introduction of new approaches and strategies offered by MCOD is necessary to address the roadblocks to diversity that many colleges and universities face. Relying on concrete tools offered by Pope (1993); Grieger (1996); Reynolds, Pope, and Wells (2002); Williams (2013); and others will assist administrators and multicultural change advocates in their efforts to assess and intervene within the college environment. Incorporating MCOD approaches and tools into institutional strategic planning is one way to ensure that multicultural change efforts are ongoing and lasting (Pope,

Reynolds, & Mueller, 2004). Finally, assessment and evaluation must be a central aspect of all multicultural interventions (Williams, 2013). Not only are such assessment efforts important to accurately assess the current breadth and depth of multicultural interventions and where the institution is on the road toward becoming a multicultural campus, they are also crucial to evaluating the effectiveness of the various programs, trainings, and strategic interventions that are introduced as part of a larger strategic effort.

Exemplars of Creating Institutional Change

Exemplars of interventions at the institutional level at both the first- and second-order levels provide specific and essential examples of effective practice as well as those that will help practitioners apply MCOD theory to their work. These exemplars are not designed to be all-inclusive or provide one-size-fits-all instructions for how to create and apply multicultural change efforts at the institutional level; rather they are intended to inspire and suggest possible approaches and competencies that are greatly needed.

A higher education professional is knowledgeable of the dynamic and emerging literature on multicultural change strategies in higher education and actively seeks out new tools, theories, and approaches. The explosion of multicultural literature in higher education in the past two decades has been tremendous and has almost created a problem of riches or abundance. Many strategies, models, and approaches to creating multicultural change are available, and professionals in higher education must sort through these available materials to find information that is useful and has heuristic value. No one need reinvent the wheel and start from scratch; however, blindly following a published model or another institution's plan without considering one's own institutional culture and context is not helpful. Reliance on research-based models and plans can be especially beneficial and can be found in general higher education–related journals such as *The Journal of Higher Education,* the *Journal of College Student Development,* or the *Journal of Student Affairs Research and Practice,* or more specialized journals such as the *Journal of Diversity in Higher Education.* Attending national conferences, such as the ACPA, the AAC&U, the Association for the Study of Higher Education (ASHE), the National Association of Diversity Officers in Higher Education (NADOHE), NASPA, and the National Conference on Race and Ethnicity in American Higher Education (NCORE) that have programming and research on diversity issues is another way to stay informed and create networks with other professionals who are engaged in multicultural change efforts on their campuses.

A higher education professional understands that multicultural change is a process and not an outcome and is fully aware of the inherent barriers and challenges that accompany such a change effort. Remaining committed to multicultural change despite the barriers and challenges that may exist on one's campus can be difficult. This is especially true when there is a lot of pressure from biased incidents, demanding students, and concerned stakeholders. However, the more patient and resilient professionals are, the more equipped they will be to address and withstand any challenges that come their way. If the focus is long-term and the goal is to engage in an open-ended process, then barriers and setbacks will not be as discouraging. If one is focused only on immediate change and satisfaction from everyone, the journey will be more stressful than it needs to be. Growth or change does not occur only in an upward or forward motion; rather, it involves periods of active growth, plateaus, and even setbacks, much as suggested by Manning and Coleman-Boatwright (1991). Creating a vision, setting short-term and long-term goals, and engaging in ongoing assessment or evaluation are effective approaches to feeling both proximate achievements and long-term successes.

A higher education professional sees the necessity and value of both programmatic and systemic interventions in the various multicultural change efforts implemented on campus. Remember that it is useful to have a diversity of multicultural interventions and that no hierarchy of interventions exists. Programmatic interventions are often highly visible and show the campus community that diversity matters. However, that is only true if those individuals, offices, or programs are allowed to have a real impact on campus. Interventions and efforts also must occur behind the scenes and truly affect how all individuals on campus do their jobs. In addition, the value of the systemic interventions is that, when instituted systematically, the entire multicultural change effort will be part of a larger plan. Moving away from haphazard, crisis-oriented, and intermittent efforts will only strengthen the effectiveness and integrity of the work.

A higher education professional is committed to addressing the underlying foundational issues of communication, organizational culture, and rewards/incentives that profoundly influence the capacity to create multicultural change. Multicultural change efforts cannot fix what already ails a department, division, or institution. If issues already exist around key issues such as communication, workforce motivation and morale, or other underlying aspects of the organizational culture, new interventions likely will not work until those issues are addressed. The MCOD suggests that organizations cannot be healthy without engaging in this type of review and revision of core structural components (e.g., policy, evaluation). Such an honest and thorough review can possibly encourage institutions to fully vet their strengths and weaknesses. When these foundational issues are in good shape and the overall health of the organization is strong, then multicultural change efforts are more likely to succeed and have a positive impact.

A higher education professional understands that context is everything, so taking into account the various cultural, geographic, historical, and institution-specific realities is essential to effective multicultural change. Every college and university is unique, and its distinctive factors must be taken into consideration when designing multicultural interventions. Learning the history of multicultural issues on one's campus is vital to any future endeavors. Past efforts and their impact, whether they are positive or negative, affect how members of the community will perceive any new approaches to addressing multicultural issues. Likewise, knowing one's local community and region and the underserved populations typically attending the college or university is also vital to addressing the diversity of the student body. Finally, knowing how the type and setting of one's campus influences any multicultural change efforts or strategic plans is vital. The various types of colleges and universities (e.g., urban, rural, or suburban institution, public or private, small liberal arts college or large public university, secular or religiously affiliated, a women's college, military institution, or a predominantly white institution or historically black college, tribal college, or institutions with significant Latino or Asian populations) shape the target of any multicultural interventions, because each of those campuses will have different underserved and underrepresented student populations. Similarly, each of these diverse campuses will have its own unique histories, challenges, and inherent strengths. Many of these types of colleges and universities have growing resources and networks for addressing diversity issues on their campuses. Any conversations or interventions around multicultural issues must be sure to address these unique realities.

A higher education professional values the use of assessment at all stages of the multicultural change process and introduces effective tools that produce results that are automatically recalculated into the multicultural change calculus. To develop an effective multicultural plan, one must incorporate assessment and evaluation at every stage of the process. Gathering information as a baseline is an important first step. Some of the data already exist, such as the diversity of the students, faculty, and staff as well as what interventions have been done in the recent past. In addition, one also must gather data about the perceptions of the various subgroups on campus. This would include students, faculty, and staff as well as any visible or invisible subgroups (e.g., students of color, LGBT staff and faculty, first-generation college students). If no climate assessment has been done, then such information about how individuals view the campus must be gathered. This can be accomplished through already designed climate tools, an instrument developed for one's campus, or qualitative means such as interviews or focus groups. All of this information can be used to develop a multicultural strategic plan. Once that plan is enacted and interventions have begun, one must evaluate the effectiveness of those efforts and then make changes as needed to improve the usefulness of any interventions. Assessment and accountability has become increasingly prevalent on college and university campuses, and sometimes campus communities grow weary of such efforts. However, assessment is less likely to be tiresome if the process is inclusive and the results, including the voices and views of many campus constituencies, are heard and incorporated.

Conclusion

More and more colleges and universities are using institutional approaches to creating multicultural change on campus. Yet, many of those efforts continue to be haphazard, crisis-oriented, shortsighted, and lacking grounding in current theories or research. As the number of theories, approaches, and tools continue to expand, one may easily become dazed and overwhelmed by all the choices. Viewing multicultural change as a long-term commitment and process, rather than a short-term outcome that can be checked off some list of accomplishments, is a valuable way to deal with information overload. Focusing on the importance of institutional context and the realities of the developmental process of multicultural change makes it easier to remember that there is no one or right way to create multicultural change at the institutional level.

Developing an effective and self-sustaining multicultural strategic plan requires a deep commitment that makes it possible to withstand the many barriers and challenges that will inevitably appear. This chapter reinforced some of the theoretical influences that are essential to creating institutional change. Theories provide an important foundation on which multicultural plans can be built. Such plans need to include both programmatic and systemic change methods to ensure that diversity efforts are both visible (as is common with adding positions or programs) and embedded (as most structural changes are). First-order change creates individuals and programs that have key responsibilities to ensuring that multicultural efforts stay constant, which continues to be a necessary reality within higher education (Manning & Munoz, 2011). Second-order change reinforces the belief that all individuals, interventions, programs, and efforts become accountable in an institution's effort to become more multicultural. Programmatic and systemic efforts build the capacity for institutional readiness, which is needed to transform organizational practices and culture (Aguirre & Martinez, 2002). The ability of colleges and universities to meet the needs of all students depends on the tools and strategies of multicultural organization development as well as the efforts to ensure that all staff, administrators, and faculty have the necessary competencies to enact meaningful and effective multicultural change.

6

ASSESSMENT AND EVALUATION OF MULTICULTURAL CHANGE EFFORTS

MAKING MULTICULTURALISM A FOUNDATION OF a higher education institution is a data-driven process (Jackson, 2006; Pope & LePeau, 2011). Assessment and evaluation are key to understanding the effectiveness of multicultural change interventions. Livingston (2006) asserts that a successful evaluation process can help an organization understand "what impact the change process has had on the organization, on the groups within the organization, and on individuals within the organization" (p. 231). Indeed, assessment and evaluation scaffold the entire process from the initiation forward, because the organization (or in our case, the college or university) must first assess where it must begin its journey and then use ongoing assessment (formative) and evaluation practices to determine its progress as it implements change plans (Jackson, 2006).

This chapter discusses the importance of assessment and evaluation as *part* of the multicultural change process, not as the final step of the process. The goal is not to provide the reader with specific assessment and evaluation strategies and techniques; those are detailed in numerous other texts. Instead, the goal of this chapter is to understand the importance of assessment and evaluation at individual, group, and institutional levels through a multicultural lens. This chapter opens with fleshing out the significance of these processes in multicultural change efforts. It also examines the processes at each of the target levels identified in the Multicultural Change Intervention Matrix (MCIM) model (individual, group, institutional) as well as campus climate assessment. Finally, it offers considerations for conducting assessment and evaluation in a multiculturally sensitive manner.

The Importance of Assessment in Multicultural Change on Campus

When approaching the topics of assessment and evaluation of multicultural change on campus, we should remind ourselves of the difference between these two terms and how they are similar to the related term, *research*. Pope, Reynolds, and Mueller (2004), citing Upcraft and Schuh (1996) and Gay and Airasian (2000), proposed the following distinctions among the three terms: *Assessment* is a measure of effectiveness of an institution or organizational unit within an institution. *Evaluation* is the application of assessment data to improve the effectiveness of interventions made by the institution or organizational unit. Whereas both assessment and evaluation relate to measuring and guiding practice, *research* is more closely related to testing and informing theory. Pascarella and Whitt (1999) proposed that because all three terms share fundamental principles, the all-encompassing term *systematic inquiry* is appropriate. Systematic inquiry is a set of processes and principles that are "focused on collecting and analyzing information both outside and inside the college or university or student affairs organization, and using that information in policymaking, planning, and decision making" (p. 94). For the purposes of this chapter and in light of the content of this book, we will use the terms *assessment* and *evaluation* interchangeably when discussing the principles and processes of systematic inquiry, except in instances in which we are explicitly distinguishing between a measure of the current conditions (i.e., assessment) and the effectiveness of interventions (i.e., evaluation).

Assessment and evaluation are critical to creating multicultural change on campus (Pope & LePeau, 2011). Assessment and evaluation allow practitioners to better understand the current state of affairs of—and to measure the effectiveness of interventions targeted at—multicultural issues at an institution. For example, assessment can help the office of admissions gain insight into why there is a revolving door of counselors of color; evaluation can measure the long-term effects of bi-annual retreats for the admissions staff to examine group dynamics, departmental goals, and decision-making processes. When considered from this perspective, the processes of assessment and evaluation should not be regarded as something that occurs at the end of the change process; instead, they are integral parts of the change process (Livingston, 2006)

Much has been written about the importance of assessment and evaluation in student affairs and in higher education (Bresciani, 2011; Love & Estanek, 2004; Pascarella & Whitt, 1999; Terenzini, 1989; Upcraft,

2003; Upcraft & Schuh, 1996). The goal of this chapter is not to discuss the importance or the techniques of assessment and evaluation as much as to discuss these forms of systematic inquiry in light of multicultural change efforts on campus. To accomplish this, we turn to literature that highlights this perspective.

Smith, Wolf, and Levitan (1994) discuss lessons learned from institutional research on diversity. We believe these lessons have important implications for assessment and evaluation of multicultural change efforts on campus. First, assessment and evaluation of diversity in higher education should not be limited to statistics on demographics of various populations. It should also focus on organizational performance, satisfaction of constituencies, and effectiveness of interventions (Comer & Soliman, 1996). Smith, Wolf, and Levitan (1994) refer to this as "reframing" (p. 3); in a similar way, we think of this in terms of a second-order perspective. Take for example, as Smith et al. do, graduation rates. Oftentimes, the study of graduation rates focuses on students and factors such as race, gender, and academic preparation (i.e., first-order). A second-order perspective to (or a reframe of) this topic might be to focus on the institution and such factors as faculty–student interaction, support for advising and teaching, and campus climate. A second lesson is that the very act of engaging in assessment and evaluation of multicultural change efforts is part of the process of change. Just the announcement of assessment and evaluation of diversity and multicultural issues opens up discussions about topic, the researchers, the methods, the potential outcomes, and so on. Third, assessment and evaluation benefit from multiple methods of data collection to get multiple perspectives. In addition to the quantitative approach to data collection and analysis gleaned from survey and institutional archives, qualitative data from interviews, focus groups, and observations can also provide a richer picture of the topic at hand. Ponterotto (2002) argued that qualitative approaches to the study of diversity equalize the power distribution between the researcher and the participants in such a way that the participants are actually the "experts" on the topic being studied. Fourth, assessment and evaluation of multicultural change in any given department or office has the tendency to reveal these issues throughout the institution. Multicultural issues on campus do not exist in silos. As Pope, Mueller, and Reynolds (2009) observe about the pervasive nature of diversity on campus, "there are few areas of university life untouched by these issues" (p. 640). For example, assessing hiring practices of faculty of color may lead to new insights on the curriculum or the campus climate. Finally, the study of diversity and multicultural change efforts can be politically charged and rife with strong emotions across a wide range of constituents (students, faculty, staff, community, and so forth). The challenge is for those conducting the assessment to engage in open communication at all stages of the process, from the design through the analysis, interpretation, and reporting. Furthermore, being as inclusive as possible in each of the design steps is essential. Inherent in each of these lessons are important implications of assessment and evaluation of multicultural change efforts when it comes to the stakeholders, the design, the inquiry approaches, and the discussion of the meanings, scope, and implementation of results.

Dimensions of Multicultural Assessment

Livingston (2006) proposes that when conducting evaluation to measure the effectiveness of organizational change efforts (including multicultural change), evaluation should occur on all levels: individual, group, and organization/institution. This "systems view" (p. 233) is necessary because organizational change cannot occur if there is not change at the group or individual levels (and vice versa). With this principle in mind, we discuss assessment and evaluation at all three levels as well as overall campus climate as a form of assessment. Again, our goal is not to detail the steps and procedures of assessment and evaluation as much as to share how these principles and potential resources (i.e., models and instruments) that are related to multiculturalism and multicultural change function across these four levels.

Assessment at the Individual Level

Assessment of multicultural change at the individual level is a measure of one's awareness, knowledge, and skills with respect to diversity-related content (first-order) or of an individual's cognitive restructuring or shift in worldview (second-order). Whereas first-order change efforts on the individual level may address (importantly) more surface awareness, knowledge, and skills, second-order change addresses a deeper consciousness, what Freire (1970) referred to as *conscientizacao*. Assessment at this level, in comparison with institutional and group levels, can be challenging because the line between awareness (first-order) and a paradigm shift (second-order) can be blurry. In theory, what one thinks and how one thinks are distinct; in practice (i.e., measurement), these are complex constructs to measure and to differentiate from one another.

Because efforts to increase knowledge about diversity-related topics (e.g., information about various racial, religious, and other cultural groups) are largely factual and content-heavy, assessments of that knowledge may be accomplished with more informal assessment. For example, the Pew Forum on Religion & Public Life (2010) has a 15-item multiple-choice online quiz on knowledge about various religions. Teaching Tolerance (n.d.) provides a 10-item online quiz to measure knowledge of Native American influences in U.S. history and culture.

Assessments of the second-order change at the individual level tap into constructs such as attitudes; one's awareness of identity with underlying assumptions and biases; knowledge about how oppression operates at the individual, group, and organizational levels; motivations for growth and change with respect to diversity issues; and ability to incorporate multicultural awareness and knowledge into multicultural skills. These characteristics may look familiar to readers as they undergird the overarching construct commonly referred to as multicultural competence (Pope & Reynolds, 1997; Pope, Reynolds, & Mueller, 2004). Models and measures of multicultural competence have become ubiquitous throughout the counseling and clinical psychology literature (see Gamst, Liang, & Der-Karabetian, 2011) and are growing in the student affairs and higher education literature (see Pope & Mueller, 2011).

Some of these instruments may not be designed for, and thus suitable for, staff assessment and evaluation of second-order change at the individual level. For example, the Multicultural Competence in Student Affairs—Preliminary Form 2 (MCSA-P2) (Pope & Mueller, 2000) in its current form is most appropriate for research purposes. The Multicultural Competence Characteristics of Student Affairs Professionals Inventory (MCCSAPI) developed by Castellanos, Gloria, Mayorga, and Salas (2007) may, however, serve the purposes of staff assessment and evaluation. In addition, an examination of the multicultural psychology and multicultural counseling fields reveals a host of measures that can be used to assess individual levels of multicultural awareness, knowledge, and skills as well as attitudes toward, perceptions of, and responses to issues of race, gender, sexual orientation, and disabilities (Gamst, Liang, & Der-Karabetian, 2011). Finally, Pope and Mueller (2011) propose, citing the multicultural counseling literature, that higher education professionals also may begin looking at individual assessment of multicultural competence through the use of portfolios (Coleman & Hau, 2003) or observer reports (Ponterotto, Mendelsohn & Belizaire, 2003).

Assessment at the Group Level

Assessment of multicultural change at the group level can be an examination of either the structural diversity of the group (first-order) or the dynamics within the multicultural group (second-order) or both. Such assessment allows us to evaluate our progress toward diversifying the group membership and the mechanisms by which we accomplish this. Similarly, these assessments can assist in measuring our efforts to restructure how the group operates in terms of the group's mission, values, goals, and norms and the involvement of all group members in planning, decision-making, managing conflict, and achieving its goals. No established instruments specifically provide for assessment of these constructs at the group level. However, some useful recommendations have been made for designing assessments to accomplish this as well as resources that can be used or adapted for the purpose. We review these.

When assessing group membership and demographics (first-order), quantitative measures of the numbers or representation of the group may be most practical and efficient. A number of considerations can be helpful to framing this type of assessment (Washington State Human Resources, 2012). These can apply to smaller groups (clubs, teams, task groups, committees, organizations, staffs) as well as larger organizational units such as departments. These considerations include:

o *Representation:* This is primarily a profile of the group and the degree to which it parallels the institution's profile, similar groups on campus, as well as like groups regionally or nationally.

o *Recruitment and hiring/appointing:* Focuses on the diversity of the pool of possible members in the pipeline and efforts to attract and include them. Here questions are raised about representation of the initial pool, those who make it to the potential candidates, and those who are actually selected or invited into the group. Also, questions about efforts to expand the pool can be examined.

o *Retention:* The emphasis here is on efforts to maintain the extant diversity within the group. Areas for assessment may include opportunities for development, advancement, and increased incentives/benefits (e.g., salary) within the group. Of particular interest is how these opportunities may differ based on group members' race, gender, sexual orientation, and so forth. For example, are the promotion rates for white group members and people of color similar? How about between women of color and men of color? Is there pay equity between men and women in the organization? Between women of color and men of color?

o *Turnover:* Similar to retention data, turnover data are important. Who is leaving the group, at what pace, and why? Of particular interest may be the voluntary versus involuntary turnover by demographic category or intersecting identities, such as lesbian, gay, bisexual, and transgender (LGBT) staff of color compared with heterosexual staff of color.

o *Resource and affinity groups:* Within an organizational unit, affinity groups for specific identity groups (e.g., women, men of color, LGBT, and so forth) can be key in attracting and retaining a diverse group (Network of Executive Women, 2006; Reed, 2011). Are there affinity groups for representative demographics? How active or involved are these subgroups? What is the participation in these groups?

For the most part, these considerations (and the associated questions) can facilitate assessment that addresses first-order change interventions. Assessment of the group from the perspective of second-order change focuses largely on the group dynamics, particularly the group's norms, communication, ability to manage conflict, and climate of interpersonal relationships. One useful instrument, developed by Halverson (2008), and which reflects the multicultural aspects of Tuckman's (1965) group development model (see Chapter 4), is the multicultural team assessment instrument. This is a 20-item measure arranged on a five-point Likert scale across the dimensions of goals, roles, procedures, and interpersonal relations. Though administered to individuals within the group, an overall assessment of the group's functioning and development can be determined.

Other than the multicultural team assessment, no specific instruments exist that measure the construct described by second-order change at the group level. However, numerous measures of specific group dynamics such as conflict, structure, power relations, and performance (Forsythe, 2006) are available, and these measures might inform efforts to address restructuring a group in terms of multicultural change interventions. For example, the Intercultural Conflict Style (ICS) inventory (Hammer, 2005) acknowledges that conflict style is "culturally contexted" (p. 677) and, as such, may vary in terms of directness of communication and expression of emotion. The ICS could be adapted for assessment at the individual, group, and organizational levels to measure fundamental approaches to conflict resolution across cultural differences.

Of course, qualitative approaches can be very effective in assessing and evaluating second-order change interventions, particularly given that more abstract constructs such as group roles, relationships, and climate are of primary interest. Data collection techniques such as focus groups, interviews, questionnaires, and even observation may, as Mueller and Cole (2009) suggest, "reveal the nuances and finer grains" (p. 334) of group dynamics. In keeping with the definition of second-order change at the group level, qualitative assessment strategies can focus on participants' perspectives of the group's mission, values, and norms; perceptions of the involvement of group members in determining goals and the plans for achieving those goals; and thoughts about how the diversity of ideas, customs, identities, worldviews, and behaviors are evident in how the group operates.

Assessment at the Institutional/Organizational Level

Assessment of multicultural change at the institutional level examines both the programmatic (first-order change) and systemic (second-order change) dimensions of the institution. This involves assessment of the institution's success at introducing new and needed multicultural programs and positions throughout the campus. At a deeper level, it also assesses the institution's ability to address institutional core values and practices with respect to budget allocations, hiring practices, policy development, curriculum, and so on, all in an effort to enhance the inclusion and diversity on campus. Both programmatic and systemic dimensions of assessment, though necessary, are challenging. As Laker and Davis (2009) note, professionals seeking "quantitative strategies for assessing the effectiveness of our progress in creating multicultural campuses need to acknowledge that the nature of the phenomena being evaluated does not lend itself, at least for now, to simple designs" (p. 259). Still, some useful measures and models do exist and can be used in actual assessment endeavors or can inform development of measures specific to an individual institution. Though we do not intend to provide an exhaustive list, we identify and discuss several examples in the following paragraphs.

The multicultural organizational development checklist (MODC) for student affairs (Grieger, 1996), for example, is 58-item checklist that specifies goals across 11 categories: (1) mission; (2) leadership and advocacy; (3) policies; (4) recruitment and retention; (5) expectations for multicultural competency; (6) multicultural competency training; (7) scholarly activities; (8) student activities and services; (9) internship and field placement; (10) physical environment; and (11) assessment. Assessment along these categories can be used for ongoing diagnosis and evaluation of a long-term systemic process of change within an organization or institution. Although designed for student affairs divisions, it can be adapted to other divisions at the institution or even the institution itself. In 2002, Reynolds, Pope, and Wells adapted the MODC in developing the multicultural organization development (MCOD) template. Less a diagnostic or evaluation tool, the MCOD provides its users with more of a strategic planning framework for integrating multicultural values and expectations into the fiber of the organization or institution, from mission to evaluation. The MCOD template can be useful to its users in structuring multicultural interventions or preparing an assessment tool to measure progress on these goals. A detailed presentation of the MCOD template can be found in Pope, Reynolds, and Mueller (2004), *Multicultural Competence in Student Affairs*.

Another organizational assessment tool is based on the multicultural organization model by Jackson and Holvino (1988). Holvino (2008) created a matrix or "lens," which she describes as a "tool that encourages analysis, discussion, and a shared assessment of where an organization is on its path towards becoming multicultural" (p. 5). The matrix examines the characteristics of an organization as it moves through three phases (from monocultural, to transitional, to multicultural) across nine dimensions of the organization: (1) mission or purpose; (2) structure and roles; (3) policies and procedures; (4) informal systems and culture; (5) people and relationships; (6) leadership; (7) environment; (8) services or products; and (9) language use. Accompanying the matrix is an open-ended questionnaire that can be used as a tool for open discussion among members of the organization to assess their organization and to identify goals and strategies to move from being monocultural to more multicultural.

A third organizational assessment, cited by Laker and Davis (2009), is the diversity scorecard (Bensimon, 2004). This assessment employs four dimensions (access, excellence, institutional receptivity, and retention) as its conceptual apparatus and measures each across three points of measure (baseline, progress toward equity, and equity achieved). Although focused largely on students and on matters of race, the framework for this scorecard can inform and be adapted for related assessment strategies.

In a departure from more quantitative assessments, Chesler (1998) proposed the use of a multicultural audit, which employs a conceptual map, developed by Chesler and Crowfoot (1997), that was later updated and repurposed by Chesler and Crowfoot (2000). The conceptual map proposes five key elements of an institution or organization: (1) mission (purpose of the institution); (2) culture (dominant belief systems); (3)

power (how decisions are made and by whom); (4) structure (patterns of positions and relationships); and (5) resources (financial, physical, technological, and human). Efforts to restructure an organization must involve careful attention to each of these elements to diagnose where and how the restructuring is to take place and to develop appropriate strategies. Although some professionals may argue that some elements are more important than others, all must be understood and attended to because each (in individual and overlapping ways) influences policies, procedures, and practices that affect the structural diversity and the operation within the organization or institution. For more details on the conceptual map and the specific steps of the institutional audit, see Chesler (1998).

From the Association of Research Libraries is an assessment to measure library staff perceptions of and attitudes toward principles of diversity. The Organizational Climate and Diversity Assessment (OCDA) (cited in Kyrillidou, Lowry, Hanges, Aiken, & Justh, 2009) is a 150-item survey that gathers demographic data on respondents as well as views on organizational climate and attitudes of the organization's workforce. Most relevant are the nine scales that measure climate for justice, leadership, deep diversity, demographic diversity, innovation, continual learning, teamwork, customer service, and psychological safety. The premise of the assessment is that organizations that wish to make diversity an imperative must foster these nine climate dimensions. Like all of the surveys and assessments discussed in this section, the OCDA may inform the development of measures of multicultural organizational change that can be used in different departments across an institution.

Finally, the most recent and perhaps most relevant entrant among conceptualizations and related assessments of multicultural change efforts at the institutional level is Flash's (2010a) Multicultural Competence in Student Affairs Organizations (MCSAO) instrument. Flash acknowledged that although some instruments measure the individual competence of student affairs practitioners, namely, the MCSA-P2 (Pope & Mueller, 2000), no such measure exists for "organizational multicultural competence" (Flash, 2010a, p. 33). Flash, in developing the MCSAO, reconceptualized and expanded on the conceptual frameworks of Grieger (1996) and Reynolds, Pope, and Wells (2002).

Following rigorous guidelines for scale development (DeVellis, 2003), Flash (2010a) has produced a measure containing 189 items across eight factors: (1) Organizational climate and culture of commitment, encouragement, and support for multicultural competence; (2) peer or colleague influence, behaviors, and expectations for multicultural engagement; (3) clear and coherent multicultural mission; (4) organizational focus on gender identity, expression, and sexual orientation; (5) multiculturally inclusive services; (6) support for and creation of diversity or multicultural programming and events; (7) incorporation of multiculturalism in strategic and formal organizational practice; and (8) multicultural recruitment practices. Flash reports strong reliabilities across the factors—ranging from 0.85 to 0.95—as well as an overall reliability of 0.98. A criterion-related validity study (Flash, 2010a) reported weak but significant correlations across each of the factors, suggesting that further validation studies are necessary for the instrument.

The MCSAO is designed for all members of a student affairs division to complete, allowing for a more comprehensive assessment of multicultural competence within the organizational or institutional unit (Flash, 2010a). The instrument, although still in development, has practical implications not only for single institution assessment and strategic planning, but also for multi-institutional assessment, which would allow for benchmark and institutional comparisons. Also, the instrument can be used in triangulated studies (i.e., combined with qualitative approaches such as focus groups, interviews, observations, and so on), allowing for a richer and deeper analysis of multicultural competence. Finally, the instrument can set the foundation for the development of measurements for other units in a college or university outside a student affairs division.

Assessment of Campus Climate

Schuh and Upcraft (2001) propose a comprehensive assessment model for student affairs comprising eight components that define various types of assessment. These types include (1) use of student services, programs, or facilities; (2) student needs; (3) student satisfaction; (4) campus environments and cultures; (5) outcomes; (6) comparable institutions; (7) use of national standards to assess; and (8) cost-effectiveness. The descriptions of each type of assessment, according to Schuh and Upcraft, allow practitioners to adopt the most appropriate assessment for their given purpose. Each of these components may have implications for assessing multicultural change on campus; however, student satisfaction, outcomes, and campus environments and cultures are arguably the most relevant. These components address the campus climate, which Rankin and Reason (2008) define as "the current attitudes, behaviors, and standards of practice of employees and students of an institution . . . that concern the access for, inclusion of, and level of respect for individual and group needs, abilities, and potential" (p. 264). To this already multidimensional definition, Hurtado, Griffin, Arellano, and Cuellar (2008) add the role of perceptions and expectations around issues of diversity as part of climate. They also propose that the internal climate of an institution must be considered in its larger sociohistorical and political context.

Hurtado, Griffin, Arellano, and Cuellar (2008) observed that early efforts to assess climate were often a reactive response to racial tensions on campus, usually tensions that attracted unwanted media attention. They were "one-shot portraits" (p. 218) that provided solutions to problems affecting women, people of color, and LGBT students. Over time, campus climate assessments have become proactive measures that serve as a catalyst for change and provide an essential understanding for institutional planning and intentional educational activity. Edgert (1994) details how campus climate can contribute to diversity goals of an institution. Indeed, campus climate assessment can reveal which programs, policies, and practices are contributing to diversity goals and which should be reconsidered, changed, or discontinued. Furthermore, assessment of campus climate can shift attention and discussion from isolated and particular diversity-related incidents to a collective and broader understanding of how diversity is perceived and experienced within the "fabric of the institution" (p. 54). In addition, the very process of campus climate assessment can create a sense of "psychological ownership" (p. 55) among campus constituents who have a stake in the end product and who may pay closer attention to their own behaviors, attitudes, and capacities to live in a more multicultural environment.

Edgert (1994) notes that multiple methods are used to examine campus climates, and some assessments may employ more than one of these: surveys, focus groups, interviews, open dialogues, outside evaluators and consultants, observation, and document analysis. Surveys tend to be the most common form of campus climate assessment. Examining the many surveys that are available is beyond the scope of this chapter. However, Hurtado, Griffin, Arellano, and Cuellar (2008) in their overview of campus climate assessment instruments cite numerous instruments that can be described in the following three categories: First, some instruments "take the 'pulse' of the institution or student body" (p. 213), typically in pursuit of obtaining information on intergroup tensions or dynamics on campus. They cite, for example, the 1994 California State University San Bernardino—Campus Diversity Issues Questionnaire, the 1995 University of North Carolina, Charlotte—Campus Climate Survey, and the University of Texas, Austin—Quality of Student Life Survey. Second, some climate assessments measure participant attitudes on a range of diversity topics, such as the 2000 Loyola Marymount University—Building and Intercultural Campus Climate Survey, the 1997 Texas A&M University—Campus

Climate Survey, and the University of Michigan, Diversity in the College Community: A Survey of Student Opinions and Experiences. A third set of instruments have combined measures of climate and outcomes that are essential for living in a multicultural and global society. These include the 2002 Preparing College Students for a Diverse Democracy Survey, the Campus Life in America Survey, the Higher Education Research Institute (HERI)'s Your First College Year and the College Senior Surveys, and the Diverse Democracy Project's Student Thinking and Interacting Classroom Surveys. Hurtado et al. also cite the Educational Benchmarking Institute's Student Climate/Diversity Assessment and the Faculty/Staff Climate/Diversity Assessment (discussed in greater detail in the next chapter). These instruments explore the experiences of and attitudes toward a range of social identity groups based on race, gender, sexual orientation, and so on. Outside of the instruments discussed by Hurtado et al., Rankin and Reason (2008), in their comprehensive transformational tapestry model, provide a multidimensional model of assessment and intervention to assist campuses to conduct inclusive climate assessments to better comprehend and respond to the challenges faced by diverse constituencies on campus. Particularly relevant to this discussion are the first two dimensions of the model, which detail assessment of the current campus climate, comprising the following areas: access and retention, research and scholarship, intergroup and intragroup relations, curriculum and pedagogy, university policies and programs, and external relations.

Assessment Across All Levels

As noted, Livingston (2006) urges that assessment be conducted across all levels of the organization (individual, group, and organizational). In the previous sections, we have demonstrated ways in which multilevel assessment, in line with the MCIM, can be conceptualized and accomplished. In doing so, we have treated each of these levels separately. Readers may have noted, however, that no overall assessment strategy has been presented that accomplishes this simultaneously for all levels of interventions (individual, group, institutional) and across the first- and second-order change dimensions, the essence of the MCIM. This is, in large part, attributable to the fact that no reliable and valid single measure of the MCIM exists. Indeed, although measures at the organizational level (or even campus climate level) may capture aspects of the sublevels of group and individual, these organization-level models and measures are insufficient to assess the finer aspects of the group and individual levels as articulated by the MCIM.

To say no such instrumentation exists is not entirely true, however. Pope (1992), in her national study of multiracial change interventions in student affairs, designed a survey based on the MCIM that contained items to assess the self-reported range of activities used by senior student affairs officers (N = 126) to address multiracial issues on campus. Using the MCIM to codify these activities, Pope identified that student affairs divisions used both first- and second-order changes targeted at the individual and group levels; however, they tended to use fewer second-order interventions than first-order, at the division level. Follow-up use of this measure has not yet occurred, so no psychometric data have been collected that would allow ongoing use of this valuable tool.

Pope (1995) proposed that the MCIM is well suited for framing the assessment of the full range of multicultural interventions in student affairs and other institutional divisions and offices on a college or university campus. Because of its versatility, the MCIM can support a variety of research designs, whether qualitative or quantitative, all in pursuit of helping practitioners understand and identify "the type and level of interventions required to ensure that a comprehensive incorporation of diverse cultures, values, norms, and ideas is developed" (p. 245).

Considerations in Assessment

We believe it is appropriate that a discussion of assessment of multicultural change interventions at the individual, group, institutional, or campus climate levels include some discussion of the importance of conducting these assessments in a multiculturally sensitive manner. We addressed this issue in great detail in a previous discussion of incorporating multicultural competence in assessment and evaluation procedures (Pope et al., 2004).

Five areas of assessment issues, framed by McEwen and Roper (1994) and Wilkinson and McNeil (1996), are useful to consider and are therefore mentioned here. Although some of these issues may be more relevant to specific types and targets of assessment, all are important in any systematic inquiry, particularly when assessment of multicultural change is involved. Readers are encouraged to review Pope, Reynolds, and Mueller (2004) for details and recommendations for each of these.

o Awareness of one's own assumptions and worldviews may have implications for the assessment and evaluation process. For example, how certain constructs are defined and measured may reflect a monocultural perspective. Similarly, one's worldview may have implications for the assessment process. One's point of reference (collective vs. individual), communication style, or time orientation may be culturally influenced and need to be considered when engaging in any systematic inquiry.

o Language used in assessments and language related to defining the population is important. Terms such as *race, ethnicity, culture, gender, gender expression, sexual orientation, religion,* and *spirituality* can be misunderstood by those being assessed, those conducting the assessment, or those interpreting the data.

o Instrumentation used in assessments must be considered with respect to their development, selection, and administration. The most common concerns have to do with cultural bias inherent in the development and with the "nonequivalence" of the measures (measures written only in the primary language of the dominant group).

o Conventional data collection techniques may have implications for multicultural assessment. Here one must consider variations in the techniques that take into account personal versus detached approaches, employing data collectors who are culturally similar to the population being assessed, use of the native language of the participants, and familiarity with the culture or cultures of those being assessed.

o Expanding the approaches to data collection is also significant. Most commonly used are "paper and pencil" surveys. However, qualitative approaches have the advantage of gathering more in-depth and finer-grain perspectives on the level of multicultural intervention being studied. In addition, qualitative approaches can empower the participants of the assessment because these approaches communicate that what the participant wants to share is more important than what the researcher wants to know.

As Pope et al. (2004) observe, when multicultural considerations and skills are infused into assessment practices, the findings and conclusions can be more valid, reliable, vivid, and useful, particularly when what is being assessed involves multicultural interventions in increasingly multicultural organizations in higher education.

Summary

Assessment of interventions at all levels within and across a college or university is essential to multicultural change efforts (Flash, 2010a; Jackson, 2006; Livingston, 2006; Pope & LePeau, 2011; Rankin &

Reason, 2008). As Jackson proposes, assessment and evaluation need to take place not only at the beginning of any change effort (to measure the start point and the necessary intervention to move forward), but also throughout the change effort to determine progress and to determine whether and where changes in the effort need to be made. We propose, in this chapter, that when it comes to multicultural change efforts, the principles of assessment and evaluation apply not only on a campus level (i.e., campus climate assessment), but also at the individual level, the group level, and the institutional level. To that end, we have examined assessment at each level more closely and present conceptual and practical tools to assist and guide practitioners in their efforts.

7

MULTICULTURAL CHANGE
IN PRACTICE

Timothy R. Ecklund and
Matthew J. Weigand

EFFECTIVE MULTICULTURAL CHANGE REQUIRES MUCH from higher education academics and administrators, from strong leadership (Kezar & Eckel, 2008) to multiculturally competent professionals at all levels (Pope, Reynolds, & Mueller, 2004), and from inclusive mission statements and clear strategies (Grieger, 1996; Reynolds & Pope, 2003; Williams, 2008) to consistent and proactive daily action (Brayboy, 2003). Although pursuing multicultural change requires considerable effort and commitment, it should not be viewed as an insurmountable challenge or a reason to wait for "perfect" conditions before starting multicultural initiatives on campus.

The purpose of this chapter is to highlight a few exemplars—campuses where multicultural change has occurred and is occurring—in an effort to demonstrate how the theories and ideas described previously in this book play out in "real life," at actual institutions of higher education operating in today's context and with the imperfect conditions that always surround our change efforts. Although not every institution type is represented, we hope readers will identify with some aspects of the campuses described in the following pages and not only be inspired by the progress each is making, but also find concrete ideas and practical approaches that can be adapted to their own work on their own campuses. By no means do these campuses claim to be perfect; they are simply trying their best to fulfill a commitment to diversity, inclusion, and social justice using multicultural organizational development (MCOD) strategies and approaches.

This chapter also emphasizes that effective multicultural change is context-specific, and that the concept of "one size fits all" does not apply to multicultural change strategies. The three institutions highlighted here—the University of Texas (UT) at Austin, the University of Vermont (UVM), and Saint Louis University (SLU)—range from mid-size to very large, span the country from New England to Missouri to Texas, and include a private Jesuit institution and two public universities. Although these exemplars are not intended to represent the entirety of higher education institutions—community colleges and small colleges are notably absent, for example—they do represent some of the variety among the over 4,000 American colleges and universities. The targets of multicultural change efforts within these institutions also vary. We highlight UT-Austin's multicultural change efforts within the Division of Housing and Food Service, UVM's efforts in University Relations and Campus Life, and SLU's efforts in their Division of Student Development. Again, the intent is to provide some examples of multicultural change efforts in various settings, not to comprehensively represent every organizational unit within higher education; however, we hope that readers from units such as academic departments, enrollment management divisions, and others can see connections and apply strategies presented here to their own unit settings. Although commonalities exist across the multicultural change efforts on these diverse campuses, it is also clear that their institutional cultures, settings, and regions influence their strategies and practices in meaningful ways. Readers are urged to consider the influences of their own regional, institutional, and departmental contexts as they ponder the multicultural change efforts that may be most effective in their settings.

Importantly, although this chapter focuses on institutional and administrative strategies, processes, and practices, the ultimate and primary beneficiaries of effective multicultural change efforts are college students. The measure of success of multicultural change efforts is not change in and of itself; rather, success is determined by the real impact of such change on students' lived experiences in college. The goal is to create welcoming environments where all students—inclusive of the growing diversity of identities in American higher education—are affirmed and supported as learners. Furthermore, multicultural change efforts create the conditions necessary to help us achieve a key higher education outcome of preparing all of our students to live and work efficaciously in our increasingly global and interdependent world.

Multicultural Change Initiatives on Campus

In this section, we present in-depth descriptions focusing on the broad range of multicultural initiatives at each of the three institutions highlighted in this chapter, UT-Austin, UVM, and SLU. Together with the book authors, we identified these campuses as exemplars based on our knowledge of their programs, our previous work with key staff members and their departments, or the recommendations of professional colleagues. We identified primary contact individuals at the three institutions, who provided foundational and descriptive documents as well as their own narratives and insights regarding their multicultural change efforts, including brief histories, current status, and assessment efforts. Initial inquiries were made with each institution's contact person via email, followed by in-depth consultations by phone, and, in the case of UT-Austin, supplemented by a site visit. Gaining an understanding of the multicultural change efforts at these campuses was an iterative process in which early conversations and document reviews led to additional follow-up conversations (by phone and e-mail) and review of more documents. Ongoing consultations with these institutional contacts occurred throughout the writing of this chapter over a period of more than nine months.

Our initial inquiries with each campus were organized around the following 10 multicultural organization development categories adapted from Grieger (1996) and further explored by Reynolds and Pope (2003) and discussed previously in Chapter 2 of this book: (1) a comprehensive definition of the term *multicultural*; (2) mission statement; (3) leadership and advocacy; (4) policy review; (5) recruitment and retention of diverse staff; (6) multicultural competency expectations and training; (7) scholarly activities; (8) departmental/division programs and services; (9) physical environment; and (10) assessment. This template was developed for strategic planning purposes, and in fact was used in that way by all three campuses we reviewed as they developed, implemented, evaluated, and revised their MCOD plans. In addition, the very practical framework provided by this MCOD model allowed for a comprehensive examination of the areas in which multicultural change efforts were taking place on these campuses. Although these categories loosely frame the descriptions of multicultural change initiatives that follow, we chose to focus on and emphasize those initiatives that the campus contacts deemed the most important or having the greatest impact.

After the descriptions of MCOD plans and initiatives on these campuses using Reynolds and Pope's (2003) 10-category template, we also reexamined some of the same initiatives using the Multicultural Change Intervention Matrix (MCIM; Pope, 1995) described at length in this book. This approach of using Reynolds and Pope's practical framework to comprehensively describe the multicultural change efforts, and then analyzing these same efforts through the more theoretical lens offered by the MCIM, allows readers to examine and contemplate real-life change efforts on campuses from both practical and more conceptual perspectives. Whereas the first model focuses on content areas such as mission statements, staffing issues, and scholarly activities, the second model focuses on targets (i.e., individual, group, or institution) and levels of intervention (i.e., first- and second-order change), helping campus leaders ensure a broad and comprehensive approach to multicultural change.

University of Texas at Austin, Division of Housing and Food Service

The University of Texas—Austin (UT) is the flagship institution of the University of Texas system. Situated in one of the most progressive and fastest growing metropolitan areas of the country, Austin, Texas, UT has one of the most diverse student populations of institutions of its size and Carnegie classification. The 2012 enrollment summary lists 39,995 undergraduate students, with Hispanics constituting 21% (8,344), Asian 18% (7,053), black 5% (1,960), and American Indian 0.03% (112). White students are no longer in the majority, constituting only 49% (19,598) of the undergraduate population (University of Texas at Austin Office of Information Management and Analysis Final Enrollment Analysis—Fall 2012). The issues surrounding student diversity at UT are particularly compelling given that its admissions practices were recently the subject of a federal Supreme Court challenge. Needless to say, UT represents the changing complexion of many colleges and universities, where the multicultural competence of the student affairs staff is essential to providing effective service to all students.

The Division of Housing and Food Services at UT (UTDHFS) encompasses services for approximately 8,000 residents with an annual operational budget of approximately 80 million dollars. The university employs 1,200 full- and part-time staff members who are responsible for this large and complex student affairs program.

At UT-Austin, Floyd Hoelting has served as the director of the Division of Housing and Food Services for the past 20 years. Hoelting is well known throughout college student housing for his progressive multicultural programming and commitment to empowering diversity in the residential setting. His trailblazing efforts to incorporate multicultural-ism began as higher education began to admit a more diverse student population in the late 1970s and early 1980s. As the pressure to meet the needs of these students became increasingly important, many colleges and universities focused primarily on programming around multicultural issues. Hoelting, as the head of residential life at Illinois State University (ISU), introduced a novel approach by requiring that multicultural skill development be included as a component of performance expectation and annual review. Under Hoelting's leadership, diversity awareness and the associated skills were viewed as integral to effective residence hall management and became an organizational priority and expectation for the Residential Life staff throughout the organization.

Another example of Hoelting's approach from ISU illustrates how cre-ating an organizational infrastructure is essential to creating a multicul-turally competent staff. At ISU, the para-professional residence life staff, including resident assistants (RAs) and desk attendants, was primarily composed of white students. The participation of students of color in staff roles was not representative of the residence hall population, although the residence life professional staff was quite diverse. To address the under-representation of students of color in the paraprofessional staff positions, Hoelting implemented a policy that required each of the residential life professional staff members to identify and mentor at least one student of color through the staff selection process for these positions. In addition, this expectation was included as a part of each staff member's annual performance review. Requiring staff to meet an expectation for which they did not yet possess the awareness, knowledge, or skills that were necessary to accomplish it could have been problematic. Instead, staff members were supported by a professional development process focused on raising staff awareness of the issues of diversity, exposing staff to the emerging scholarship of race, gender, and ethnicity, and teaching mentor-ing skills to increase their abilities.

"A SPIRIT OF HARMONY" ORGANIZATIONAL DEVELOPMENT MODEL. The "Spirit of Harmony" Organizational Development Model currently being used at the UTDHFS is a culmination of Hoelting's work to use a multicultural competence model for the staff that was inspired by the MCOD model proposed by Reynolds and Pope (2003). Reynolds and Pope created a template to be used by student affairs divisions or units in developing a strategic plan for MCOD. The UTDHFS created a Ten-Point Plan and Model for Organizational Development and Diversity. All mem-bers of the UTDHFS staff, full-time and part-time, front line and executive management, are required to meet the expectations of the plan, which focuses on diversity awareness, training, knowledge enhancement, and skill building. The 10 points of this comprehensive plan are as follows.

1. Start at the top with leadership and advocacy

   For a successful diversity program to exist, leaders must model and champion behaviors they expect employees to demonstrate and advocate for the diversity initiatives within the organization.

   a. Make sure all employees are familiar with the UTDHFS diversity plan

   b. Establish short- and long-term goals annually

   c. Set expectations for the organization

   d. Seek additional diversity training to support mission efforts

   e. Support training of staff

   f. Recognize efforts of those who go above and beyond expectations

   g. Review assessment results and implement changes

2. Create a comprehensive definition of organizational diversity and multiculturalism

   Managing organizational diversity requires a common definition for organizational diversity. UTDHFS uses a definition created by Dr. R. Roosevelt Thomas, which states, organizational diversity is an organizational environment in which everyone can contribute to their fullest to achieve organizational goals.

   a. Provide a clear and inclusive definition of organizational diversity

   b. Educate staff on multiculturalism and include multiculturalism terms in publications, interviews, training

   c. Make sure the diversity statement addresses cultural groups, ethnicities, genders, socioeconomic levels, religions, abilities, and sexual orientations

3. Create and publicize mission statement and diversity plan

   The mission statement and diversity model provide direction for how the diversity plans will be implemented throughout the organization. It promotes greater involvement and trust that the program is working and keeps members of the organization aware of the diversity initiatives.

   a. Post diversity plans and goals

   b. Publicize organizational newsletters

   c. Highlight diversity accomplishments

4. Recruit, hire, and retain diverse staff

Recruiting, hiring, and retaining a diverse staff is critical to the diversity goals of UTDHFS. The organization is constantly working to improve its commitment to diversity and encourages all staff members to provide feedback for how UTDHFS can improve.

a. Ensure hiring committees/teams are diverse

b. Ensure diverse hiring pools

c. Review recruitment practices, strategies, and advertising sources

d. Include multicultural awareness, competence, knowledge, and skills as an integral part of the job description and evaluate candidates using these criteria

e. Solicit feedback from all staff for constant improvement

f. Encourage exit interviews and ongoing supervision to explore retention-related issues

5. Review policies, activities, forms, and services

Developing practical policies for an entire organization can be a daunting task, but these policies inspire staff to support the organization's diversity program.

a. Create a hate incident guide/policy and educate staff on content

b. Establish clear minimum diversity training requirements for all staff and publicize them

c. Create an organizational diversity statement

d. Conduct a full review of departmental policies/procedures/forms to assess their impact on diverse populations and make appropriate changes where needed

6. Develop multicultural/diversity expectations and evaluations

Establishing clear expectations for participation in the Organizational Diversity Program ensures that each employee understands what is required of him or her and provides a means to establish accountability. Employees are expected to be an agent of organizational diversity. This includes using their position and influence to confront, teach, and learn about issues of diversity.

a. Clearly outline diversity training expectations; include in annual evaluations, and explain how unachieved expectations will be addressed

b. Provide effective multicultural supervision for all professional and student staff

   c. Require diversity goals for each staff area and encourage each individual to establish at least one diversity goal each year

   d. Publicize and support employee participation in local, state, and national conferences or workshops that address multicultural diversity issues

7. Implement and maintain a diversity/multicultural training program

The Division of Housing and Food Service understands the importance of inclusion. We believe that diversity awareness and appreciation improves the effectiveness of our daily operations.

   a. Create opportunities for staff to attend training programs

   b. Ensure that diversity training programs are multicultural in content and values

   c. Explain how diversity and multicultural training and development benefit the work environment and individual employee

8. Schedule and publicize scholarly activities, outreach, and celebrations

UTDHFS has the resources and activities to educate, collaborate, and celebrate the multicultural entities of the people of the division, the university, and the world.

   a. Share diversity and multicultural information through flyers, books, and articles

   b. Present workshops on multicultural topics at local, state, regional, and national conferences, and at employee team days

   c. Collaborate with other departments and organizations to reach larger audiences and to share current efforts and successes

   d. Write diversity articles for departmental newsletters and other publications

   e. Subscribe to a wide range of cultural publications

9. Perform physical environment reviews

Socially inclusive spaces encourage a sense of comfort, belonging, and common purpose. They are accessible to everyone and represent the diversity of the people who use them. The UTDHFS plan for maintaining a physically inclusive environment is to:

   a. Review individual offices and public spaces to make sure they are void of offensive or insensitive language and materials

   b. Ensure that offices, programs, and activities are welcoming to all students

   c. Include accessibility for students with disabilities

   d. Display culturally inclusive and diverse artwork, music, and publications in public spaces

   e. Provide education to staff on how to respond to insensitive or offensive verbal and nonverbal conduct and remarks

10. Survey and assess programs, initiatives, and services

   Measuring the effectiveness of the organizational diversity program is critical to its continued success. This is accomplished through:

   a. Evaluating programs, workshops, and activities for effectiveness

   b. Assessing employee and student satisfaction with services and with the level of multicultural competence demonstrated by peers and supervisors

   c. Gathering demographic information on those who attend diversity programs and those who use diversity-related services

   d. Setting goals to increase participation numbers, overall satisfaction level, and cultural representation in workshops and classes (UTDHFS, "A spirit of harmony. . ." Organizational Diversity and Development Model, 2012, pp. 3–5)

According to Hoelting, the establishment of this plan was not enough to ensure its success (personal communication, October 19, 2012). Therefore, the Office of Organization Diversity and Development was established within the Division of Housing and Food Service to implement and enforce the Ten Point Plan. The office coordinates professional development and training, mediation, and facilitated discussions, customer service, and wellness and serves as an internal resource on diversity-related management issues with the UTDHFS and is led by a senior-level director. Vision, mission statement, and values are articulated to express this commitment to diversity and to guide the Ten-Point Plan (UTDHFS "A spirit of harmony. . ." Organizational Diversity and Development Model, 2012):

> **Vision:** Create an inclusive community that fosters cultural understanding, respect, and appreciation among division staff and students and allows each person to grow and contribute to their full potential in pursuit of the division's mission.
>
> **Mission:** Our mission is to provide opportunities that:
> o Educate staff and students on the terminologies associated with diversity

o Promote and cultivate a positive understanding of global culture and heritage

o Provide educational opportunities for staff and students that empower them to acknowledge their personal values and actions

o Support the recruitment and retention of diverse and inclusive staff

o Encourage cultural celebrations

Values: Equality, Fairness, Respect, Inclusiveness, Excellence, Empowerment, Celebrations, Service, and Integrity

Hoelting realized that the MCOD plan was incomplete without a comprehensive assessment component. To address this, UTDHFS partnered with the Educational Benchmarking Institute (EBI) in the development of an assessment instrument, EBI Faculty/Staff Organizational Climate/Diversity Assessment. The survey, which is administered to all employees, measures organizational climate across 20 different factors. These factors include areas such as "Work Environment: Represent Others" and "Elements of Organizational Diversity: Feedback Regarding Diversity." According to the EBI website (http://www.webebi.com/assessments/campus-diversity), this assessment is described as a "powerful Climate Assessment tool to assess the diversity climate on your campus." It is designed to:

o Identify specifically where improvement efforts should be focused to improve overall quality and performance

o Benchmark your institution's performance with our existing community of institutions

o Evaluate performance over time to monitor the impact of improvement efforts and inform future improvement initiatives

o Provide evidence of how your department contributes to the fulfillment of the institutional mission

o Create/enhance continuous improvement methodology for Student Affairs on your campus

The survey has 179 items that rate performance over a series of 20 factors related to the climate of diversity within the organization, including relationships with fellow employees; respect, friendship, and tolerance among racial/ethnic groups; work environment; equal treatment of diverse faculty/staff; expressions of insensitivity and prejudice among supervisor and fellow employees; impact of organizational diversity; elements of organizational diversity (e.g., accessibility, leadership, feedback); and overall evaluation. The survey questions are both qualitative and quantitative and result in a score by factor. The scores are assigned to each factor in one of three rating categories: 0%–70%, Issue; 71%–74%, Needs Work; 75%–100%, Good (http://www.webebi.com/assessments/campus-diversity).

The UTDHFS has administered the assessment with employees on two occasions, once in 2008 and again in 2011. The 2011 survey was offered to all full-time staff to complete. They achieved a 52% participation rate (214/413). The comparative results have demonstrated continued overall progress and improvement in specific areas. In addition, areas of poor performance have been identified and are beginning to be addressed. The 2008 to 2011 comparison reveals that overall performance improved from a rating of Needs Work (74.7%) in 2008 to the top rating of Good (76.1%) in 2011. Some of the specific areas of strength identified were Factor 8, "Work Environment: Represent Others" (89%); Factor 10, "Expressions of Insensitivity and Prejudice: Supervisors" (88.5%); and Factor 7, "Work Environment: Value of Contributions" (86.3%). Some of the areas needing work were Factor 5, "Relationships: Tolerance Among Racial Ethnic Groups" (73.5%); Factor 1, "Relationships with Fellow Employees: Respect and Trust" (73.3%); and Factor 12, "Impact of Organizational Diversity: Personal Development" (73.2%). The only areas of concern identified were Factor 13, "Impact of Organizational Diversity: Working Effectively with Others" (66.3%) and Factor 15, "Elements of Organizational Diversity: Accessibility" (56.9%). Armed with these data and using the tenets of the 10-point plan, which includes the establishment of annual diversity plans by supervisors, focused initiatives to address the areas needing improvement have been developed and implemented, thus creating a cycle of continuous improvement. The EBI Faculty/Staff Organizational Climate/Diversity Assessment is available to colleges and universities through EBI (http://www.webebi.com/assessments/campus-diversity).

Gloria Allen, Director of Diversity for UT, identified the following initiatives that were developed to respond to the survey results:

1. Diversity educator Lee Mun Wah was brought to campus to address the importance of communication and civility within groups and between groups.

2. Learning outcomes for each diversity program were included on the program feedback form and emphasized at the beginning of each program. This also aided in assessing program effectiveness.

3. The diversity program feedback forms ask for suggestions to improve future programs. These suggestions were used to enhance program offerings.

4. Programs that offer historical background information on diversity and a broader definition of terms used in diversity education were added to help staff have a better understanding and appreciation of their peers and their own pathway.

5. All foundational programs are now offered in Spanish.

6. The required number of diversity education hours for nonsupervisory staff was increased from three to four, increasing their participation to two programs per year instead of only one.

7. The diversity programs that were offered were modified to include an interactive segment that allows staff to share their thoughts and learn from each other.

8. The resources in the Staff Library on various cultures/ethnicities (books, videos, activities, and so forth) have been reviewed and expanded.

9. More intentional assessment efforts have been developed.

10. A DHFS-wide civility campaign has been developed and launched. The campaign includes speakers and presenters.

The MCOD program developed by UTDHFS is quite impressive in its structure, confluence, and comprehensiveness, but this multicultural mission can only be accomplished through the work of a staff that believes in the program and is willing to follow the plan at all levels. Several of the UTDHFS staff volunteered for interviews regarding their experience participating in the program. The interviews were conducted during a visit to UT in the fall of 2012. As evidenced in the following comments from the staff, the MCOD program appears to be working at all levels:

> When I first came here, I was told you are going to take some diversity training. I thought that's interesting—it's getting shoved down my throat. As I started going, I loved the classes. The whole thing has to start at the top, one person at the very top, and on and on, and continue down. Everyone doesn't love each other and are not in a good mood every day, but it helps us to understand differences.

---o---

> I supervise 40 staff and I didn't think I needed the training but it really opened my eyes to other things—never thought about prejudices according to age, gender, etc., only color. A lot of staff doesn't speak English and so there are Spanish-speaking classes. I recently attended a class that was in Spanish and wore English

headphones, so I got to understand how it felt to have to be in a class where it is translated.

———— o ————

We have the wonderful privilege of researching and designing the program. A few years ago, we did an assessment of the program and realized that one particular program was very successful, so we made a radical shift—"awareness, knowledge, skill-building" was the theme—where we asked about awareness of self and how we interact with others, and incorporated new orientation about roles and identities. Knowledge—Provide information to become familiar, engage in conversations related to topic. Skill-building—how to navigate the nuances in the workplace with some savvy . . . has been the most interesting aspect of presentation. As it relates to specific training, it's a way to reduce incidents . . . focus on the front end so you do not have to deal in a reactive way with the time and expense needed to resolve. It has been quite a journey.

———— o ————

When I was thrown into classes, I felt like I was a pendulum swinging and it made me nervous—didn't mean to insult anyone. Eventually it just became educational and fun. It is definitely a top-down approach and that makes the difference. This is a healthy department. This is one aspect of the openness and communication. If you do something good, you are told, and if bad, you are told and also told how to do better. I am actually a better person with this style of management and process. We are thinking how can we do this better? How can we grow and develop? What I like in this group, is open conversations—not seen as confrontational. Have we found the best solution? That's what I treasure about the organization.

As can be seen through these statements, Floyd Hoelting's vision to employ an organizational model to develop and sustain multicultural development in the UTDHFS staff is working. This is a true example of theory in practice and has allowed the MCOD model to be tested and evaluated. Although still in its beginning stages of development, the MCOD model at UTDHFS gives us the opportunity to learn from implementation strategies. It is also quite striking that the development of this model has led to the creation of a benchmarking assessment instrument that is now being used by several institutions across the nation.

University of Vermont

The University of Vermont (UVM) is a public research university enrolling over 10,000 undergraduates and nearly 2,000 graduate and medical students (About UVM, n.d.). Located on the shores of Lake Champlain in the small New England city of Burlington, UVM's commitment to diversity may at first seem unlikely, given that the state's population is over 95% white (compared with 78% nationally; U.S. Census Bureau, 2012). Although UVM's student body is more racially/ethnically diverse (82% white; University of Vermont Office of Institution Research, 2012) than the state population, it is significantly less diverse than the population of students enrolled in college nationally (60.5% white; U.S. Department of Education, 2011). However, despite the limited structural diversity, the university's multicultural change efforts are in fact broad and deep.

A statement on diversity adopted by the Board of Trustees addresses why diversity is an academic and institutional strategic priority:

> The University of Vermont holds that diversity and academic excellence are inseparable. An excellent university, particularly one that is a public land grant, needs to actively seek to provide access to all students who can excel at the institution, without respect to their backgrounds and circumstances, including, among other differences, those of race, color, gender, gender identity and expression, sexual orientation, national and ethnic origin, socio-economic status, cultural and/or geographical background, religious belief, age, and disability. (University of Vermont and State Agricultural College Board of Trustees, 2009, February, para. 1)

The statement further argues that attending to diversity is necessary to accomplishing some of the most basic purposes of the university, namely, educating students about the world in which they live and preparing them for successful and productive lives:

> It is not possible to accomplish this without the strong presence of three critical things. The first is maintaining a safe and respectful climate for all members of our University community. The second is achieving diversity among the university community of faculty, staff, and students. The third is providing a curriculum that teaches critical thinking and engages learners of different multicultural perspectives across our various programs and disciplines. (University of Vermont and State Agricultural College Board of Trustees, 2009, February, para. 4)

This statement from the highest level of leadership of UVM clearly articulates a commitment to pluralism and multicultural values, and positions diversity work as being essential to excellence. Support from top leadership is typically viewed as a necessary precursor to multicultural change (Reynolds & Pope, 2003; Williams, Berger, & McClendon, 2005). Moreover, the statement explicitly defines diversity in more inclusive terms, specifically mentioning differences such as race, ability, sexual orientation, and geographical background, among others. The existence of five presidential commissions focused on diversity issues further illustrates this commitment from senior leadership: President's Commission on Diversity & Inclusion; President's Commission on Racial Diversity; President's Commission on The Status of Women; President's Commission on Lesbian, Gay, Bisexual, and Transgendered Equity; and President's Commission on Social Change (Presidential Commissions, n.d.). Each of these commissions was charged with "acting as a catalyst and advocate" in its respective areas by making recommendations to the president. Examples of these recommendations include expanding the recruitment "geomarket" for students of color, encouraging diversity topics throughout curricula, and modifying policies related to campus blood drives because of the categorical exclusion of gay men as potential donors (Presidential Commissions, n.d.).

The University of Vermont's commitment to diversity has historical roots, including "firsts" such as the first university admitting women into Phi Beta Kappa honor society in 1875 to their response to incidents of racial tensions on campus in the early 1990s (Our History of Diversity, n.d.). In more recent decades, administrators carefully examined data that showed how new hires were almost exclusively white, and even white students began expressing disappointment in the lack of diversity interactions on campus (L. Flash, personal communication, November 13, 2012). These data points and other sources of information reinforced and catalyzed current multicultural change initiatives at UVM.

UNIVERSITY RELATIONS AND CAMPUS LIFE—DIVERSITY AND SOCIAL JUSTICE: VALUES, COMMITMENT, VISION. Within this institutional context, UVM's Dean of Students office (a unit of University Relations and Campus Life) has led much of the work related to multicultural change at UVM (A. Stevens, personal communication, October 13, 2012). One of the five goals of the Dean of Students office's strategic initiative is "advancing diversity," and this commitment is demonstrated by specific actions in several of the 10 MCOD categories described by Reynolds and Pope (2003). In describing the UVM context, we have already illustrated UVM's efforts and actions in the first three categories: comprehensive definition of the term *multicultural,* mission statement, and leadership and advocacy. Next, we describe efforts within the Student Affairs division toward the remaining seven categories: policy review, recruitment and retention of diverse staff, multicultural competency expectations and training, scholarly activities, departmental/ division programs and services, physical environment, and assessment.

POLICY REVIEW. On at least a bi-annual basis, each of the nine departments within Student Affairs (including Academic Support Programs, Career Services, Center for Health & Wellbeing, Center for Student Ethics & Standards, Dining Services, Residential Life, Student Life, Student & Community Relations, and Dean of Students office) reviews their policies and procedures through the lens of inclusion and multiculturalism (Diversity & Social Justice, n.d.). In collaboration with other university offices, Student Affairs also developed a campus bias protocol to effectively respond to reported incidents. Furthermore, several Student Affairs staff members now serve as commissioners on the aforementioned Presidential Commissions focused on diversity, which review campus-wide policies and practices and make recommendations to improve the overall campus climate (Diversity & Social Justice, n.d.).

RECRUITMENT AND RETENTION OF DIVERSE STAFF. Of significant note are UVM's practices related to the next two categories of MCOD: recruiting and retaining a diverse staff, and setting expectations for and providing training on multicultural competence. Reynolds, Pope, and Wells (2002), as cited in Pope, Reynolds, and Mueller (2004), stated "to have a truly multicultural department/division, it is essential that the staff be culturally diverse. Without a diversity of voices, life experiences, and cultural backgrounds, staff may be limited in their ability to meet the needs of some students" (p. 66). With this in mind, UVM's University Relations and Campus Life (URCL) division sets affirmative hiring goals and measures progress against those goals on an annual basis. Over the past decade, the URCL division has filled approximately 20% of their annual position openings with people of color (T. Gustafson, personal communication, September 7, 2012). Keeping in mind the racial demographics of the state, clearly UVM's diversity hiring strategies are helping to realize significant outcomes related to structural diversity, one component of multicultural change. The vice president of URCL notes that if they expanded the definition of diversity to include differences such as sexual orientation, ability, and gender, their success in achieving structural diversity would be even more apparent. To support that claim, recent census data about the makeup of the division's staff includes 61% women; 15% differently abled people—physically, cognitively, or emotionally; and 17% lesbian, gay, bisexual, or queer individuals (T. Gustafson, personal communication, September 7, 2012).

Success in recruiting a diverse staff, according to UVM's URCL leadership, is an ongoing effort that involves intentional networking through conference attendance, listservs, and other means so that when a position does become available, staff members are able to reach out to other professionals to encourage diversity among potential applicants (T. Gustafson, personal communication, September 7, 2012). Moreover, informational interviews are offered to potential candidates, and the Dean of Students Office maintains a potential candidate resource file for future vacancies. In addition, all position descriptions, rather than merely including an affirmative action statement, include "demonstrated comfort with and commitment to issues of diversity and social justice" as a minimum qualification, communicating the division's expectation and commitment to inclusion to potential applicants from the very beginning of the recruitment process (T. Gustafson, personal communication, September 7, 2012). A focus on multicultural competence is evident in later stages of the hiring process as well, as interviews include questions related to diversity and social justice, and regular awareness training is provided to search committee members to minimize the impact of bias during search processes (T. Gustafson, personal communication, September 7, 2012). Finally, URCL partners with UVM's Higher Education and Student Affairs academic program to recruit and retain a diverse class of graduate assistants (GAs) who work in various URCL departments, typically resulting in over 40% of GAs being people of color (T. Gustafson, personal communication, September 7, 2012).

MULTICULTURAL COMPETENCY EXPECTATIONS AND TRAINING. Achieving and maintaining diversity among their staff is not only the result of these recruitment and hiring practices; instead, it is the result of the division's overall commitment to diversity and inclusion (T. Gustafson, personal communication, September 7, 2012). Thus, efforts to recruit and retain a diverse staff cannot be separated from URCL's concurrent efforts to set expectations for multicultural competence among staff members and to provide ongoing and comprehensive training for their staff. As previously mentioned, multicultural competence is written as a minimum requirement for all positions, highlighting UVM's position that it is an expectation for all staff members in all areas of the division, not simply a specialized competency required of a few. Moreover, multicultural competence is incorporated into staff performance appraisals (T. Gustafson, personal communication, September 7, 2012), further institutionalizing URCL's multicultural change efforts by requiring regular evaluation and discussion of staff members' performance in this area.

Staff members are also expected to seek out sessions related to multicultural competence while attending conferences, and to attend several full- and half-day diversity professional development sessions each semester at UVM, all in an effort to increase their multicultural awareness, knowledge, and skills (Diversity & Social Justice, n.d.; T. Gustafson, personal communication, September 7, 2012). For example, twice a year URCL offers a full-day training titled "Understanding Our Differences: An Introduction to Multicultural Competencies at UVM" that is attended by all new staff members as well as those seeking a refresher course (T. Gustafson, personal communication, September 7, 2012). URCL has partnered with nationally recognized scholars and consultants to provide additional trainings on campus throughout the academic year, and their "ALLY-ances" mentoring program supports professional development of staff, particularly from historically marginalized communities (Diversity & Social Justice, n.d.).

SCHOLARLY ACTIVITIES. With respect to the multicultural change category of scholarly activity, several staff members have written or presented on topics of multiculturalism, diversity, and social justice in a variety of local and national venues (Diversity & Social Justice, n.d.). For example, the Assistant Dean for Conduct, Policy and Climate at UVM developed *Components of Multicultural Competency in Student Affairs Organizations* (Flash, 2010b) and the *Multicultural Competence in Student Affairs Organizations Questionnaire* (Flash, 2010c), designed to help student affairs organizations assess and implement strategic and sustained multicultural organizational change (L. Flash, personal communication, November 30, 2012). Several other UVM staff members have presented sessions at meetings of major student affairs professional organizations. For example, a staff member from UVM's ALANA (African, Latino[a], Asian, and Native American) Student Center presented "Layered Identities: Campus Climate and QPOC (Queer People of Color) Students" at a recent American College Personnel Association (ACPA) College Student Educators International annual convention (ACPA, 2012), and a team of Student Life staff members and residence directors presented "Building Multicultural Competence with Professional Development" at the most recent National Association of Student Personnel Administrators

(NASPA) Student Affairs Administrators in Higher Education conference (NASPA, n.d.).

DEPARTMENTAL/DIVISION PROGRAMS AND SERVICES. The Division of Student Affairs at UVM supports a variety of programs and services focused on multicultural change, including the "Next Step" weekend retreat, which guides students and faculty/staff in their social justice journey, and sponsoring a national mentoring program for underrepresented students (Diversity & Social Justice, n.d.). Student Affairs staff also teach Inter-Group Dialogue courses through their Center for Student Ethics and Standards (T. Gustafson, personal communication, September 7, 2012).

PHYSICAL ENVIRONMENT. In an initiative related to the next category of multicultural change efforts, the physical environment, the newly constructed Davis Campus Center was intentionally built to exude an ethos that fosters social justice. This is evident throughout the building, from the multicultural art on the walls to the gender-neutral bathrooms (Discover Our Values, n.d.; Diversity & Social Justice, n.d.). Moreover, the division promotes the use of universal design principles—that is, environments designed "to be usable by all people, to the greatest extent possible, without the need for adaptation or special design" (AHEAD, 2010)—in remodeling or building new facilities (Diversity & Social Justice, n.d.).

ASSESSMENT. To assess progress related to multicultural change initiatives, the final category described by Reynolds and Pope (2003), the Divisional Diversity Council conducts regular, comprehensive multicultural competence assessments every three years within all student affairs departments (T. Gustafson, personal communication, September 7, 2012). Results are used to provide each unit with areas of strengths and opportunities for improvement that help inform future goal setting and planning. Most recently, in May 2012, all student affairs units completed an organizational multicultural competency assessment, examining the following seven organizational components: (1) organizational culture of commitment, encouragement, and support for multicultural engagement; (2) peer/colleague influence, behaviors, and expectations for multicultural engagement; (3) clear and coherent multicultural organizational mission; (4) provision of multiculturally inclusive services; (5) support for and creation of diversity/multicultural programming and events; (6) incorporation of multiculturalism in strategic and formal organizational practice; and (7) multicultural recruitment practices (Flash, 2010a). In addition, and as mentioned previously, the URCL assesses progress in multicultural change efforts through an annual staffing census examining the success of recruitment and retention strategies in terms of structural diversity, and individuals are assessed and provided feedback on their multicultural competence through annual performance programs and appraisals.

The University of Vermont, and particularly the division of URCL, has clearly articulated a commitment to MCOD. More than that, however, the attitudes and actions of staff members have allowed MCOD to become a reality on this campus. Whether walking through their Davis Center or talking with staff—from graduate students through senior-level administrators—UVM's vision of being a multicultural campus that truly values and embraces diversity is almost palpable. There is a notable passion when talking to members of the community that truly demonstrates their values, commitment, and vision, focusing on creating an environment in which all students are welcomed, valued, and supported in their educational journeys.

St. Louis University, Division of Student Development

Saint Louis University (SLU) is a private, Catholic/Jesuit–affiliated university located in St. Louis, Missouri. It was founded in 1818 and in 2011–2012 enrolled 8,670 undergraduate students and 5,403 graduate students. Of its undergraduates, 64.3% are white, non-Hispanic; 7.3% are black, non-Hispanic; 7.2% are Asian/Pacific Islander; 3.9% are Hispanic/Latino, 3.6% are multi-racial; 0.1% are American Indian/Alaskan Native; 40.9% are males, and 59% are females (The Saint Louis University Fact Book, 2011–2012. The Division of Student Development at SLU is led by Kent Porterfield, Vice President for Student Development, and includes Business and Auxiliary Services, Campus Recreation, Housing and Residential Life, Student Support and Parent & Family Programs, Cross Cultural Center, Student Health and Counseling, Center for Service and Community Engagement, Student Responsibility and Community Standards, Student Involvement Center, Career Services, Academic Advising and Support, Housing and Residence Life, Cross Cultural Center, and Athletics.

During the spring semester of 2010, SLU encountered several racially motivated bias incidents on campus, which alarmed the university community and gained national media attention. According to a document entitled "Saint Louis University Application of MCOD: A Case Study," prepared by the Division of Student Development, the events prompted an immediate response to address safety and security needs of the campus. According to Leanna Fenneberg, Assistant Vice President for Student Development, the document outlines the application of an MCOD framework to promote diversity and inclusion on their campus (personal communication, October 29, 2012). A more robust and proactive focus on a holistic approach to promoting diversity and inclusion on campus was then initiated. As a result, the SLU Division of Student Development created and implemented the following MCOD plan based on the work of Reynolds and Pope (2003) (Saint Louis University Division of Student Development, 2012):

COMPREHENSIVE DEFINITION OF THE TERM *MULTICULTURAL*. The following University-level definition of diversity was established by a campus-wide President's Diversity Council:

> "Diversity" defined can be very broad in scope and includes each member of the University community, with the understanding that each individual possesses unique social identities. The principles of diversity and inclusion, however, move beyond understanding the characteristics of each social identity and lead to creating an inclusive community and environment. The University's commitment to diversity and inclusion requires a set of conscious practices that involve:
>
> Building alliances across social identities to work together to eradicate all forms of individual and institutionalized discrimination and oppression, including, but not limited to, discrimination and oppression based on race, ethnicity, national origin, immigrant status, gender, sex, sexual orientation, gender identity, age, physical ability, cognitive ability, mental illness, religious beliefs, physical appearance, income, military experience, geographic location, marital status, education, and parental status.
>
> Instilling in all members of the University community the values and tools necessary to empower them to combat all forms of discrimination and oppression that will prepare each individual to be a responsible local and global citizen and leader.
>
> Recognizing that personal, cultural, institutionalized, and organizational discrimination and stigmatization along social identities creates and sustains privileges for some while creating and sustaining oppression for others. Practicing mutual respect for our own identities, as well as identities different from our own. Exploring differences and similarities in a safe and nurturing environment.

Moving beyond tolerance to embracing and celebrating the identities each individual possesses. (Saint Louis University Application of MCOD: A case study, 2012, p. 1)

A campus-wide University diversity and inclusion vision statement was established as well:

University Diversity and Inclusion Vision Statement: Faithful to its values of promoting social justice and the dignity of all human beings, Saint Louis University is committed to fostering an inclusive environment that welcomes and celebrates all expressions of diversity and identity that advance the Jesuit mission of forming women and men for and with others. This commitment inspires and prepares students, faculty, and staff to create communities unburdened by discrimination and oppression. (Saint Louis University Division of Student Development, 2012)

The Division of Student Development created the following Divisional Statement on Diversity:

In support of Saint Louis University's Jesuit mission, the Division of Student Development is committed to maintaining an environment of mutual respect and dignity for people of all backgrounds and cultures. It is our mission to encourage and support a thriving and diverse community among our staff and students.

We honor the differences in our community, whether they be age, ability, race, religion, gender identity and expression, sexual orientation, or socio-economic background, and prepare our students to thrive in a multicultural, diverse society. Our efforts are grounded in cultivating awareness, inclusion, and engagement through intentional experiences, events, and programs that demonstrate our commitment to excellence.

LEADERSHIP AND ADVOCACY. The Diversity Core working group was established in 2010 and included staff from Student Development as well as other key campus partners, with the goal of developing a framework for multicultural competence that would be used as a foundation for all pro-grammatic and educational efforts. This framework is based on the MCOD philosophy, and it has been the basis for work since its establishment.

STUDENT DEVELOPMENT EQUITY, DIVERSITY, AND INCLUSION SERIES. Professional development efforts for Student Development staff have continued on an annual basis. In 2010–2011, a comprehensive series, the Student Development Equity, Diversity, and Inclusion Series, provided robust opportunities for staff to engage in this education. During the 2010–2011 academic year, staff who participated in at least 60% of the offered professional development sessions were awarded publicly at the end-of-the-year in-service with a plaque acknowledging their commitment. Staff members who significantly demonstrated a commitment to diversity and inclusion have been recognized through the annual staff leadership award for commitment to diversity and inclusion. Efforts to promote professional development related to diversity and inclusion have continued since 2011, with at least one workshop annually designed specifically for staff in student development. Staff members are regularly encouraged to participate in other campus-sponsored dialogues.

POLICY REVIEW. One specific policy that has been developed as part of the MCOD strategic plan is the hate crime and bias incident response protocol (Fall 2010). Through the hate crime and bias incident response protocol, all reports of incidents involving students and within the scope of the policy are tracked in the incident report log. An e-mail notification is immediately sent to the University community when a new report is received, to promote transparent communication. Additional consideration of policy and procedures that support diverse needs has been done at the departmental level.

RECRUITMENT AND RETENTION OF A DIVERSE STAFF. A working group was established in student development to specifically consider the aspects of the MCOD framework that address recruiting and retaining a diverse staff. The Recruiting and Retaining a Diverse Staff Working Group reviewed the tenets and efforts related to these areas of MCOD and considered the most pressing needs and opportunities to infuse action throughout the Division of Student Development. In spring 2011, listening groups were conducted within Division of Student Development for staff members of underrepresented identities (including people of color, non-Christian or non-religious, women, and lesbian, gay, bisexual, and transgender [LGBT]) as a way to learn from their experiences. Divisional leadership considered and incorporated suggestions in future planning for staff hiring and training and general staff support and morale initiatives. Specific efforts aligned with recruiting a diverse staff have included (1) reviewing and identifying expanded locations to post position openings; (2) developing a marketing plan for recruiting a diverse pool of qualified candidates; (3) establishing a website that espouses the university's values of diversity and inclusion; (4) developing a staff recruitment

video; (5) hosting two undergraduate interns affiliated with a professional student affairs organization; (6) aligning staff selection process
materials (e.g., interview questions, search committee representation)
with values of diversity and inclusion; (7) training divisional staff on
how to facilitate an inclusive search process; and (8) reviewing position descriptions to insure that relevant multicultural competencies are
included.

PHYSICAL ENVIRONMENT. One important consideration in the area
of physical environment was the implementation of the bias incident
response protocol, which assures prompt and appropriate follow-up for
any reports of bias-related incidents such as graffiti. This provides transparency in communication regarding threats to University safety and
security. Efforts to reflect diversity in the physical environment on campus have included efforts to infuse artwork reflecting various cultures in
displays in the Busch Student Center, campus bookstore, and the Cross
Cultural Center. Additionally, the students initiated the following "Oath
of Inclusion" statement, which is displayed prominently in many Student
Development locations, including the Student Involvement Center, Student Success Center, and Campus Recreation:

> We, as students, form a diverse and vibrant university community.
>
> We do not enter into this community by proximity, but by virtue of a
> shared Jesuit vision—to pursue higher truths, obtain greater knowledge,
> and strive for a better world. In this endeavor, we do not succeed by
> our individual ambitions, but by our discovery of each other.
>
> We find higher truths when we seek to understand the complexity
> of our neighbors' identities, we obtain greater knowledge when we
> consider the perspectives of our fellow students, and we begin to
> strive for a better world when we build a stronger community.
>
> As a student and a member of the SLU community, I will live by
> this oath.
>
> I will embrace people for the diversity of their identities, creating
> a community inclusive of race, ethnicity, sex, age, ability, faith,
> orientation, gender, class, and ideology.
>
> I will challenge my worldview through education inside and
> outside the classroom.
>
> I will show that I am proud to be a Billiken by enriching the
> culture of our University.
>
> I will foster a community that welcomes all by recognizing the
> inherent dignity of each person.

I will work for social justice in the Saint Louis community and
beyond.
This is the SLU I believe in.
This is the community I am building.
This is our SLU.
(Saint Louis University, *Oath of Inclusion*, 2012)

The Oath was created by students separately from the creation of the
MCOD efforts but during the same time period. According to Leanna
Fenneberg, the Oath has been actively used in their educational efforts
for students (personal communication, October 29, 2012).

ASSESSMENT. All programmatic initiatives outlined to meet learning
goals associated with multicultural competences for students are evaluated on a regular basis to contribute to the overall understanding of
learning in this area. Assessment efforts are in their infancy stages and
are currently occurring more at a departmental level, with the hope of
developing some cross-departmental analysis. According to Leanna Fenneberg, some assessment of student learning on multicultural competence
skills per specific programs and departments has been completed; conversations regarding hiring practices with the Diversity & Affirmative
Action office have begun; and the student government has completed a
campus climate assessment specifically related to the Oath of Inclusion
(personal communication, October 29, 2012).

The creation of a comprehensive multicultural organizational development plan by Saint Louis University demonstrates an excellent response
to unforeseen circumstances. Many times in higher education, situations
arise that draw our attention to issues in our communities that we may
not see. In these situations, we are often judged by how well we respond.
In response to a difficult time of bias-related incidents at SLU, this new
program galvanized the community in the pursuit of a more just environment consistent with the Jesuit values of the institution. Using MCOD as
the cornerstone of the plan has resulted in a program that clearly articulates the values of the Division of Student Development and has allowed
for the program to develop and grow.

Campus Change Initiatives and the Multicultural Change
Intervention Matrix

The three campus examples presented in this chapter are intended to provide readers with insight into how multicultural change is currently happening, in "real life" contexts, in an effort to ultimately inspire and model

change at campuses across the country. The differences in approaches, emphases, and priorities at UT Austin, UVM, and SLU demonstrate that there is no one "right" or "best" way to initiate or advance multicultural change; rather, what is most effective depends on the context and the people involved. What is also demonstrated, through these three unique examples, is that each campus tends to make multicultural efforts using multiple approaches and a variety of initiatives.

Effective multicultural organizational change, as argued throughout this book, requires a comprehensive approach that is systemic, planned, and sustained. Using the MCIM (Pope, 1995) as a framework, we can see how the units (e.g., Residence Life, Student Affairs division) at these three campuses are transforming into multicultural organizations by focusing their efforts on multiple targets of intervention—this is, individual, group, and institutional—and on both first-order and second-order change for each target. The examples that follow, while not exhaustive, will serve to illustrate how these three campuses are promoting multicultural change by intentionally addressing each cell of the MCIM.

Individual Level of Intervention

AWARENESS. This cell (Table 7.1) describes first-order change at the individual level, and usually involves content-based education focusing on various groups or particular skills involved in working with diverse students (Pope, 1995). The University of Texas's Division of Housing and Food Services offers workshops and activities each year to their staff members; examples of topics covered recently include bystander training, microaggressions, transgender identity, and generational differences in the workplace (Organizational Diversity and Development, 2012). Similarly, University Relations and Campus Life at the UVM offers a full-day training on "Understanding Our Differences: An Introduction to Multicultural Competencies at UVM" twice a year for new employees and continuing employees who would like a refresher (T. Gustafson, personal communication, September 7, 2012). At SLU, interventions focused on the awareness cell include programs such as Safe Zone, focusing on erasing prejudice and providing support to the LGBT community, and hosting speaker Touré for a talk entitled "How Racism Functions Today and Ways to Deal with It to Get Success" (Diversity Calendar of Events, 2013 February). Each of these workshops and programs focus on building awareness, knowledge, or skills related to working with diverse others.

Table 7.1   Multicultural change intervention matrix (MCIM)

	Type of change	
Target of change	First-order change	Second-order change
Individual	A. Awareness	B. Paradigm shift
Group	C. Membership	D. Restructuring
Institutional	E. Programmatic	F. Systemic

© Raechele L. Pope (1993)

PARADIGM SHIFT. This cell of the MCIM (Table 7.1) describes second-order change at the individual level. Such initiatives move beyond learning particular content and instead focus on processes and experiences that challenge individuals' underlying assumptions or worldview (Pope, 1995). The University of Vermont's Next Step retreat is an initiative aimed at shifting participants' worldviews. The goal of the program is to develop participants' effectiveness as social activists through an intensive personal and collective experience (The Next Step 2013, n.d.). By focusing on exploring one's own social identity and background, genuinely listening to others' experiences, and learning about roots of oppression and privilege, faculty, staff, and student participants "discover ways to address everyday bias, stereotypes, and discrimination as an ally (or someone who is not personally impacted, but who is responsible based on their privilege)" (The Next Step 2013, para 3).

At UT, their self-awareness workshops and their improvement initiative (based on assessment results) to modify diversity programs to include greater reflection and interaction among staff may be an example of an individual-level, second-order change. The UT leadership is intentionally trying to help staff members recognize their assumptions, biases, and worldviews and to encourage greater reflection and interaction among staff members, allowing for the opportunity to share with and learn from one another. The "aha" moment that is often characteristic of paradigm shifts is evident in the statement of one staff member, who said, "I supervise 40 staff and I didn't think I needed the training but it really opened my eyes to other things—never thought about prejudices according to age, gender, etc., only color."

The Intergroup Dialogue Program at SLU is another example of a program focusing on cognitive restructuring, or shifting paradigms. The semester-long face-to-face dialogues, facilitated by trained students, provide a safe space for students from different identity groups to honestly discuss issues related to diversity and social justice, while fulfilling one of SLU's general education requirements (Intergroup Dialogue Program, 2013). Through conversations on topics that are often difficult, controversial, or even taboo, participants learn from and teach one another by exploring differing cultures, backgrounds, and worldviews.

Group Level of Intervention

MEMBERSHIP. This cell (Table 7.1) describes first-order change at the group level, usually involving a change toward a more multicultural composition of a group (Pope, 1995). In other words, members of traditionally underrepresented groups are "invited to the table" of existing committees or staffs. In the Division of Housing and Food Service at UT Austin, recruiting, hiring, and retaining a diverse staff is one of the strategies specifically addressed in their Ten-Point Plan. By ensuring diverse hiring pools and hiring committees and by regularly soliciting feedback from all staff—including exit interviews—for continual improvement, the division is intentionally focusing on diversifying the membership of its staff.

Similarly, Student Affairs at the UVM has focused on increasing the diversity of their staff through intentional and sustained efforts, including ongoing networking with potential future employees, including multicultural competence as a requirement for all positions, and reducing bias in the hiring process, to name just a few efforts. Despite the relative lack of (racial) diversity in the state, URCL at UVM has succeeded in bringing traditionally underrepresented voices to their table, filling an average of 20% of open positions with people of color and creating a staff that consists of over 60% women, 15% who identify as differently abled, and over 15% identifying as LGBT (T. Gustafson, personal communication, September 7, 2012).

At SLU, Student Development facilitated listening groups for members of underrepresented identities as a way to learn about their experiences as staff members, and then used what they learned to improve future hiring, training, and support initiatives in their division. Their working group that was established to examine this aspect of MCOD identified expanded opportunities for job postings; developed a marketing plan for recruiting a diverse pool of candidates; aligned staff selection tools, materials, and processes with their value of inclusion; and began fostering the career development of potential future student affairs professionals.

RESTRUCTURING. This cell (Table 7.1) focuses on moving beyond increasing the diversity of a group, and instead emphasizes transformation of the group at its core. Beyond simply adding underrepresented people to the existing group or organization, restructuring involves reconceiving of the organization itself, frequently involving reexamining mission statements, values, and goals. University Relations and Campus Life at UVM did just that, by reflecting on who they were as a group and ultimately developing new goals. Today, one of their five strategic initiatives is advancing diversity. Moreover, the infusion of multicultural themes is evident in their other strategic initiatives; for example, in their promotion of health and safety, one goal is for students to "act to end incidents of harm or injustice" (Promoting Health and Safety, 2013). At SLU, the Division of Student Development reflected on and redefined their values as an organization and subsequently articulated them in a statement on diversity, stating in part that

> "In support of [our] Jesuit mission, [we are] committed to maintaining an environment of mutual respect and dignity for people of all backgrounds and cultures. It is our mission to encourage and support a thriving and diverse community among our staff and students. We honor the differences in our community, whether they be age, ability, race, religion, gender identity and expression, sexual orientation, or socioeconomic background, and prepare our students to thrive in a multicultural, diverse society." (Saint Louis University, Divisional Statement on Diversity, n.d.)

All three campuses' efforts aimed at retaining a multicultural staff (not just recruiting from traditionally underrepresented groups) are also examples of restructuring. That is, each campus moved beyond increasing numerical or structural diversity and instead examined and ultimately changed their expectations, processes, and assumptions related to working in their institutions. They sought to learn about the experiences of underrepresented staff members, revised their expectations and reward structures for all staff members, and expanded what is included in their definition of good supervision, to name just a few efforts toward multicultural change. In so doing, each campus redefined and reorganized their organization to some extent, moving it closer to being a truly multicultural organization.

Institutional Level of Intervention

PROGRAMMATIC. The change efforts of this cell (Table 7.1) involve first-order change at the institutional level. At UT, an example of a programmatic intervention is the development of the annual diversity education requirement, required of all full-time (benefits-eligible) staff members in the Division of Housing and Food Service. Each year, central management staff must complete 16 hours of diversity training, supervisors and managers must complete 12 hours, assistant supervisors and team leaders complete 8 hours, and staff complete 4 hours. The Division provides clear guidelines for staff members regarding what "counts" as a diversity education credit, and they provide a comprehensive set of workshop options each year addressing the three learning categories of self-awareness, knowledge building, and skill development. The Organizational Diversity and Development staff members record each staff member's diversity credits earned, and provide quarterly reports to supervisors to help everyone meet their annual requirement (Diversity Workshop Guidelines, 2012).

An example of a programmatic change at UVM is their appointment of an Assistant Dean for Conduct, Policy, and Climate, whose role is to help realize the division's "vision of having a staff who are multiculturally competent and offices that are welcoming and inclusive to all students and staff" (Dean of Students Office, n.d.). St. Louis University's Student Development Equity, Diversity, and Inclusion Series is another example of a programmatic change. The changes and programs at SLU are intended to have an overall impact on the climate of diversity at the institution. This is particularly true for the student body and those who experienced the bias-related incidents, and it led to the strategic plan, which has been endorsed for the university by the President. Although not required, all staff members in the division are encouraged to participate, and those who demonstrate significant and sustained participation are publically acknowledged and rewarded.

SYSTEMIC. This cell (Table 7.1) involves second-order change efforts focused on the institutional level. Both programmatic and systemic efforts are institutional (or divisional) level initiatives. Systemic efforts involve second-order change and thus have an impact on underlying institutional values or goals, whereas programmatic efforts may be more of "add-on" initiatives (Pope, 1995). Because each of the MCIM cells are related to each other in fluid and dynamic ways, the programmatic efforts previously described were likely necessary for some of these campuses' systemic changes. For example, UTDHFS's annual diversity education requirement is described as an example of first-order change, but increasing the staff's overall awareness, knowledge, and skills related to diversity (programmatic effort) may have been prerequisite for the staff to buy into and ultimately promulgate the division's vision to create an inclusive community (systemic effort), ultimately leading to an overall increase in staff members' rating of the organization as a whole. Moreover, whereas

UVM hiring an assistant dean for conduct, policy, and climate in itself may be a first-order programmatic change, the work that Dr. Flash has done, for example, helping to meaningfully infuse multicultural competence into hiring decisions and every staff member's performance program and review, is an example of systemic, or second-order, change.

Summary and Challenges

Based on these examples, clearly each of these campuses is employing a comprehensive, multi-pronged approach to creating multicultural organizations. Each campus has initiated efforts targeted toward individuals, groups, and the division/institution, and each has initiated efforts that support both first-order and second-order change as categorized and described by the MCIM (Pope, 1995). Readers are encouraged, as they begin or continue this work on their own campuses, to think, plan, and act comprehensively and systemically, using the MCIM as a framework for guidance.

Importantly, we do not suggest that creating a strategic plan using the MCIM is a panacea and that there will not be significant challenges to creating multicultural change, even with the best-laid plans. On the contrary, the campuses highlighted in this chapter have all faced myriad challenges over time as they have engaged in MCOD work. We share a few examples from each of these institutions to demonstrate that effective MCOD requires consistent and sustained attention and efforts, to help readers anticipate challenges they may face as they work for multicultural change in their own contexts, and to share some of the lessons learned from these institutions.

UNIVERSITY OF TEXAS–AUSTIN. The MCOD program in the UTDHFS is designed to meet the needs of a very large and diverse staff. With approximately 1,200 full- and part-time employees, it is one of the largest departments of its kind across the nation. The programs that are offered as a part of diversity education have been designed to cover as wide a set of areas as possible. As a result, the scope of the program may be limited to meet the general needs of the staff. Although the staff are provided individual assessments to help identify their specific needs, meeting these specific needs through existing programs is quite challenging.

Requiring participation also creates some challenges. UTDHFS has a "Code of the Road," which is provided to each employee. The Code states, "You are expected to be an agent of organizational diversity. This includes using your position and influence to confront, teach, and learn about issues of diversity." This clear and concise proclamation from the top sets the expectation that the diversity education program is a requirement and not a voluntary initiative. According to Gloria Allen, although requiring diversity education is necessary to achieve the division's diversity goals, it is challenging to have everyone embrace this requirement. Additionally, the programs are designed to "push staff beyond their comfort level," and some of the staff "are not willing to take on that kind of risk" (personal communication, October 19, 2013).

Higher education has faced across-the-board budget constriction in recent years, requiring campuses to prioritize funding. This has also been a challenge at the UTDHFS. Although the diversity program is well supported, as the program has grown the need for additional funding for keynote speakers and presenters has also grown. The division leadership will need to examine this challenge more closely to chart a sustainable course for the future.

UNIVERSITY OF VERMONT. When staff members from the Dean of Students Office at UVM meet with their student affairs colleagues to discuss expectations for and training on multicultural competence, they state "challenges cannot be our excuses" (Flash, Stevens, & Whitworth, 2013). This statement both acknowledges that real challenges exist and conveys the expectation that the work is important and will continue in spite of roadblocks or speed bumps. UVM faces challenges in affirmative recruitment, including the lack of racial diversity in the state, the challenge of deconstructing biases in hiring practices, and a lack of universal buy-in that diversification of staff will benefit the university (Flash, Stevens, & Whitworth, 2013; T. Gustafson, personal communication, September 7, 2012). In response, they cultivate relationships with professional colleagues across the nation (even before positions are open), they include bias awareness activities in their hiring trainings, and they meet regularly with their staff to openly discuss any hesitations and to remind one another that diversity is an institutional priority and strategic goal (Flash, Stevens, & Whitworth, 2013; T. Gustafson, personal communication, September 7, 2012).

Staff at UVM also acknowledge limited resources as a challenge to achieving multicultural change, noting that staff members' time to participate in educational and other training opportunities must be balanced with daily workload needs, and that limited funds are available to send staff members to conferences, professional meetings, and other networking opportunities. They have implemented strategies to prioritize MCOD work in terms of both time and money, and enhance flexibility by diversifying training times and options and offering division-level funding for staff to attend conferences (T. Gustafson, personal communication, September 7,

2012). Moreover, student affairs staff members at UVM realize that their commitment to multicultural change may not be shared by every other unit within the University or by the community external to UVM, therefore creating the possibility of varied experiences by students and staff as they navigate these communities. University Relations and Campus Life staff thus continue to explore ways to partner with others on and off campus to expand and deepen these broader communities' commitment to MCOD (T. Gustafson, personal communication, September 7, 2012).

Finally, despite all of these efforts, UVM is still not a "perfect" multicultural environment. For example, in May 2012, a student painted graffiti on a concrete wall on the campus that included a racially offensive comment (*Burlington Free Press*, 2012). The University responded by quickly investigating the incident and removing the graffiti, by intervening with the responsible student, and by issuing a statement from the president condemning "this hateful, hurtful deed" and reminding the campus community that "when any member of our community is threatened, our entire community is threatened" and that "incidents involving violence, hatred, or bias have no place in our community" (*Burlington Free Press*, 2012). As their president said, "this ugly stain reminds us that the hard work must continue."

ST. LOUIS UNIVERSITY. Student affairs divisions on many campuses are reliant on entry-level staff in their departments. This is also true at SLU and creates a challenge when orienting the staff to the MCOD efforts. Training and development of staff related to multicultural competence is an ongoing challenge. To address this need, SLU offers regular workshops, which include 1~HF-day workshops with nationally known diversity trainers. The workshops are designed to continue the in-depth conversations around MCOD and to address different levels of needs (e.g., basic, more advanced leadership techniques in applying MCOD).

In an environment that includes many entry-level staff, a fairly high rate of staff turnover results in the need for regular staff hiring. According to Leanna Fenneberg, staff appreciation and understanding regarding the hiring practices and valuing hiring for diversity is sometimes challenging (personal communication, October 29, 2012). In response, a standing committee to discuss these issues has been formed. The committee has also initiated all-Division staff workshops to provide context, information, resources, and a time to reflect about the issues. In addition, a Google site has been established that includes resources for hiring managers.

Finally, SLU faces challenges in working with campus partners who do not necessarily have the same commitment, values, or exposure to training in this area, which can cause frustration for staff who rely on these partnerships to move programs forward. In an initial attempt to address this issue, key stakeholders including departments such as Enrollment & Retention Management and Academic Advising have been invited to attend social justice workshops.

Conclusions

The purpose of this chapter was to provide several in-depth examples of how multicultural change is happening on college campuses in the United States, to demonstrate ways in which MCOD may manifest in real-life contexts. That is, using MCOD concepts described in previous chapters, we presented the current experiences of three diverse institutions that are committed to making their campuses welcoming and affirming to all students. The UT-Austin's Division of Housing and Food Services, UVM's Division of University Relations and Campus Life, and SLU's Division of Student Development have created and implemented wide-ranging strategies for making progress toward this goal that are appropriate for their institutions and regions. Recognizing that multicultural change in diverse contexts is possible is an important first step in creating multicultural change (Pope, 1995), and thus we hope these exemplars inspire readers to lead or contribute to MCOD efforts on their own campuses. We further hope that readers identify some concrete ideas and practical approaches used by these institutions to adapt on their own campuses.

At the same time, we tried to paint a realistic picture, demonstrating that real multicultural change that makes a difference for college students does not happen overnight, is not easy, and cannot be accomplished by just one person. Instead, "creating multicultural environments and attaining a multicultural perspective is a process that requires expertise, focused reflection, commitment, specific competencies, and purposeful action" (Pope, 1995, p. 235). Multicultural change requires sustained, consistent, and dynamic efforts that range from increasing individuals' awareness to affecting institutional systems (Pope, 1995). As evidenced by the campuses highlighted here, there will be challenges to the process (such as individual resistance), and there will be setbacks in achieving intended outcomes (such as hate crimes or biased incidents). However, we must work through these challenges, knowing that the efforts put forth in creating multicultural environments help us affirm and support all students as learners and help all students live and work effectively in our increasingly global world.

8

CONCLUSION

TEN YEARS AGO, WE PUBLISHED *Multicultural Competence in Student Affairs* (Pope, Reynolds, & Mueller, 2004). The purpose of that book was to expand the concept of multicultural competence, initially introduced by Pope and Reynolds (1997). In our 2004 book, we detailed how multicultural awareness, knowledge, and skills can and should be incorporated into the core competencies of theory and translation, administration and management, helping and advising, assessment and research, ethics and professional standards, and teaching and training. The emphasis of that book was individual practitioners and their multicultural competence.

Since the publication of that book, we have each had numerous opportunities to speak, research, and continue writing about multicultural competence and the student affairs profession. In nearly every conversation about the topic, two questions are commonly asked: (1) Will you be developing a measure for multicultural competencies of students and paraprofessionals? and (2) Can the principles of multicultural competence be applied to organizations? To the first question, we have responded that we have not developed such an assessment because the principles of multicultural competence, as we define them, were not designed for students or paraprofessionals. Multicultural competence is an integrated skill set that all student affairs and higher education professionals must bring to their practices to create and maintain diverse and inclusive campus environments. Although the notion of multicultural competence (and any associated measures) for students and paraprofessionals is an important area to explore, it has not been the focus of our work.

The second question, however, has given us reason to pause. Over the years, we have discussed the idea of a multiculturally competent organization or institution. We have considered the idea that an organization (as an organism) can strive to be multiculturally competent in the same way that an individual can. Indeed, other scholars have discussed the idea in ways that have informed our thinking (Flash, 2010a; Wilcox & McCray, 2005). Several years before the publication of this book, when we were approached about the possibility of writing a second edition to *Multicultural Competence in Student Affairs,* we concluded that one was not warranted at the time. However, the idea of extending the concept of multicultural competence from the individual to the organization did, we believed, have potential. Interestingly, the seed for the idea was contained within our own 2004 book (page 57 to be exact): The Multicultural Change Intervention Matrix (MCIM; Pope, 1993; 1995). The MCIM illustrates how the principles of multicultural organization development (MCOD) can be applied to student affairs and higher education.

That has become the goal of this book. Whereas our first book was an expansion on the Pope and Reynolds model (1997) of multicultural competence of student affairs practitioners, this book is an expansion on the Pope (1993; 1995) model of multicultural organizational change or, perhaps, a multiculturally competent organization or institution in a higher education context. As such, the goal of this book is to more deeply examine systemic and systematic multicultural change on college and university campuses. Our goal is to integrate theory with practice, policy, and program assessment and interventions in pursuit of creating campus environments that are inclusive, welcoming, and affirming for all who work, teach, and learn on college and university campuses. In this final chapter, we summarize the key points from the core chapters of this book and present emergent themes and insights from these chapters. Finally, we close with suggestions in response to some of the challenges inherent in multicultural change efforts on campus.

Summary of Key Points

The thrust of this book has been that to effect multicultural change on campus, higher education professionals must be equipped with viable theories, tools, and strategies. In the process of identifying numerous specific theories and models, we did so with two overarching constructs in mind: multicultural competence and MCOD. Combined, these two overlapping and mutually reinforcing constructs become the foundation for the core theory of this book: the MCIM. As Flash (2010a) proposed, and we wholeheartedly agree, the principles of multicultural competence are necessary not only on the individual level but also on the organizational level. The MCIM allows us to examine more deeply how we can better understand and design multicultural change intervention strategies that target the individual level (students, faculty, staff, administrators, and so forth), the group level (staff teams, committees, student groups, task groups, and so forth), and the organizational level (departments or divisions within an institution or the institution as a whole). In addition, the MCIM challenges us to consider different types of change efforts: those that address more external aspects and the composition of the target (first-order change) and those that address the more internal features and the structure of the target (second-order change). Said another way, "First-order change involves doing better what we already do, while second-order change alters the core ways we conduct business or even the basic business itself" (Lorenzi & Riley, 2000, p. 119).

To further review the MCIM, let us briefly examine each of these target levels (and the associated types of change) and summarize the key points.

Multicultural Intervention at the Individual Level

The chorus of Michael Jackson's 1988 hit song "Man in the Mirror" challenges listeners with a pithy message: "If you want to make the world a better place, take a look at yourself and then make a change." This compelling lyric gets to the heart of multicultural change at the individual level; it involves looking at oneself honestly and engaging the will and courage to make changes as necessary. Several theoretical perspectives, identified in Chapter 3, describe conditions that can facilitate individual change. These include awareness of self, readiness for change, willingness to explore and cross familiar interpersonal boundaries, the ability to deconstruct one's ways of seeing the world, and ongoing self-reflection. Interestingly, although the emphasis is on the individual at this level, central to all of the conditions are the interactions one has with others. First-order interventions, then, focus on efforts to enhance one's awareness, content knowledge, sensitivity, and behaviors that are consistent with valuing diversity. Second-order interventions target one's capacity for deeper change, such as examining core beliefs and assumptions, exploring one's intersecting identities and the attendant privileges and obstacles, and as a consequence shifting one's view of self and the world—the core of transformation. Both first- and second-order change are necessary components of change at the individual level.

Multicultural Intervention at the Group Level

Margaret Mead famously said, "Never doubt that a small group of thoughtful, committed, citizens can change the world. Indeed, it is the only thing that ever has." Mead's quote acknowledges the power of individuals coming together and working with one another to accomplish great things. This idea is central to group theory: A group is not simply a collection of individuals; it is a collection of people interacting and working interdependently in pursuit of common goals. When diversity of the group becomes a focus, group theory takes on a new significance. First-order change at the group level addresses the makeup and character (i.e., the membership) of the group in terms of race, gender, sexual orientation, language, religion, class, and so on. As the group develops beyond the formation of the group into the operation of the group, aspects of second-order change become pronounced. Here, the structure of the group becomes focused as the diverse set of group members work through setting norms, negotiating conflict, making decisions, and meeting goals. Interventions to facilitate both group membership and structure (or operation) are essential to multicultural change.

Multicultural Intervention at the Institutional Level

As once uttered by Reverend Martin Luther King, "Change does not roll in on the wheels of inevitability but comes through continuous struggle." His thought-provoking quote not only is a reminder of the ongoing process involved with multicultural change but also highlights some of the challenges faced when cultivating change at the institutional level. First-order change at the institutional level focuses on programmatic changes (i.e., adding new programs or positions to address diversity). As those changes are enacted, the institution does begin to look more attentive to diversity issues; however, the additions still place the bulk of the responsibility for multicultural change with a few individuals and offices. Second-order change involves infusing multicultural values, structures, and practices throughout the institution so that soon every individual, program, department, and unit becomes accountable for the multicultural mission of the institution. Once there are programs, policies, and practices that inculcate multiculturalism in systematic and ongoing ways, such as found in a multicultural strategic plan that was not separate but rather rolled into the university or college overall plan, then a palpable and enduring transformation has occurred.

Themes and Insights

As we have unpacked multicultural interventions at these three levels (individual, group, and institutional) across the dimensions of first-order change and second-order change, several themes and insights have emerged that warrant closer attention as we close this book. First, the concepts of first- and second-order change, while unique to the MCIM, are reflected in other related scholarship. Second, the targets of intervention, while treated separately in the model (and in this book), are actually more integrated that they appear. And finally, we must resist the temptation to regard first-order change as somehow deficient with respect to second-order change. We look at these three points more closely below.

Complementary Conceptualizations

Pope (1993; 1995), in developing the MCIM for student affairs and higher education, cited Lyddon (1990) and Watzlawick, Weakland, and Fisch (1974) and the concepts of first-order and second-order change. As noted earlier in this book, first- and second-order change has been explored in other contexts such as counseling (Reynolds, 1997), leadership development (Waters, Marzano, & McNulty, 2003), and medical information systems (Lorenzi & Riley, 2000). Likewise, the fundamental idea of first- and second-order change has also been examined from other angles, which can only add further insight to our own understanding.

Watt (2014), for example, in her discussion on implementing multicultural initiatives on campus, proposes that when designing and implementing these initiatives, we must examine our underlying assumptions and approaches. Are we approaching the initiative as a "social good" or a "social value"? Viewing diversity as social good, according to Watt (2014), "requires a surface level commitment to systemic change with a focus on outcomes without attempting to assess or dismantle the underlying problems that contribute to marginalization" (p. 8). This approach *is* beneficial in that it can provide direct support (i.e., programs and service) to marginalized groups; still, the intervention usually becomes the responsibility of the marginalized group and occurs within the cultural norms of the institution, with little effect on those norms. When diversity is viewed as a social value, however, strategies are developed that "disrupt systematic oppression on a deeper level" and "fundamentally question[s] the underlying structures that bind the way campus community members interact" (p. 9). In this case, marginalized *and* privileged groups share responsibility for the change and are both affected by the change. These perspectives parallel first-order change (i.e., diversity as a social good) and second-order change (i.e., diversity as a social value). To detail Watt's analysis and recommendations would go beyond the scope of this chapter and book. Suffice it to say, though, her work serves as a reminder that the work of other scholars on this topic can expand and add further depth to existing conceptualizations of multicultural change.

Another example of a model that complements MCIM is Palmer's (1989) three-paradigm model that describes an organization's approach to diversity and organizational change: (1) The Golden Rule; (2) Right the Wrongs; and (3) Value the Differences. In the first paradigm, the assumption is that diversity is about individual differences in characteristics and that people are more alike than different and, therefore, everyone should be treated fairly and the same regardless of differences. If there are any problems in the organization when it comes to race or gender, for example, they are isolated incidents or the result of a few bad people. The second paradigm acknowledges differences more broadly and recognizes that certain groups in the organization may have been systematically disadvantaged. The objective then is to correct, through recruitment, retention, and reward efforts, the injustices that one or two target groups have experienced. The third paradigm acknowledges and emphasizes the various cultures and heritages of the different groups within the organization. As such, diversity is not viewed as a problem but as an opportunity to work synergistically and more effectively with other organizational members. The diversity within the organization is thus maximized through hiring practices, new norms, inclusive decisions, rewards, and communication. Palmer's model provides us with another way to consider the range of intervention strategies across a continuum similar to the first-order and second-order conceptualization.

Intersections and Permeability of the Model

The utility of the MCIM model lies in its capacity to clearly illustrate the 3 × 2 dimensions of target level (individual, group, and organizational) and the type of change (first-order and second-order). Indeed, this book has employed this model as the conceptual apparatus to present multicultural competence in organizations in terms of the distinct cells: (A) awareness; (B) paradigm shift; (C) membership; (D) restructuring; (E) programmatic; and (F) systemic. At the same time, we remind the reader, as we conclude this book, of a point made earlier in the book: The illustration of the model and its use of dotted lines between the cells is intended to depict the dynamic and fluid nature of the model. Interventions anchored in one cell of the model may impact, overlap, or may even be relevant to interventions in other cells of the model, particularly adjacent cells.

Looking more closely at the relationship between target levels, we find that although each differs structurally from the other (organizations are larger than groups, which are larger than a single individual), each is an organism, and each shares and is influenced by similar dynamics. Smith (2009) observed that each level is complex and dynamic because each level has its own source of culture, identity, and values and that each operates within its own context. Although in this book we discuss these levels separately (i.e., by chapters), we must think of them as interacting with and influencing one another. For example, an individual's paradigm shift may be the direct result of the individual's interaction in a diverse group, particularly in one that has restructured itself to effectively accommodate and meaningfully incorporate its diversity. Furthermore, this paradigm shift and restructuring may be fostered by an institution that has intentionally addressed systematic change. Similarly, changes at the individual level and group level (particularly second-order changes) may inspire, if not compel, systemic change at the institutional level. Institutions and organizations are made of groups and groups are made of individuals; a connection always exists between and among these distinct entities.

In a similar way, we can look at the permeable lines between first-order change and second-order change at any of the three levels. Not all interventions can be neatly defined as either first-order or second-order. Lorenzi and Riley (2004) consider definitions of first- and second-order changes as extremes on a continuum. They cite Golembiewski, Billingsley, and Yeager (1976), who suggest "middle-order change," a compromise of sorts in which "the magnitude of change is greater than first-order change, yet it neither affects the critical success factors nor is strategic in nature" (p. 66). For example, at the group level, efforts may be made to not only diversify the group but to ensure that leadership roles, traditionally held by white men, are also occupied by women and people of color. Still, efforts by this new leadership to examine the goals and norms of the group may be stifled and resisted. Although the group has made significant efforts to diversify staff and leadership, little progress has been made in the actual functioning of the group. Similarly, a single intervention may not fit neatly into one type of change, because it may have an equal impact on both first-order and second-order change. For example, providing ongoing diversity training for a staff group that focuses on a deeper level meant to challenge the way each individual understands diversity clearly is individually oriented second-order paradigmatic change. However, because the change effort is occurring within an intact group, it also may affect how that group functions and works together. In that way, there is a blending of the type of intervention that is being provided.

First Things First

As we examine the differences between first- and second-order change, the inclination is to assume that second-order change is "better" than first-order and that the goal is to graduate from first-order to second-order change. Furthermore, one may believe that once second-order change efforts are established, first-order change efforts can cease. We must shift from this "either/or" thinking and consider first- and second-order change as a "both/and" arrangement.

First-order change may, at first glance (or in comparison with second-order change), be viewed as superficial, easy, passive, and uninspiring. Not so. Depending on where an individual, a group, or organization is in their development, first-order change may be providing just the challenge and change that is needed (e.g., it opens up one's eyes, it changes the composition of the group, or it brings an important new position to the organization). It may even bring about changes that prepare the target for the type of challenge that comes with second-order change. We maintain that first-order change is valuable and necessary, but it is not sufficient, and it cannot sustain itself without second-order change. It may be difficult to resist thinking about this in hierarchical terms (i.e., higher is better), but it is as important to do so. Perhaps an analogy of a building would be helpful. When constructing a building, the cornerstone is the first stone that is set, and all other stones in the structure are set in reference to the cornerstone. The cornerstone, then, determines the structure of the entire building. First-order change serves the same purpose as the cornerstone of a building. It can establish and set the foundation for the second-order change that follows. As a result, there is, and always will be, a constant need to provide ongoing interventions that target both first- and second-order change. As noted earlier in discussions of the transtheoretical model of change (Prochaska & DiClemente, 1984), attending to the process of change is likely more important than focusing energy on moving individuals, groups, or individuals along some imaginary linear trajectory.

Another assumption about the MCIM is that interventions begin at the individual level and work their way up to the organizational or institutional level. The other perspective might be more "trickle down," wherein successful interventions at the organizational level work their way down through the group level to the individual level. This debate over a top-down or bottom-up approach to the MCIM creates a cause-and-effect question: Which causes which? Wilber (2000) provides some useful insight on this "chicken or egg" dilemma that can help us understand the non-hierarchical and interactive nature of the MCIM (i.e., three levels of interventions). He uses "holons" as a way to explain how each part is unto itself (i.e., autonomous) while simultaneously being a part of the whole. For example, "a word is a *part* of a sentence, but a *whole* with regard to the letters that compose it" (italics added) (Sattler, 2008, p. 10). Though far more complex than introduced here, the concept of holons can help us recognize and appreciate the mutual interaction effect of the levels of intervention. That is, interventions at one level (e.g., the group) can simultaneously and positively affect the other levels (e.g., individual and institutional) and vice versa.

A Call to Action

The MCIM can be a very useful tool to guide higher education professionals in their mission to create more multicultural campuses, but as noted earlier, it is not a cure-all, and it can be fraught with resistance and challenges. Although multicultural change efforts have promise, they also shake the foundation of an individual, a group, or an organization. Oppressive attitudes and behaviors are so deeply engrained in individuals, structures, and cultures of higher education organizations that multicultural change requires courage, consciousness, vision, assessment, strategic planning, and deployment of key resources to be most effective (Chesler & Crowfoot, 1997; Harper & Antonio, 2008; Pope & LePeau, 2012). A significant challenge to this process is overcoming the hostility and controversy that have historically characterized these efforts. Chesler and Crowfoot propose that rooting out racism and other forms of discrimination poses more of a challenge to institutions than major curriculum transformation or overhauling financial plans.

As we conclude this book, we provide readers with a call to action to address these challenges and to move forward with multicultural change efforts. Nothing in this book is intended to be prescriptive, because multicultural change efforts occur in context with many different variables, depending on the history, the players, the issues, and the politics of the institution. Still, broad questions may linger, such as "How do I start?" or "What I should be mindful of?" or "How do I keep the momentum going?" We offer several thoughts on how to address these and other questions. We draw on the work of Chesler, Lewis, and Crowfoot (2005) and other scholars (Kline, 2013; Nash, Bradley, & Chickering, 2008;

Petitt & McIntosh, 2011; Watt, 2007, 2012) as a foundation for recommendations that can lead to more successful beginnings and outcomes.

o *Think long-term and big picture.* Viewing multicultural change as a short-term project—perhaps a priority goal for the upcoming year—can have some short-term benefits for an organization. However, this approach overlooks the long-engrained effects of monoculturalism within an organization once that short-term effort comes to a close. Multicultural change needs to be viewed as an ongoing change effort. Similarly, organizations may respond to a crisis or an immediate condition and believe that the problem is resolved. Focusing on crises and overlooking underlying conditions and deeper issues will do little to promote lasting multicultural change. What *is* needed are long-term vision, a concrete plan, and accountability measures.

o *Identify and rally resources.* Approaching the enormous task of multicultural change can be overwhelming and can lead to retreat, fear, failure, pessimism, doubt, and defeat. Tap into the numerous resources that are already available on your campus and at other institutions; ones that can be adapted to your institution's or organization's needs. In addition, although those who are most vocal (e.g., grassroots level) or who have the most influence (e.g., leadership) can bring needed energy, knowledge, direction, and even resources to organizational change, it is unwise to pin all hope on a single person or group within an institution. Sustained efforts must involve the "middle dwellers" (p. 192) who represent various identity groups and organizational levels and should, as Petitt and McIntosh (2011) propose, be the result of "systems and processes that are not person-dependent" (p. 203) and which outlast the tenure of any single change agent.

o *Be coordinated and nimble.* Too often, change efforts are sporadic, isolated, or marginalized within the organization—they only occur at certain times (e.g., crises) or are the responsibility of a few (e.g., Assistant Dean of Multicultural Affairs). If the efforts are not baked into the organization at all levels and a part of everyone's responsibility, it is difficult to monitor them, build in accountability and reward measures, and evaluate their impact. Also, as much as planned and coordinated efforts are necessary, so too is flexibility and adaptation. Sticking to a rigid plan that fails to acknowledge how fluid and dynamic multicultural change is (and resistance to it) may lead to less than effective outcomes.

o *Expect and address resistance.* Resistance or differing opinions will emerge when an organization introduces multicultural change efforts. A healthy balance of rational debate and emotional confrontation will help to engage a wider range of participants in strategies to persuade, problem-solve, resolve conflict, converse, and negotiate. Relying only on a "logical" approach denies the existence of strong emotions associated with a history of racism and other forms of discrimination experienced by individual members, groups, or the organization itself that need to be rooted out and addressed. Conversely, focusing only on emotions may hinder cooperative consensus-building strategies that are needed for long-term and sustained change. Finally, with respect to resistance, although it is likely to occur and it is prudent to be aware of it, to overstate its significance or to expect complete support before moving forward is naïve. The entire institution need not be on board for change to start. A critical mass of colleagues as individuals, groups, and organizational units can work to create and maintain the structural change needed.

o *Monitor, evaluate, and reward.* Efforts to restructure the organization from within involve hard work and require developing innovative strategies to build into the organization's policies, practices, and culture. To sustain this, ongoing assessment to monitor progress is needed, and drawing attention to success is essential. Institutionalizing the assessment and rewards processes to the organization is as important as institutionalizing the diversity change efforts themselves. Chapter Six of this book provides multiple tools and resources for conducting assessment at all levels of the institution, including assessment of the overall campus climate.

o *Reflect and engage in difficult dialogues.* Revitalizing as change might be, it is often difficult. The process of multicultural change can expose (within the individual, group, or institution) long-held assumptions, biases, and privileges that in turn can raise feelings of shame, guilt, discomfort, resentment, and anxiety. Likewise, when change occurs in response to and in the context of challenging social issues such as diversity and multiculturalism, the potential to, as Nash, Bradley, and Chickering (2008) call it, "ignite the fire" (p. 3) is strong. All of this can be overwhelming and may lead to conversations that are polarizing or immobilizing. In these instances, we urge professionals to lean into that discomfort, to reflect on and make meaning of theory, practice, training, and research, to seek critical consciousness, and to engage in those difficult dialogues (Kline, 2013; Watt, 2007). Watt (2012) proposes that two key conditions must be in place for productive dialogues: mutual purpose (a shared understanding of the goal) and mutual respect (reassurance that all engaged will be treated fairly).

Summary

Levine and Dean (2012) in their book characterizing today's college student and college campuses call on higher education professionals to examine notions of diversity and visions of what a multicultural higher education institution truly looks like. In doing so, the authors argue, professionals can turn those visions into action plans that are incorporated across all dimensions of the campus, including facilities, budgets, staff, services, and programs. The ultimate goal? To define a quality education as one that "facilitates students' ability to interact effectively with diversity" (Katz, 1989, p. 1).

We believe that *Creating Multicultural Change on Campus* can help higher education professionals achieve this goal. In this book we have drawn connections between individual multicultural competence and MCOD, mutually reinforcing constructs that yield a range of principles, strategies, and tools to effect multicultural change. It is our hope that in doing so, we honor the optimism of Cheatham (1991), whose own scholarly work was devoted to helping higher education professionals realize their individual and institutional commitments to cultural pluralism, inclusion, and social justice.

REFERENCES

About UVM. (n.d.). Fast facts. Retrieved from http://www.uvm.edu/about_uvm/?Page=facts.html

ACPA. (2012). ACPA 2012 Annual Convention: Create Possibilities [Program book]. Washington, DC: Author. Retrieved from http://www2.myacpa.org/docs/ACPA_2012_Program_Book.pdf

Adler, N. J. (2008). *International dimensions of organizational behavior.* Mason, OH: Thomson.

Aguirre, A., & Martinez, R. (2002). Leadership practices and diversity in higher education: Transitional and transformational frameworks. *Journal of Leadership Studies, 8,* 53–62.

Allport, G. W. (1954). *The nature of prejudice.* Reading, MA: Addison Wesley.

American College Personnel Association and National Association of Student Personnel Administrators. (1997). *Principles of good practice.* Washington, DC: authors.

Antonio, A. L., Chang, M. J., Hakuta, K., Kenny, D. A., Levin, S., & Milem, J. F. (2004). Effects of racial diversity on complex thinking in college students. *Psychological Science, 15,* 507–510.

Argyris, C., & Schon, D. (1974). *Theory in practice: Increasing professional effectiveness.* San Francisco, CA: Jossey-Bass.

Arredondo, P. (1996). *Successful diversity management initiatives: A blueprint for planning and implementation.* Thousand Oaks, CA: Sage Publications.

Arredondo, P., & Perez, P. (2006). Historical perspectives on the multicultural guidelines and contemporary applications. *Professional Psychology: Research and Practice, 37,* 1–5.

Association of American Colleges and Universities (AAC&U) (1995). *The drama of diversity and democracy: Higher education and American commitments.* Washington, DC: Author.

Association on Higher Education and Disability (AHEAD). (2010). *Universal design in higher education* [Brochure]. Huntersville, NC: Author.

Astin, A. W. (1993). *What matters in college? Four critical years revisited.* San Francisco: Jossey-Bass.

Bales, R. F. (1999). *Social interaction systems: Theory and measurement.* New Brunswick, NJ: Transaction.

Barcelo, N. (2007). Transforming our institutions for the twenty-first century: The role of the chief diversity officer. *Diversity Digest, 10,* 5–6.

Baxter Magolda, M. B. (1997). Facilitating meaningful dialogues about race. *About Campus, 2,* 14–18.

Bensimon, E. M. (2004). The diversity scorecard: A learning approach to institutional change. *Change, 36,* 44–52.

Blimling, G. S., & Whitt, E. J. (1999). *Good practice in student affairs: Principles to foster student learning.* San Francisco: Jossey-Bass.

Bok, D. (2006). *Our underachieving colleges: A candid look at how much students learn and why they should be learning more.* Princeton, NJ: Princeton University Press.

Bonebright, D. A. (2010). 40 years of storming: A historical review of Tuckman's model of small group development. *Human Resource Development International, 13,* 111–120.

Bowman, N. A. (2010). College diversity experiences and cognitive development: A meta-analysis. *Review of Educational Research, 80,* 4–33. doi:10.3102/0034654309352495

Bowser. B. P., & Baker, O. (1995). Toward a multicultural university: Using strategic planning for change. In B. P. Bowser, T. Jones, & G. A. Young (Eds.), *Toward the multicultural university* (pp. 125–134). Westport, CT: Praeger.

Brayboy, B.M.J. (2003). The implementation of diversity in predominantly white colleges and universities. *Journal of Black Studies, 34,* 72–86.

Bresciani, M. J. (2011). Assessment and evaluation. In J. H. Schuh, S. R. Jones, & S. R. Harper (Eds.), *Student services: A handbook for the profession* (5th ed.) (pp. 321–334). San Francisco, CA: Jossey-Bass.

Bunker, B. B., & Alban, B. T. (2006). Large group methods: Developments and trends. In B. B. Jones & M. Brazzel (Eds.), *The NTL handbook of organization development and change: Principles, practices, and perspectives* (pp. 287–301). San Francisco, CA: Pfeiffer.

Burke, B. L. (2011). What can motivational interviewing do for you? *Cognitive and Behavioral Practice, 18,* 74–81.

Burlington Free Press. (2012, May 10). University of Vermont condemns racist graffiti; student to be cited. BurlingtonFreePress. com. Retrieved from http://www.burlingtonfreepress.com/article/20120511/NEWS02/120510037/University-Vermont-condemns-racist-graffiti-student-cited

Caban, A. R. (2010). *Development and initial validation of the multicultural competence change scale for psychology trainees.* (Order No. 3435762, University of Oregon). *ProQuest Dissertations and Theses, 187.* Retrieved from http://search.proquest.com/docview/816348942?accountid=14169 (prod.academic_MSTAR_816348942).

Castellanos, J., Gloria, A. M., Mayorga, M., & Salas, C. (2007). Student affairs professionals' self-report of multicultural competence: Understanding awareness, knowledge, and skills. *NASPA Journal, 44,* 643–663.

Chang, M. J. (2001). Is it more than getting along? The broader educational relevance of reducing students' racial biases. *Journal of College Student Development, 42,* 93–105.

Chang, M. J. (2005). Reconsidering the diversity rationale. *Liberal Education, 91,* 6–13.

Chang, M. J. (2007). Beyond artificial integration: Reimagining cross-racial interactions among undergraduates. *New Directions for Student Services, 120,* 25–37.

Chang, M. J., Astin, A. W., & Kim, D. (2004). Cross-racial interaction among undergraduates: Some causes and consequences. *Research in Higher Education, 45,* 527–551.

Chang, M. J., Chang, J. C., & Ledesma, M. C. (2005). Beyond magical thinking: Doing the real work of diversifying our institutions. *About Campus, 10,* 9–16.

Chavez, A. F., Guido-DiBrito, F., & Mallory, S. L. (2003). Learning to value the "other": A framework of individual diversity development. *Journal of College Student Development, 44,* 453–469.

Cheatham, H. E. (1991). *Cultural pluralism on campus.* Alexandria, VA: ACPA Media.

Cheng, D. X., and Zhao, C. M. (2006). Cultivating multicultural competence through active participation: Extracurricular activities and multicultural learning. *NASPA Journal, 43,* 13–38.

Chesler, M. A. (1994). Organizational development is not the same as multicultural organization development. In E. Y. Cross, J. H. Katz, F. A. Miller, & E. W. Seashore (Eds.), *The promise of diversity: Over 40 voices discuss strategies for eliminating discrimination in organizations* (pp. 240–251). Burr Ridge, IL: Irwin.

Chesler, M. A. (1998). *Planning multicultural audits in higher education.* (To Improve the Academy Paper #400). Retrieved from: http://digitalcommons.unl.edu/cgi/viewcontent.cgi?article=1399&context=podimproveacad

Chesler, M. A., & Crowfoot, J. (1997). *Racism in higher education II: Challenging racism and promoting multiculturalism in higher education organizations.* (Center for Research on Social Organization Working Paper #558). Retrieved from http://141.213.232.243/handle/2027.42/51322

Chesler, M. A., & Crowfoot, J. (2000). An organizational analysis of racism in higher education. In M. C. Brown (Ed.), *Organization & governance in higher education* (5th ed.) (ASHE Reader Series, J. L. Ratcliffe, Ed.), pp. 436–469. Boston, MA: Pearson Custom Publishing.

Chesler, M. A., Lewis, A. E., & Crowfoot, J. E. (2005). *Challenging racism in higher education: Promoting justice.* Lanham, MD: Rowman & Littlefield.

Cilente, K. (2009). An overview of the social change model of leadership development. In S. R. Komives and W. Wagner (Eds.), *Leadership for a better world: Understanding the social change model of leadership development* (pp. 43–77). San Francisco: Jossey-Bass.

Coleman, H.L.K., & Hau, J. M. (2003). Multicultural counseling competency and portfolios. In D. B. Pope-Davis, H.L.K. Coleman, W. M. Liu, & R. L. Toporek (Eds.), *Handbook of multicultural competencies in counseling and psychology* (pp. 168–182). Thousand Oaks, CA: Sage Publications.

Comer, D., & Soliman, C. (1996). Organizational efforts to manage diversity: Do they really work? *Journal of Management Issues, 8,* 470–483.

Corey, G. (2011). *Theory and practice of group counseling* (8th ed.). Belmont, CA: Cengage Learning.

Cox, T. (2001). *Creating the multicultural organization: A strategy for capturing the power of diversity.* San Francisco: Jossey-Bass.

Coyne, R. K. (1991). Organization development: A broad net intervention for student affairs. In T. Miller & R. Winston (Eds.), *Administration and leadership in student affairs. Actualizing student development in higher education* (2nd ed.) (pp. 72–109). Muncie, IN: Accelerated Development.

Cuyjet, M. J. (2011). Environmental influences on college culture. In M. J. Cuyjet, M. F. Howard-Hamilton, & D. L. Cooper (Eds.), *Multiculturalism on campus: Theory, models, and practices for understanding diversity and creating inclusion* (pp. 37–63). Sterling, VA: Stylus.

Daloz, L.A.P. (2000). Transformative learning for the common good. In J. Mezirow (Ed.), *Learning as transformation: Critical perspectives on a theory in progress* (pp. 103–124). San Francisco: Jossey-Bass.

Dean of Students Office (n.d.). *Lacretia Johnson Flash*. Retrieved from http://www.uvm.edu/~dos/?Page=office/lacretia.php&SM=office/ officemenu.html

Deardorff, D. K. (2011). Assessing intercultural competence. *New Directions for Institutional Research, 149*, 65–79.

DeVellis, R. F. (2003). *Scale development: Theory and applications* (2nd ed.). Thousand Oaks, CA: Sage.

DiClemente, C. C., & Prochaska, J. O. (1998). Toward a comprehensive, transtheoretical model of change: Stages of change and addictive behaviours. In W. R. Miller & N. Heather (Eds.), *Treating addictive behaviours* (2nd ed., pp. 3–24). New York: Plenum Press.

Discover Our Values (n.d.). *Discover our values & history: Not just a building*. Retrieved from http://www.uvm.edu/~davis/?Page=discover .php&SM=menu_history.html

Diversity & Social Justice (n.d.). *Diversity & social justice: Values, commitment, vision*. Retrieved from http://www.uvm.edu/~dos/ advancing_diversity/SCL_Diversity_Brochure.pdf

Diversity Calendar of Events (2013, February). *Diversity at SLU: Diversity Calendar of Events*. Retrieved from http://www.slu.edu/ diversity/about-diversity-at-slu/diversity-calendar-of-events

Diversity Workshop Guidelines (2012). *Diversity workshop guidelines*. Retrieved from http://www.utexas.edu/student/housing/index .php?site=6&scode=0&id=1268

Dose, J. J., & Klimoski, R. J. (1999). The diversity of diversity: Work values effects on formative team processes. *Human Resource Management Review, 9*(1), 82–108.

Drake, M. J. (2006). Ambivalence at the academies: Attitudes toward women in the military at the federal service academies. *Social Thought and Research, 27*, 43–68.

Drechsler, M. J., & Jones, W. A. (2009). In S. R. Komives and W. Wagner (Eds.), *Leadership for a better world: Understanding the social change model of leadership development* (pp. 397–443). San Francisco: Jossey-Bass.

Eckel, P., Hill, B., & Green, M. (1998). *On change: En route to transformation*. Washington, DC: American Council on Education.

Edgert, P. (1994). Assessing campus climate: Implications for diversity. In D. G Smith, L. E. Wolf, & T. Levitan (Eds.), *Studying diversity in higher education* (New Directions for Institutional Research, No. 81, pp. 51–62). San Francisco, CA: Jossey-Bass.

Einfeld, A., & Collins, D. (2008). The relationships between service-learning, social justice, multicultural competence, and civic engagement. *Journal of College Student Development, 49*, 95–109.

El-Khawas, E. (2003). The many dimensions of student diversity. In S. R. Komives & D. B. Woodard (Eds.), *Student services: A handbook for the profession* (4th ed.) (pp. 45–62). San Francisco, CA: Jossey-Bass.

Ely, R. J., & Roberts, L. M. (2008) Shifting frames in team-diversity research: From difference to relationships. In A. P. Brief (Ed.), Diversity at work (pp. 175–201). New York, NY: Cambridge University Press.

Ely, R. J., & Thomas, D. A. (2001). Cultural diversity at work: The effects of diversity on work group processes and outcomes. *Administrative Science Quarterly, 46,* 229–273.

Flash, L. J. (2010a). *Developing a measure of multicultural competence in student affairs organizations* (Unpublished doctoral dissertation). University of Vermont, Burlington, VT.

Flash, L. J. (2010b). *Components of multicultural competency in student affairs organizations.* Unpublished manuscript.

Flash, L. J. (2010c). *Multicultural competence in student affairs organizations (MCSAO) questionnaire: Research summary.* Unpublished manuscript.

Flash, L. J., Stevens, A., & Whitworth, P. E. (2013, March). *Voices of inclusion medallion exemplary program: Innovations in diversity and multicultural competency professional development for student affairs professionals.* Presented at annual convention of the American College Personnel Association, Las Vegas, NV.

Flowers, L. A. (2004). (Ed.). *Diversity issues in American colleges and universities: Case studies for higher education and student affairs professionals.* Springfield, IL: Charles C. Thomas.

Foldy, E. G. (2004). Learning from diversity: A theoretical explanation. *Public Administration Review, 64*(5), 529–538.

Forsythe, D. R. (1990). *Group dynamics* (2nd ed.). Pacific Grove, CA: Brooks/Cole.

Forsythe, D. R. (2006). *Group dynamics* (4th ed.). Belmont, CA: Thomson Wadsworth.

Freire, P. (1970). *Pedagogy of the oppressed.* New York: Continuum.

Frey, L. R. (2000). Diversifying our understanding of diversity and communication in groups. *Group Dynamics: Theory, Research, and Practice, 4,* 222–229.

Gallant, S. M., & Rios, D. (2006). Entry and contracting phase. In B. B. Jones & M. Brazzel (Eds.), *The NTL handbook of organization development and change: Principles, practices, and perspectives* (pp. 177–191). San Francisco, CA: Pfeiffer.

Gamst, G. C., Liang, C.T.H., & Der-Karabetian, A. (2011). *Handbook of multicultural measures.* Washington, DC: Sage.

Gay, L. R., & Airasian, P. (2000). *Educational research: Competencies for analysis and application* (6th ed.). Upper Saddle River, NJ: Merrill.

Gayles, J. G., & Kelly, B. T. (2007). Experiences with diversity in the curriculum: Implications for graduate programs and student affairs practice. *NASPA Journal, 44,* 193–208.

Golembiewski R. T., Billingsley, K., & Yeager, S. (1976). Measuring change and persistence in human affairs: Types of change generated by OD designs. *Journal of Applied Behavioral Science, 12,* 133–157.

Gloria, A. M., Rieckmann, T. R., & Rush, J. D. (2000). Issues and recommendations for teaching an ethnic/culture-based course. *Teaching of Psychology, 27,* 102–107.

Good, G. E., & Beitman, B. D. (2006). *Counseling and psychotherapy essentials: Integrating theories, skills, and practices.* New York: Norton.

Grieger, I. (1996). A multicultural organizational development checklist for student affairs. *Journal of College Student Development, 27,* 561–573.

Gurin, P., Dey, E. L., Hurtado, S., & Gurin, G. (2002). Diversity and higher education: Theory and impact on educational outcomes. *Harvard Educational Review, 72,* 330–366.

Gurin, P., & Nagda, B. A. (2006). Getting to the *what, how,* and *why* of diversity on campus. *Educational Researcher, 35,* 20–24.

Gurin, P., Nagda, R., & Lopez, G. (2004). The benefits of diversity in education for democratic citizenship. *Journal of Social Issues, 60,* 17–34. doi:10.1111/j.0022–4537.2004.00097.x

Hale, F. W. (2004). Introduction. In F. W. Hale (Ed.), *What makes racial diversity work in higher education: Academic leaders present successful policies and strategies* (pp. 2–23). Sterling, VA: Stylus.

Halverson, C. B. (2008). Team development. In C. B. Halverson & S. A. Tirmizi (Eds.), *Effective multicultural teams: Theory and practice* (pp. 81–110). New York, NY: Springer.

Hammer, M. R. (2005). The intercultural style conflict style inventory: A conceptual approach and measure of intercultural conflict resolution approaches. *International Journal of Intercultural Relations, 29,* 675–695.

Harper, S. R. (2008). (Ed.). *Creating inclusive campus environments for cross-cultural learning and student engagement.* Washington, DC: NASPA.

Harper, S. R., & Antonio, A. L. (2008). Not by accident: Intentionality in diversity, learning and engagement. In S. Harper (ed.), *Creating Inclusive Campus Environments for Cross-Cultural Learning and Student Engagement.* Washington, DC: NASPA.

Harper, S. R., & Hurtado, S. (2007). Nine themes in campus racial climates and implications for institutional transformation. *New Directions for Student Services, 120*, 7–22.

Heath, C., & Heath, D. (2010). *Switch: How to change things when change is hard.* New York: Broadway Books.

Higher Education Research Institute (HERI). (1996). *A social change model of leadership development* (version III). Los Angeles: UCLA HERI.

Holvino, E. (2008). Developing multicultural organizations: A change model. http://www.chaosmanagement.com/images/stories/pdfs/MCODmodel.pdf

Howard-Hamilton, M. F., Cuyjet, M. J., & Cooper, D. L. (2011). Understanding multiculturalism and multicultural competence among college students. In M. J. Cuyjet, M. F. Howard-Hamilton, & D. L. Cooper (Eds.), *Multiculturalism on campus: Theory, models, and practices for understanding diversity and creating inclusion* (pp. 11–18). Sterling, VA: Stylus.

Howard-Hamilton, M. F., Richardson, B. J., & Shuford, B. (1998). Promoting multicultural education: A holistic approach. *College Student Affairs Journal, 18*, 5–17.

Hu, S., & Kuh, G. D. (2003). Diversity experiences and college student learning and personal development. *Journal of College Student Development, 44*, 320–334.

Hunt, J. A., Bell, L. A., Wei, W., & Ingle, G. (1992). Monoculturalism to multiculturalism: Lessons from three public universities. *New Directions for Teaching and Learning, 52*, 101–114.

Hurtado, S. (2005). The next generation of diversity and intergroup relations research. *Journal of Social Issues, 61*, 595–610.

Hurtado, S., Dey, E. L., Gurin, P., & Gurin, G. (2003). The college environment, diversity, and student learning. In J. Smart (Ed.), *Higher education: Handbook of theory and research* (pp. 145–189). Amsterdam: Kluwer Academic Press.

Hurtado, S., Griffin, K. A., Arellano, L., & Cuellar, M. (2008). Assessing the value of climate assessment: Progress and future directions. *Journal of Diversity in Higher Education, 1*, 204–221.

Hurtado, S., Milem, J., Clayton-Pedersen, A., & Allen, W. (1999). *Enacting diverse learning environments: Improving the climate for racial/ethnic diversity in higher education.* ASHE-ERIC Higher Education Report, Vol. 26, No. 8. Washington, D.C.: The George Washington University, Graduate School of Education and Human Development.

Intergroup Dialogue Program (2013). *Cross Cultural Center: Intergroup Dialogue Program.* Retrieved from http://www.slu.edu/cross-cultural-center/ccc-initiatives/intergroup-dialogue-program

Iverson, S. V. (2012). Multicultural competence for *doing* social justice: Expanding our awareness, knowledge, and skills. *Journal of Critical Thought and Praxis, 1,* 62–87.

Jackson, B. W. (2005). The theory and practice of multicultural organization development in education. In M. L. Ouellett (Ed.), *Teaching inclusively: Resources for course, department & institutional change in higher education* (pp. 3–20). Stillwater, OK: New Forums.

Jackson, B. W. (2006). Theory and practice of multicultural organization development. In B. B. Jones & M. Brazzel (Eds.), *The NTL handbook of organization development and change: Principles, practices, and perspectives* (pp. 139–154). San Francisco, CA: Pfeiffer.

Jackson, B. W., & Hardiman, R. (1981). *Organizational stages of multicultural awareness.* Amherst, MA: New Perspectives.

Jackson, B. W., & Hardiman, R. (1994). Multicultural organizational development. In E. Y. Cross, J. H. Katz, F. A. Miller, & E. W. Seashore (Eds.), *The promise of diversity: Over 40 voices discuss strategies for eliminating discrimination in organizations* (pp. 231–239). Burr Ridge, IL: Irwin.

Jackson, B. W., & Holvino, E. (1988). Developing multicultural organizations. *The Journal of Religion and Applied Behavioral Sciences, 9,* 14–19.

Jackson, L. C. (1999). Ethnocultural resistance to multicultural training: Students and faculty. *Cultural Diversity and Ethnic Minority Psychology, 5,* 27–36.

Johnson, D. R., & Longerbeam, S. D. (2007). Implications for the privileged identity exploration model student affairs theory and practice. *College Student Affairs Journal, 26,* 216–221.

Jones, J. E., & Bearly, W. (2001). Facilitating team development: A view from the field. *Group Facilitation, 3,* 56–64.

Jones, S. R., & Abes, E. S. (2011). The nature and uses of theory. In J. Schuh, S. Jones, & S. Harper (Eds.), *Student Services: A handbook for the profession* (5th ed.) (pp. 149–167). San Francisco: Jossey-Bass.

Jones, S. R., & McEwen, M. K. (2000). A conceptual model of multiple dimensions of identity. *Journal of College Student Development, 41,* 405–414.

Katz, J. H. (1989). Facing the challenge of diversity and multiculturalism. In C. Woolbright (Ed.), *Valuing diversity on campus:*

A multicultural approach (pp. 1–22). Bloomington, IN: Association of College Unions–International [ACU-I].

Katz, J. H., & Miller, F. A. (1996). Coaching leaders through culture change. *Consulting Psychology Journal: Practice and Research, 48,* 104–114.

Kayes, P. E. (2006). New paradigms for diversifying faculty and staff in higher education: Uncovering cultural biases in search and hiring processes. *Multicultural Education, 14,* 65–69.

Kelly, B. T., & Gayles, J. G. (2010). Resistance to racial/ethnic dialog in graduate preparation programs: Implications for developing multicultural competence. *College Student Affairs Journal, 29,* 75–85.

Kezar, A. (2007). Learning from and with students: College presidents creating organizational learning to advance diversity agendas. *NASPA Journal, 44,* 578–609.

Kezar, A., & Carducci, R. (2009). Revolutionizing leadership development: Lessons from research and theory. In A. Kezar (Ed.), *Rethinking leadership practices in a complex, multicultural, and global environment: New concepts and models for higher education* (pp. 1–38). Sterling, VA: Stylus.

Kezar, A., & Eckel, P. (2007). Learning to ensure the success of students of color: A systemic approach to effecting change. *Change, 39,* 18–24.

Kezar, A., & Eckel, P. (2008). Advancing diversity agendas on campus: Examining transactional and transformational presidential leadership styles. *International Journal of Leadership in Education, 11,* 379–405.

King, P. M., & Baxter Magolda, M. B. (2005). A developmental model of intercultural maturity. *Journal of College Student Development, 46,* 571–592.

King, P. M., & Howard-Hamilton, M. (2003). An assessment of multicultural competence. *NASPA Journal, 40,* 119–133.

King, P. M., & Shuford, B. C. (1996). A multicultural view is a more cognitively complex view: Cognitive development and multicultural education. *American Behavioral Scientist, 40,* 153–164. doi:10.1177/0002764296040002006

Kline, K. A. (2013). Implications for daily practice and life. In K. A. Kline (Ed.), *Reflection in action: A guidebook for student affairs professionals and teaching faculty* (pp. 155–165). Sterling, VA: Stylus.

Komives, S. R. (2007). The social change model: A decade of practice and progress. *NASPA Leadership Exchange, 5,* 23.

Komives, S. R., & Wagner, W. (2009) (Ed.). *Leadership for a better world: Understanding the social change model of leadership development*. San Francisco: Jossey-Bass.

Krishnamurthi, M. (2003). Assessing multicultural initiatives in higher education institutions. *Assessment and Evaluation in Higher Education, 28,* 263–277.

Krumboltz, J. D. (1966). Promoting adaptive behavior: Behavior approach. In J. D. Krumboltz (Ed.), *Revolution in counseling*. Boston: Houghton-Mifflin.

Kyrillidou, M., Lowry, C., Hanges, P., Aiken, J. & Justh, K. (2009, March). *ClimateQUAL: Organizational Climate and Diversity Assessment*. Paper presented at ACRL Fourteenth National Conference, Seattle, WA.

Kuhn T. S. (1970). *The structure of scientific revolutions*. Chicago: Chicago University Press.

Kupo, V. L. (2011). Remembering our past to shape our future. In D. L. Stewart (Ed.), *Multicultural student services on campus: Building bridges, re-visioning community* (pp. 13–28). Sterling, VA: Stylus.

Laker, J. A., & Davis, T. L. (2009). Continuing the journey toward multicultural campus communities. In G. S. McClellan & J. Stronger (Eds.), *The handbook of student affairs administration* (3rd ed.) (pp. 242–264). San Francisco, CA: Jossey-Bass.

Levine, A., & Cureton, J. S. (1998). *When hope and fear collide: A portrait of today's college student*. San Francisco: Jossey-Bass.

Levine, A., & Dean, D. R. (2012). *Generation on a tightrope: A portrait of today's college student*. San Francisco: CA: Jossey-Bass.

Linnehan, F. & Konrad, A. M. (1999). Diluting diversity: Implications for intergroup inequality in organizations. *Journal of Management Inquiry, 8,* 399–414.

Livingston, R. E. (2006). Evaluation and termination phase. In B. B. Jones & M. Brazzel (Eds.), *The NTL handbook of organization development and change: Principles, practices, and perspectives* (pp. 231–245). San Francisco, CA: Pfeiffer.

Loden, M. (1995). *Implementing diversity*. Chicago, IL: Irwin.

Lorenzi, N. M., & Riley, R. T. (2004). *Managing technological change: Organizational aspects of health informatics* (2nd ed.). New York, NY: Springer Science+Business Media, Inc.

Lorenzi, N. M., & Riley, R. T. (2000). Managing change: An overview. *Journal of the American Medical Informatics Association, 7,* 116–124.

Love, P. G., & Estanek, S. M. (2004). *Rethinking student affairs practice*. San Francisco, CA: Jossey-Bass.

Lyddon, W. J. (1990). First- and second-order change: Implications for rationalist and constructivist cognitive therapies. *Journal of College Student Development, 69*, 122–127.

Manning, K., & Coleman-Boatwright, P. (1991). Student affairs initiatives toward a multicultural university. *Journal of College Student Development, 32*, 367–374.

Manning, K., & Munoz, F. M. (2011). Conclusion: Re-visioning the future of multicultural student services. In D. L. Stewart (Ed.), *Multicultural student services on campus: Building bridges, re-visioning community* (pp. 282–299). Sterling, VA: Stylus.

Maples, M. F. (1988). Group development: Extending Tuckman's theory. *Journal for Specialists in Group Work, 13*, 17–23.

Marchesani, L. S., & Jackson, B. W. (2005). Transforming higher education institutions using multicultural organizational development: A case study of a large northeastern university. In M. L. Ouellett (Ed.), *Teaching inclusively: Resources for course, department & institutional change in higher education* (pp. 241–257). Stillwater, OK: New Forums.

Marquis, J. P., Lim, N., Scott, L. M., Harrell, M. C., & Kavanagh, J. (2007). *Managing diversity in corporate America: An exploratory analysis.* New York: Rand Corporation.

Marshak, R. J., & Grant, D. (2008). Organizational discourse and new organization development practices. *British Journal of Management, 19*, S7–19.

Maurer, R. (2006). Resistance and change in organizations. In B. B. Jones & M. Brazzel (Eds.), *The NTL handbook of organization development and change: Principles, practices, and perspectives* (pp. 121–138). San Francisco, CA: Pfeiffer.

McClellan, G. S., & Larimore, J. (2009). The changing student population. In G. S. McClellan & J. Stringer (Eds.), *The handbook of student affairs administration* (3rd ed.), (pp. 225–241). San Francisco, CA: Jossey-Bass.

McEwen, M. K., & Roper, L. D. (1994). Incorporating multiculturalism into student affairs preparation programs: Suggestions from the literature. *Journal of College Student Development, 35*, 46–53.

McGrath, J. E. (1984). Groups: Interaction and performance. Englewood Cliffs, NJ: Prentice-Hall.

Mezirow, J. (2009). An overview on transformative learning. In K. Illeris (Ed.), *Contemporary theories of learning. Learning theorists . . . in their own words* (pp. 90–105). New York: Routledge.

Miklitsch, T. A. (2006). *The relationship between multicultural education, multicultural experiences, racial identity, and multicultural competence among student affairs professionals.* (Unpublished doctoral dissertation). University at Buffalo, Buffalo, NY.

Mildred, J., & Zúñiga, X. (2004). Working with resistance to diversity issues in the classroom: Lessons from teacher training and multicultural education. *Smith College Studies in Social Work 74,* 359–375.

Milem, J. F., Chang, M. J., & Antonio, A. L. (2005). *Making diversity work on campus: A research-based perspective.* Washington, DC: Association of American Colleges and Universities.

Miles, J. R., & Kivlighan, D. M. (2012). Perceptions of group climate by social identity group in intergroup dialogue. *Group Dynamics: Theory, Research, and Practice, 16,* 189–205.

Miller, D. (2003). The stages of group development: A retrospective study of dynamic team processes. *Canadian Journal of Administrative Sciences, 20,* 121–143.

Miller, F. A. (1998). Strategic culture change: The door to achieving high performance and inclusion. *Public Personnel Management, 27,* 151–160.

Miller, F. A., & Katz, J. H. (2002). *The inclusion breakthrough: Unleashing the real power of diversity.* San Francisco: Berrett-Koehler Publishers.

Miller, W. R., & Rose, G. S. (2009). Toward a theory of motivational interviewing. *American Psychologist, 64,* 527–537.

Moody, J. (2001). Race, school segregation, and friendship segregation in America. *American Journal of Sociology, 107,* 679–717.

Mueller, J. A., & Cole, J. C. (2009). A qualitative examination of heterosexual consciousness among college students. *Journal of College Student Development, 50,* 320–336.

Mueller, J. A., & Pope, R. L. (2001). The relationship between multicultural competence and white racial consciousness among student affairs practitioners. *Journal of College Student Development, 42,* 133–144.

Musil, C. M. (1996). The maturing of diversity initiatives on American campuses. *American Behavioral Scientist, 40,* 222.

Nagda, B. A., & Zuniga, X. (2003). Fostering meaningful racial engagement through intergroup dialogues. *Group Process and Intergroup Relations, 6,* 111–128. doi:10.1177/1368430203006001015

Nash, R. J., Bradley, D. L., & Chickering, A. W. (2008). *How to talk about hot topics on campus: From polarization to moral conversation.* San Francisco, CA: Jossey-Bass.

NASPA. (n.d.). *Annual Conference Archives.* Retrieved from http://www.naspa.org/membership/mem/archives/conf/default.cfm

Network of Executive Women (2006). Affinity networks: New insights and productivity from within. *Affinity networks: Building organizations stronger than their parts.* Retrieved from http://www.newnewsletter.org/bestpractices/newreport3_affinity_0407.pdf

Norcross, J. C., Krebs, P. M., & Prochaska, J. O. (2011). Stages of change. *Journal of Clinical Psychology: In Session, 67,* 143–154. doi:10.1002/jclp.20758

O'Neil, M. E. (2010). *Development and initial validation of a measure of multicultural competence stage of change.* (Order No. 3435774, University of Oregon). *ProQuest Dissertations and Theses, 149.* Retrieved from http://search.proquest.com/docview/816350096?accountid=14169. (prod.academic_MSTAR_816350096).

Orfield, G. (Ed.). (2001). *Diversity challenged: Evidence on the impact of affirmative action.* Cambridge, MA: Civil Rights Project, Harvard Education Publishing Group.

Orfield, G., Bachmeier, M. D., James, D. R., & Eitle, T. (1997). Deepening segregation in American public schools: A special report from the Harvard Project on School Desegregation. *Equity & Excellence in Education, 30,* 5–24.

Organizational Diversity and Development (2012). *Diversity education and professional development calendar.* Unpublished manuscript.

Ortiz, A. M., & Patton, L. D. (2012). Awareness of self. In J. Armino, V. Torres, & R. Pope (Eds.), *Why aren't we there yet? Taking personal responsibility for creating an inclusive campus* (pp. 9–32). Sterling, VA: Stylus.

Ortiz, A. M., & Rhoads, R. A. (2000). Deconstructing whiteness as part of a multicultural educational framework: From theory to practice. *Journal of College Student Development, 41,* 81–93.

Our History of Diversity (n.d.). *Our history of diversity.* Retrieved from http://www.uvm.edu/~diversit/?Page=history.html

Palmer, J. D. (1989). Diversity: Three paradigms for change leaders. *OD Practitioner: Journal of the National Organization Development Network, 21,* 15–18.

Pascarella, E. T., & Whitt, E. J. (1999). Using systematic inquiry to improve performance. In G. S. Blimling and E. Whitt (Eds.), *Good practice in student affairs: Principles to foster student learning* (pp. 91–112). San Francisco, CA: Jossey-Bass.

Passmore, J. (2011). Motivational interviewing: A model for coaching psychology practice. *The Coaching Psychologist, 7*, 36–40.

Patton, L. D., & Hannon, M. D. (2008). Collaboration for cultural programming: Engaging culture centers, multicultural affairs, and student activity offices as partners. In S. R. Harper (Ed.), *Creating inclusive campus environments for cross-cultural learning and student engagement* (pp. 139–154). Washington, DC: NASPA.

Pedersen, P. (1988). *A handbook for developing multicultural awareness*. Alexandria, VA: American Counseling Association

Petitt, B., & McIntosh, D. (2011). Negotiating purpose and context. In D. L. Stewart (Ed.), *Multicultural student services on campus* (pp. 201–217). Sterling, VA: Stylus Publishing.

Pettigrew, T. F. (1998). Intergroup contact theory. *Annual Review of Psychology, 49*, 65–68. doi:10/1146/annurev.psych.49.1.65

Pettigrew, T. F., & Tropp, L. R. (2006). A meta-analytical test of intergroup contact theory. *Journal of Personality and Social Psychology, 90*, 751–783. doi:10.1037/0022–3514.90.5.751

Pew Forum on Religion & Public Life (2010). Retrieved from: http://www.pewforum.org/U-S-Religious-Knowledge-Survey-FAQs-About-Measuring-Religious-Knowledge.aspx

Ponterotto, J. G. (2002) Qualitative research methods: A fifth force in psychology. *The counseling psychologist. 30*, 394—406.

Ponterotto, J. G., Mendelsohn, J., & Belizaire, L. (2003). Assessing teacher multicultural competencies, self-report instruments, observer report evaluations, and a portfolio assessment. In D. B. Pope-Davis, H.L.K. Coleman, W. M. Liu, & R. L. Toporek (Eds.), *Handbook of multicultural competencies in counseling and psychology* (pp. 191–210). Thousand Oaks, CA: Sage Publications.

Pope, R. L. (1992). *An analysis of multiracial change efforts in student affairs.* (Order No. 9305881, University of Massachusetts Amherst). *ProQuest Dissertations and Theses*, pp. 156–156. (prod.academic_MSTAR_304034270). Retrieved from http://search.proquest.com/docview/304034270?accountid=14169

Pope, R. L. (1993). Multicultural organization development in student affairs: An introduction. *Journal of College Student Development, 34*, 201–205.

Pope, R. L. (1995). Multicultural organizational development: Implications and applications for student affairs. In J. Fried (Ed.),

Shifting paradigms in student affairs: A cultural perspective (pp. 233–249). Washington, DC: ACPA Media.

Pope, R. L., & LePeau, L. A. (2011). The influence of institutional context and culture. In J. Arminio, V. Torres, & R. L. Pope (Eds.), *Why aren't we there yet? Taking personal responsibility for creating an inclusive campus* (pp. 103–130). Sterling, VA: Stylus Publishing.

Pope, R. L., & Mueller, J. A. (2000). Development and initial validation of the Multicultural Competence in Student Affairs-Preliminary 2 Scale. *Journal of College Student Development, 41,* 599–607.

Pope, R. L., & Mueller, J. A. (2011). Multicultural competence. In J. Schuh, S. Jones, & S. Harper (Eds.), *Student Services: A Handbook for the Profession* (5th ed.) (pp. 339–352). San Francisco: Jossey-Bass.

Pope, R. L., Mueller, J. A., & Reynolds, A. L. (2009). Looking back and moving forward: Future directions for diversity in student affairs. *Journal of College Student Development (50th Anniversary Special Issue), 50,* 640–658.

Pope, R. L., & Reynolds, A. L. (1997). Student affairs core competencies: Integrating multicultural awareness, knowledge, and skills. *Journal of College Student Development, 38,* 266–277.

Pope, R. L., Reynolds, A. L., & Mueller, J. A. (2004). *Multicultural competence in student affairs.* San Francisco: Jossey-Bass.

Presidential Commissions (n.d.). *Presidential commissions.* Retrieved from http://www.uvm.edu/president/?Page=commissions/presidentialcommissions.html&SM=submenu5.html

Prochaska, J. O. (1979). *Systems of psychotherapy.* Homewood, IL: The Dorsey Press.

Prochaska, J. O., & DiClemente, C. C. (1984). *The transtheoretical approach: Crossing traditional boundaries of change.* Homewood, IL: Dorsey Press.

Prochaska, J. O., & Norcross, J. C. (2009). *Systems of psychotherapy: A transtheoretical analysis* (7th ed.). Pacific Grove, CA: Brooks/Cole.

Prochaska, J. O., Norcross, J. C., & DiClemente, C. C. (2007). *Changing for good: A revolutionary six-stage program for overcoming bad habits and moving your life positively forward.* New York: William Morris.

Prochaska, J. M., Prochaska, J. O., & Levesque, D. A. (2001). A transtheoretical approach to changing organizations. *Administration and Policy in Mental Health, 28,* 247–261.

Prochaska, J. O., Velicer, W. F., Rossi, J. S., Goldstein, M. G., Marcus, B. H., Rakowski, W., Fiore, C., Harlow, L. L., Redding, C. A., Rosenbloom, D., & Rossi, S. R. (1994). Stages of change and decisional balance for 12 problem behaviors. *Health Psychology, 13,* 39–46. doi:10.1037/0278–6133.13.1.39

Promoting Health and Safety (2013). *Promoting health and safety.* Retrieved from http://www.uvm.edu/~dos/?Page=health_safety/default.php&SM=health_safety/health_safetymenu.html

Quillian, L., & Campbell, M. E. (2003). Beyond black and white: The present and future of multiracial friendship segregation. *American Sociological Review, 68,* 540–566.

Rankin, S. R., & Reason, R. D. (2005). Differing perceptions: How students of color and white students perceive campus climate for underrepresented groups. *Journal of College Student Development, 46,* 43–61.

Rankin, S., & Reason, R. (2008). Transformational Tapestry Model: A comprehensive approach to transforming campus climate. *Journal of Diversity in Higher Education, 1,* 262–274.

Ramos, M. C., & Chesler, M. A. (2010). Reflections on a cross-cultural partnership in multicultural organization development efforts. *OD Practitioner, 42,* 4–9.

Reed, B. G., & Peet, M. R. (2005). Faculty development and organizational change: Moving from "minority relevant" to intersectionality and social justice. In M. L. Ouellett (Ed.), *Teaching inclusively: Resources for course, department & institutional change in higher education* (pp. 473–491). Stillwater, OK: New Forums.

Reed, S. E. (2011). *The diversity index: The alarming truth about diversity in corporate America . . . and what can be done about it.* New York, NY: Amacon.

Reynolds, A. L. (1997). Using the multicultural change intervention matrix (MCIM) as a counseling training model. In D. Pope-Davis, & H.L.K. Coleman (Eds.), *Multicultural counseling competence: Assessment, education and training, and supervision* (pp. 209–226). Thousand Oaks, CA: Sage.

Reynolds, A. L. (2011). Understanding the perceptions and experiences of faculty who teach multicultural counseling courses: An exploratory study. *Training and Education in Professional Psychology, 5,* 167–174. doi:10.1037/a0024613

Reynolds, A. L., & Baluch, S. (2001). Racial identity theories in counseling: A literature review and evaluation. In C. L. Wijeyesinghe & B. W. Jackson (Eds.), *New perspectives on racial identity: A*

theoretical and practical anthology (pp. 153–181). New York, NY:
New York University Press.

Reynolds, A. L., & Pope, R. L. (2003). Multicultural competencies in
counseling centers. In D. B. Pope-Davis, H.L.K. Coleman, W. M. Liu,
& R. L. Toporek (Eds.), *Handbook of multicultural competencies in
counseling and psychology* (pp. 365–382). Thousand Oaks, CA: Sage.

Reynolds, A. L., Pope, R. L., & Wells, G. V. (2002). *Creating a student
affairs diversity action plan: Blueprint for success.* Paper presented at the
meeting of the American College Personnel Association, Long Beach, CA.

Rodriguez, R. A. (1998). Challenging demographic reductionism: A
pilot study investigating diversity in group composition. *Small Group
Research, 29*, 744–759.

Rudenstine, N. L. (2001). Student diversity and higher learning. In
G. Oldfield (Ed.), *Diversity challenged: Evidence on the impact of
affirmative action* (pp. 31–48). Cambridge, MA: Civil Rights Project,
Harvard Education Publishing Group.

Saint Louis University Division of Student Development (n.d.).
Divisional Statement on Diversity. Retrieved from https://www.slu
.edu/division-of-student-development/divisional-statement-on-diversity

Saint Louis University Division of Student Development (2012). *Saint
Louis University application of MCOD: A case study.* Unpublished
document.

Saint Louis University (2012a). *Oath of Inclusion.* Retrieved from
http://www.slu.edu/diversity/students/oath-of-inclusion

Saint Louis University (2012b). *Saint Louis University Fact Book
2011–2012.* Retrieved from https://www.slu.edu/Documents/provost/
oir/Fact%20Book%202011–2012%20Final%2010.09.2012%
2020130509.pdf

Saint Louis University (2012c). *University diversity and inclusion vision
statement.* Retrieved from http://www.slu.edu/x47273.xml

Sammons, C. C., & Speight, S. L. (2008). A qualitative investigation of
graduate-student changes associated with multicultural counseling
courses. *The Counseling Psychologist, 36*, 814–836.

Sandeen, C. A., & Barr, M. J. (2006). *Critical issues for student affairs:
Challenges and opportunities.* San Francisco, CA: Jossey-Bass.

Sanford, N. (1967). *Where colleges fail.* San Francisco: Jossey-Bass.

Sattler, R. (2008). *Wilber's AQAL map and beyond.* Retrieved from:
http://www.beyondWilber.ca

Schuh, J. H., & Upcraft, M. L. (2001). *Assessment practice in student
affairs: An applications manual.* San Francisco, CA: Jossey-Bass.

Senge, P. (1990). *The fifth discipline.* New York: McGraw Hill.

Shaw, J. B., & Barrett-Power, E. (1998). The effects of diversity on small group work processes and performance. *Human Relations, 51,* 1307–1325.

Shuford, B. C. (2011). Historical and philosophical development of multicultural student services. In D. L. Stewart (Ed.), *Multicultural student services on campus: Building bridges, re-visioning community* (pp. 29–37). Sterling, VA: Stylus.

Smith, D. G. (1997). *Diversity works: The emerging picture of how students benefit.* Washington, DC: AAC&U.

Smith, D. G. (2009). *Diversity's promise for higher education: Making it work.* Baltimore: Johns Hopkins University Press.

Smith, D. G., & Parker, S. (2005). Organizational learning: A tool for diversity and institutional effectiveness. *New Directions for Higher Education, 131,* 113–125.

Smith, D. G., & Wolf-Wendel, L. E. (2005). *The challenge of diversity: Involvement or alienation in the academy?* ASHE Higher Education Report: Vol. 31, No. 1. San Francisco, CA: Jossey-Bass.

Smith, D., Wolf, L., & Levitan, T. (1994). Studying diversity in higher education. *New Directions for Institutional Research, 81,* 1–8.

Sodowsky, G. R., Taffe, R. C., Gutkin, T. B., & Wise, S. L. (1994). Development of the Multicultural Counseling Inventory (MCI): A self-report measure of multicultural competencies. *Journal of Counseling Psychology, 41,* 153–162.

Sorensen, N., Nagda, B. A., Gurin, P., & Maxwell, K. E. (2009). Taking a "hands on" approach to diversity in higher education: A critical-dialogic model for effective intergroup interaction. *Analyses of Social Issues and Public Policy, 9,* 3–35.

Stearns, E., Buchmann, C., & Bonneau, K. (2009). Interracial friendships in the transition to college: Do birds of a feather flock together once they leave the nest? *Sociology of Education, 82,* 173–195.

Steward, R. J., Morales, P. C., Bartell, P. A., Miller, M., & Weeks, D. (1998). The multiculturally responsive versus the multiculturally reactive: A study of perceptions of counselor trainees. *Journal of Multicultural Counseling and Development, 26,* 13–27.

Stewart, D. L., & Bridges, B. K. (2011). A demographic profile of multicultural student services. In D. L. Stewart (Ed.), *Multicultural student services on campus: Building bridges, re-visioning community* (pp. 38–60). Sterling, VA: Stylus.

Strange, C. C., & Banning, J. H. (2001). *Educating by design: Creating campus learning environments that work.* San Francisco: Jossey-Bass.

Sue, D. W. (1995). Multicultural organization development: Implications for the counseling profession. In J. Ponterotto, M. Casas, L. Suzuki, & C. Alexander (Eds.), *Handbook of multicultural counseling* (pp. 474–492). Thousand Oaks, CA: Sage.

Sue, D. W. (2001). Multiple dimensional facets of cultural competence. *The Counseling Psychologist, 29*, 790–821.

Sue, D. W., Bernier, J. E., Durran, A., Feinberg, L., Pederson, P., Smith, E. J., & Vasquez-Nuttall, E. (1982). Position paper: Cross-cultural counseling competencies. *The Counseling Psychologist, 10*, 45–52.

Swarns, R. L. (2012, November 18). Out of the closet and still in uniform. *New York Times*, p. ST1.

Tatum, B.D. (2000). The ABC approach to creating climates of engagement on diverse campuses. *Liberal Education, 86*, 22–30.

Teaching Tolerance (n.d.). Retrieved from http://www.tolerance.org/ activity/native-american-influences-us-history-and-culture

Terenzini, P. T. (1989). Assessment with open eyes. *Journal of Higher Education, 60*, 644–664.

The Next Step 2013 (n.d.). *The Next Step 2013: A Social Justice Retreat*. Retrieved from http://www.uvm.edu/~lce/?Page=nextstep .php&SM=ns_menu.html

Tuckman, B. W. (1965). Development sequence in small groups. *Psychological Bulletin, 63*, 384–399.

Tuckman, B. W., & Jensen, M. (1977). Stages of small group development revisited. *Group and Organizational Studies, 2*, 410–427.

University of Texas Austin, Division of Housing and Food Service. (2012). *"A spirit of harmony. . ." Organizational Diversity and Development Model*.

University of Vermont and State Agricultural College Board of Trustees (2009, February). *Diversity: Why diversity is an academic and institutional strategic priority for the University of Vermont*. Retrieved from http://www.uvm.edu/president/?Page=whydiversity_ statement.html

University of Vermont Office of Institutional Research (2012, September). *Fall 2012 student body diversity*. Retrieved from http:// www.uvm.edu/~isis/consumer/divecomp.pdf

Upcraft, M. L. (2003). Assessment and evaluation. In S. R. Komives & D. B. Woodard (Eds.), *Student services: A handbook for the profession* (pp. 555–572). San Francisco, CA: Jossey-Bass.

Upcraft, M. L., & Schuh, J. H. (1996). *Assessment in student affairs: A guide for practitioners*. San Francisco, CA: Jossey-Bass.

U.S. Census Bureau (2012, December 6). *State and county quickfacts.* Retrieved from http://quickfacts.census.gov/qfd/states/50000.html

U.S. Department of Education (2011, November). *Total fall enrollment in degree-granting institutions, by level of student, sex, attendance status, and race/ethnicity: Selected years, 1976 through 2010.* National Center for Education Statistics. Retrieved from http://nces .ed.gov/programs/digest/d11/tables/dt11_237.asp

Wageman, R. (2001). The meaning of interdependence. In M. E. Turner (Ed.), *Groups at work: Theory and research* (pp. 197–217). Mahwah, NJ: Lawrence Erlbaum Associates.

Wagner, W. (2009). What is social change? In S. R. Komives and W. Wagner (Eds.), *Leadership for a better world: Understanding the social change model of leadership development* (pp. 7–41). San Francisco: Jossey-Bass.

Waters, J. T., Marzano, R. J., & McNulty, B. A. (2003). *Balanced leadership: What 30 years of research tells us about the effect of leadership on student achievement.* Aurora, CO: Mid-continent Research for Education and Learning.

Washington State Human Resources (2012). *Measuring diversity.* Retrieved from http://www.dop.wa.gov/diversity/ diversitymanagement/pages/measuringdiversity.aspx

Watt, S. K. (2007). Difficult dialogues, privilege and social justice: Uses of the privileged identity exploration (PIE) model in student affairs practice. *College Student Affairs Journal, 26,* 114–126.

Watt, S. K. (2012). Moving beyond the talk: From difficult dialogue to action. In J. Arminio, V. Torres, & R. L. Pope (Eds.), *Why aren't we there yet? Taking personal responsibility for creating an inclusive campus* (pp. 131–144). Sterling, VA: Stylus Publishing.

Watt, S. K. (2014). Designing and implementing multicultural initiatives: Guiding principles. In Watt, S. K & Linley, J. (Eds.), *Creating successful multicultural initiatives in higher education and student affairs: New directions for student services.* (pp. 5–16). San Francisco, CA: Jossey-Bass.

Watzlawick, P., Weakland, J., & Fisch, R. (1974). *Change: Principles of problem formation and problem resolution.* New York: W. W. Norton & Company.

Weigand, M. J. (2005). *The relationships between multicultural competence, racial identity, and multicultural education and experiences among student affairs professionals responsible for first-year student orientation.* (Unpublished doctoral dissertation). University at Buffalo, Buffalo, NY.

Wilber, K. (2000). *Sex, ecology, spirituality: The spirit of evolution* (2nd ed.). Boston, MA: Shambhala.

Wilcox, D. A., & McCray, J. Y. (2005). Multicultural organization competence through deliberative dialogue. *Organization Development Journal, 23,* 77–85.

Wilkinson, W. K., & McNeil, K. (1996). *Research for the helping professions.* Cincinnati, OH: Brooks/Cole.

Williams, D. A. (2008). Beyond the diversity crisis model: Decentralized diversity planning and implementation. *Planning for Higher Education, 36,* 27–41.

Williams, D. A. (2013). *Strategic diversity leadership: Activating change and transformation in higher education.* Sterling, VA: Stylus.

Williams, D. A., Berger, J. B., & McClendon, S. A. (2005). *Toward a model of inclusive excellence and change in postsecondary institutions.* Washington, DC: AAC&U.

Williams, D. A., & Wade-Golden, C. (2007). *The chief diversity officer: A primer for college and university presidents.* Washington, DC: American Council on Education.

Wilson, A. (2011). The relationship between multicultural competence, and the use of the social change model. (Doctoral Dissertation, University at Buffalo, 2011). Digital Dissertations, 3169117.

Workman, N. (2009). Change. In S. R. Komives and W. Wagner (Eds.), *Leadership for a better world: Understanding the social change model of leadership development* (pp. 101–143). San Francisco: Jossey-Bass.

Yalom, I. D., & Leszcz, M. (2005). *The theory and practice of group psychotherapy* (5th ed.). New York: Basic Books.

Zimmerman, G. L., Olsen, C. G., & Bosworth, M. F. (2000). A 'stages of change' approach to helping patients change behavior. *American Family Physician, 61,* 1409–1416.

Zuniga, X., Nagda, B. A., Chesler, M., & Cytron-Walker, A. (2007). (Eds.). *Intergroup dialogue in higher education: Meaningful learning about social justice.* ASHE-ERIC Higher Education Report, no. 32(4). San Francisco: Jossey-Bass.

Zuniga, X., Nagda, B. A., & Sevig, T. D. (2002). Intergroup dialogues: An educational model for cultivating engagement across differences. *Equity & Excellence in Education, 35,* 7–17.

NAME INDEX

A

Abes, E. S., 39
ACPA, 93, 132
Adler, N. J., 73
Aguirre, A., 4, 8, 19, 20, 84, 86, 92, 98
AHEAD, 133
Aiken, J., 108
Airasian, P., 100
Alban, B. T., 74
Allen, G., 125, 146
Allen, W., 67
Allport, G. W., 43
American Association of Colleges and Universities (AAC&U), 93
American College Personnel Association (ACPA), 93
Antonio, A. L., 3, 5, 157
Arellano, L., 109–111
Argyris, C., 82, 83–84
Arredondo, P., 64, 91–92
Association of American Colleges and Universities, 6
Association of Research Libraries, 108
Association on Higher Education and Disability (AHEAD), 133
Astin, A. W., 10–11, 43

B

Bachmeier, M. D., 9
Baker, O., 6
Bales, R. F., 60
Baluch, S., 65
Banning, J. H., 11
Barcelo, N., 7
Barr, M. J., 66
Barrett-Power, E., 63
Bartell, P. A., 53

Baxter Magolda, M. B., 6, 12, 39, 40, 41, 52
Bearly, W., 63
Beitman, B. D., 15
Belizaire, L., 103
Bell, L. A., 30
Bensimon, E. M., 107
Berger, J. B., 7–8, 129
Bernier, J. E., 12
Billingsley, K., 155
Blimling, G. S., 93
Bok, D., 5
Bonebright, D. A., 61, 63
Bonneau, K., 3
Bosworth, M. F., 15, 40, 42
Bowman, N. A., 40, 41
Bowser, B. P., 6
Bradley, D. L., 157, 159
Brayboy, B.M.J., 7, 115
Bresciani, M. J., 100
Bridges, B. K., 89
Buchmann, C., 3
Bunker, B. B., 74
Burke, B. L., 15, 42
Burlington Free Press, 147

C

Caban, A. R., 51
Campbell, M. E., 9
Carducci, R., 11, 86
Castellanos, J., 5, 103
Chang, J. C., 3, 8, 71
Chang, M. J., 2, 3, 4, 5, 8, 13, 18, 43, 47, 71
Chavez, A. F., 39, 40–41, 48
Cheatham, H. E., 19, 160
Cheng, D. X., 12

SUBJECT INDEX

A

Acceptance, 7, 24, 71–73
Access, 2, 24, 107, 124–125
Action-oriented change, 85
Action *vs.* reflection, 45
Adjourning stage, 62, 73–74
Administration. *See* Leadership
Advocacy, 136
Affinity groups, 105
Affirmative action, 3, 8, 18, 130, 146
Affirming system, 24
Alliances, 44, 135
Assessment: challenges to, 149;
   considerations in, 112–113;
   examples of, 121, 123, 125,
   133–134, 139; group-level,
   104–106; individual-level, 102–103;
   institutional-level, 106–111,
   124; multi-level, 111–112; of
   multicultural competency, 133; *vs.*
   other inquiry, 100–101; value of, 2,
   4, 26, 94, 96, 99, 100
Assumptions, 141
Attitudes, 12, 41, 44, 103, 108–110,
   110–111. *See also* Multicultural
   awareness
Authority figures. *See* Leadership
Awareness, multicultural. *See*
   Multicultural awareness

B

Behavioral change, 15, 42–43, 48, 120,
   151. *See also* Individual change
Beliefs. *See* Multicultural awareness
Bias incident response protocol, 137
Biases, identification of, 46–48, 141,
   146, 159. *See also* Multicultural
   awareness

Bottom-up approach, 156–157
Budgeting, 90, 146
Buy-in, 74, 144, 146–147

C

Campus climate: assessment of, 28,
   97, 108–111, 124–125; definition
   of, 109–110; effects of, on diversity
   goals, 5, 22, 33, 110, 130–132,
   144–147
Campus Diversity Initiative Project,
   84
Campus incidents, 147
Campus safety, 134–135
Centralization, 9
Change. *See also* First-order change;
   Group-level change; Individual
   change; Institutional change;
   Second-order change: barriers to,
   19, 31, 51–52, 95; requirements
   for, 15, 26, 95, 116, 145–146,
   158; types and levels of, 29–34,
   95 (*See also* specific types of
   change)
Change agents, 25–27, 86
Chief diversity officers, 7–8
Climate, campus. *See* Campus
   climate
Cognitive change, 32, 41, 49–52,
   141
Cohesiveness, group, 60–62
Committed action, 50
Competence, multicultural. *See*
   Multicultural competence
Competencies for change. *See* specific
   levels of change
Compliance system, 24
Conflict in groups, 61–62